DATE DUE

MAY 3 0 1989		
SEP 7 1989		
JAN 8 1990 1989		
APR 5 1990		
DEC 5 1991		
FEB 2 0 1998		
NOV 2 6 2002		
NOV 0 7 2008		

Wall Systems

Wall Systems
Analysis by Detail

Herman Sands
Professor of Architectural Technology
New York City Technical College of the
City University of New York
Partner, Sands and Sperling Architects

McGraw-Hill Book Company

New York St. Louis San Francisco Auckland Bogotá
Hamburg Johannesburg London Madrid
Mexico Montreal New Delhi Panama
Paris São Paulo Singapore
Sydney Tokyo Toronto

Library of Congress Cataloging in Publication Data

Sands, Herman.
  Wall systems.

  Includes index.
  1. Walls. 2. Buildings—Details. I. Title.
TH2201.S26 1985   721′.2   85-12830
ISBN 0-07-054665-7

1234567890 HAL/HAL 898765

ISBN 0-07-054665-7

The editors for this book were Joan Zseleczky, Olive Collen, and Jim Bessent,
the designer was Naomi Auerbach, and the production
supervisor was Tom Kowalczyk. It was set in Auriga
by University Graphics, Inc.
Printed and bound by Halliday Lithograph.

*This book is dedicated to my wife, Phyllis,
and in memory of my father, Morris.*

Contents

Preface

Shortly after graduating from college, I purchased a foreign car and decided that I was going to service it myself. I picked up a maintenance manual and fell in love with it. The manual was lucidly written, and its illustrations were primarily three-dimensional drawings on which all the automobile's parts were clearly labeled and numbered. Exploded isometric views of the vehicle's systems helped me understand the relation of the components to each assembly and supplied me with pertinent information for ordering replacements. The car (a lemon) has long been forgotten. The manual, with its clear, easily read drawings, still occupies a warm spot in my heart and was a factor in my decision to write this book.

An automobile manual reflects a manufacturing system that owns, controls, or has agreements with many companies that supply it with parts. This type of industry is known as a *vertical industry;* it manages many elements of production, from the gathering of raw materials to the assembly of component systems. By controlling many aspects of production, from bolts to gaskets, the automobile industry ensures that its parts are fully interchangeable, can be used in different automobile models, and can be warehoused and supplied to repair shops throughout the world.

The building industry, however, is based upon a horizontal model that reflects the involvement of thousands of different manufacturers who provide the construction materials used in building. Here there is no assembly line, no organization controlling production, but there are innumerable contractors trying to assemble noncoordinated products into whole buildings. In spite of this, the construction industry is very successful, and it is a never-ending marvel of variety and innovation. It is composed of a myriad of component industries producing a vast number of products

that must be carefully surveyed and tested by those who use them. There are hundreds of thousands of workers involved in the manufacturing of materials, the design of structures, and the fabrication of new and renovated buildings. Basic materials in use today are reliable; many of them have been used since ancient times. Stone, brick, mortar, and wood are examples of materials that have been in use since before the advent of written history. To these have been added a host of relatively new products—steel, reinforced concrete, glass, aluminum, plastics, and so forth. In addition to the industries supplying these basic building materials are whole systems controlling pure-water delivery, waste disposal, power distribution, vertical transportation, and environmental control. A glance through *Sweet's Catalogue File* can be both breathtaking and alarming. How do we negotiate our way through the approximately 6500 trade names and countless products found in this catalog, which is only one of many available compilations listing product sources?

Manufacturers of construction materials generate hundreds of thousands of pages of literature describing their output. An architect must become familiar with a host of products, models, and sizes in order to make even the simplest assembly work properly. For example, in order to design a window in a masonry curtain wall, the architect must be knowledgeable about window sash sections, glass types, glazing details, lintels, sills, flashing, sealants, and an assortment of hardware clips and bolts. The reference material for this assembly is spread out over hundreds of pages of literature that the architect must collect and absorb before making even tentative detailing decisions. The durability of materials—their effective life span and expected period of maintenance-free utilization—becomes another demanding area of exploration that the architect must satisfy if a given assembly is to work well and indeed satisfy the design intent of the architect and the expectations of the client. There are few things worse than leaky windows; they literally dampen a client's respect for an architect's ability.

As a practitioner and principal of my own firm, I have had the opportunity of working on a variety of building types, some large and some small. Despite my extensive experience in detailing and in assembly analysis, I have had firsthand acquaintance with only a partial range of technological innovations and procedures. I suspect that many of my colleagues find themselves in a similar situation. It is unfortunate that architectural schools generally do not prepare us for the demands of technical detailing and systems design. Acquiring skills in detailing is, at best, an informal process, catch-as-catch-can; this learning method is totally inappropriate to the rigid demands of today's construction industry. The preparation of this book has allowed me to explore the design and technical solutions developed by some extremely fine firms in response to the requirements of challenging projects.

It is the purpose of this book to explore building assemblies by analyzing their details. The scope has been confined to the investigation of curtain wall or cladding systems and their relation to a building's structure. Examples of other related forms of construction are explored here, but the book deals primarily with various curtain wall systems such as metal, precast concrete, masonry, and glass in low- and high-rise buildings.

Ten buildings executed by architects with established reputations for outstanding professional performance are described. These architects are listed in the acknowledgments and individual chapters of this book, and it is because of the cooperation of their firms that I was able to develop the material used here. It was essential to work with actual buildings and their contract documents to avoid producing a book that was overly theoretical in nature. Common sense indicated the necessity of a pragmatic text, dealing with actual case studies, so that the reader would encounter only real solutions to detailing and design problems. The term *design* in this book does not necessarily imply aesthetic considerations. *Design* is employed here in much the same way engineers use it to describe the development of an assembly or system that "works" and satisfies a problem.

It is not my intention to dwell on the aesthetic properties of the buildings used as examples in this book. These buildings were chosen because each one demonstrates a particular method of construction. The various materials described reflect contemporary construction reality and demonstrate actual building conditions. The inclusion of details in this book does not imply approval or an endorsement on my part; the selected details should be viewed by the reader as a general guide to curtain wall assemblies and a basis upon which greater technical knowledge may be developed.

My drawings are the compilation of materials provided by the various architectural firms: working drawings, specifications, and the fabricator's shop drawings. The first two items, constituting the contract documents, are readily available. These are carefully stored by the architect and are accessible even years after construction on a given project is completed. The shop drawings, on the other hand, are not always available. Most often they are lost or misfiled, making an exact analysis or study of a building very difficult.

Many architects design the overall requirements of an assembly but do not specify exactly how it is to be put together. Instead they call for a *performance* submission by the contractors bidding for the job, who then provide details and design data. The material submitted, if approved, becomes the basis of the construction contract for that element of the work. The assembly or system is fabricated in accordance with the architect's technical and design requirements but remains a reflection of the technical virtuosity and experience of the contractor. Chapters 6 and 11 describe buildings constructed with this type of contract variation. The pertinent material supplied by the contractor or manufacturer is incorporated into the architect's contract documents and is therefore relatively easy to locate.

Each chapter of this book, with the exception of Chapter 1, addresses a particular type of building and system of curtain wall construction that is primarily non-load-bearing. It is not the purpose of this book to explain the whole building but to deal with the architect's integration of its structure and cladding. An example of an integrated structural cladding system can be found in Chapter 9. Photographs of the projects used as examples are included in the text. These should be studied with respect to the building's overall impact and design. The structure and cladding are explored in isometric drawings and detail sections. Included are separate diagrams of typical fascia and soffit details, floor and parapet spandrels, and roof conditions, as well as detailed horizontal and vertical section cuts through the various assemblies. When further clarification is required, large-scale detail studies are used to explain an assembly thoroughly.

This book presupposes that the reader has a basic ability to understand technical isometric drawings and architectural details in section analysis. Following is a construction example that demonstrates how this book functions. Figure 1 is an isometric drawing of a shelf angle and hung lintel assembly in a masonry cavity wall. This is not a random detail selection. It illustrates a point with respect to the design of this assembly. In spite of the fact that this detail is used repeatedly, serious problems occur when it is mishandled.

Several years ago New York City newspapers reported that segments of brick were falling to the street in lower Manhattan. Witnesses reported that bricks appeared to be shot explosively from the face of certain buildings. The structures involved were not the older load-bearing buildings but had contemporary

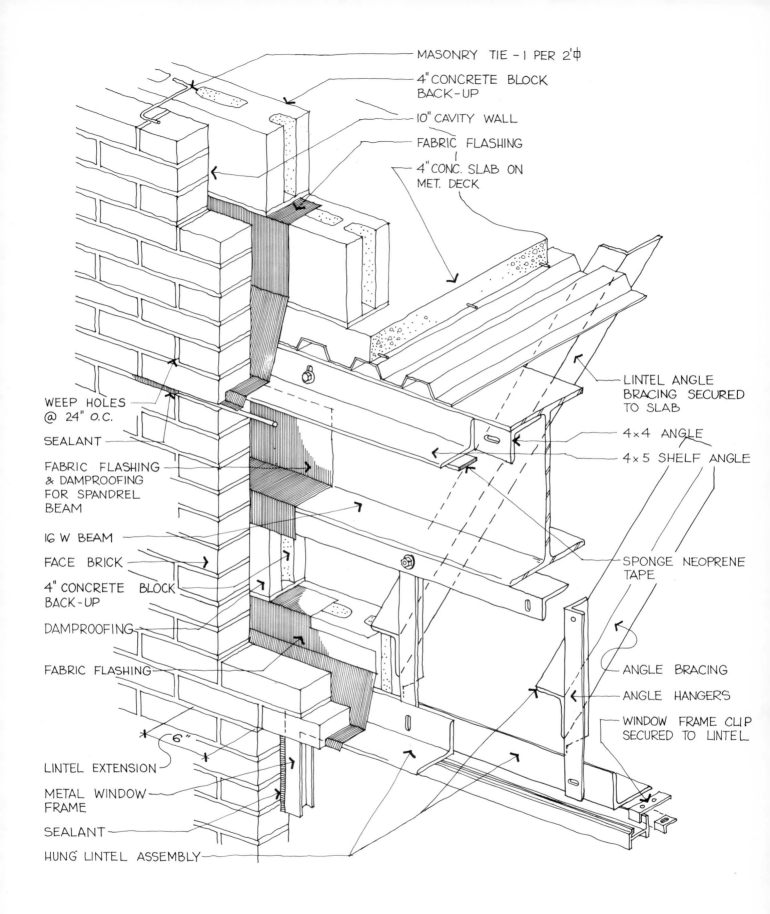

MASONRY TIE - 1 PER 2'□

4" CONCRETE BLOCK BACK-UP

10" CAVITY WALL

FABRIC FLASHING

4" CONC. SLAB ON MET. DECK

LINTEL ANGLE BRACING SECURED TO SLAB

4 x 4 ANGLE

4 x 5 SHELF ANGLE

SPONGE NEOPRENE TAPE

ANGLE BRACING

ANGLE HANGERS

WINDOW FRAME CLIP SECURED TO LINTEL

WEEP HOLES @ 24" O.C.

SEALANT

FABRIC FLASHING & DAMPROOFING FOR SPANDREL BEAM

16 W BEAM

FACE BRICK

4" CONCRETE BLOCK BACK-UP

DAMPROOFING

FABRIC FLASHING

6"

LINTEL EXTENSION

METAL WINDOW FRAME

SEALANT

HUNG LINTEL ASSEMBLY

Fig. 1   A hung lintel and relieving angle.

steel or concrete skeleton frames with masonry and glass walls. The origin of the problem became apparent after some engineering studies had been performed. It appears that the shelf angles (also called *relieving angles*) which were designed specifically to carry the exterior face brick from floor to floor were not performing as designed. The bricks installed above and below the relieving angles were mortared into place, and the joint below the angle was filled with a combination of mortar debris and sealant which, over the years, hardened. The shelf angle no longer transmitted the weight of the face brick to the spandrel beam, and the pressure of the loading moved downward until certain segments of brick finally became overstressed and failed. The bricks involved were "shot" from the face of the building in much the same way a watermelon seed can be turned into a projectile by merely squeezing the seed between the index finger and thumb.

Figure 1 illustrates a simple combination of shelf angle and hung lintel in a typical masonry curtain wall system. The 16-inch beam supports the slab, the shelf angle, and the hung lintel assembly. The exterior brick is shown seated on shelf and lintel angles. The assembly is made watertight by applying fabric flashing and sealants in the appropriate places. An enlarged view of the shelf angle is shown in Figure 2, which demonstrates the designer's solution to the problem of masonry curtain wall overloading. The critical element in this assembly is the pressure-sensitive sponge neoprene tape on the underside of the relieving angle. All other aspects of this assembly are conventional. The neoprene tape will maintain its flexibility indefinitely, and the detailer may be assured that vertical forces generated by the curtain wall face brick will be directed to the beam rather than downward. This example illustrates how important it is for the designer to be aware of a potential problem and how it may be solved.

When a simple lintel is not structurally adequate to span a wide window opening, a hung lintel is suspended from the spandrel beam and braced back to the structural slab as shown in Figure 3. The hung lintel allows the designer to develop unbroken lines of horizontal glass at a height appropriate for a hung ceiling installation. Note the fabric flashing, dampproofing, and weep holes that effectively protect the steel and the inner cavity wall from moisture buildup that might cause rust and structural failure.

This book may be studied for the sake of the illustrations alone. However, I would recommend that the photographs, isometric sketches, details, and written material be studied together and compared if the reader is to derive maximum benefit. Understanding this book and its illustrations will require concentration and will depend to a certain degree upon the reader's background. Those who make the effort should acquire not only a fuller understanding of the systems shown here but a generally enhanced ability to deal with the larger subjects of technical design and construction practices.

Herman Sands

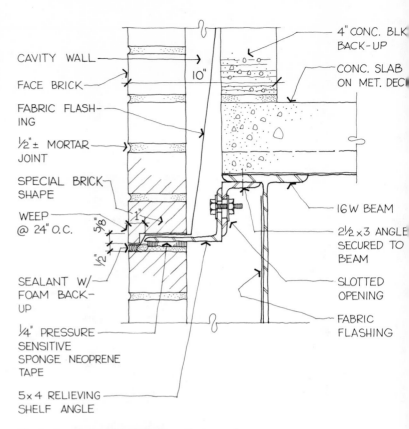

Fig. 2   A vertical section through a relieving angle.

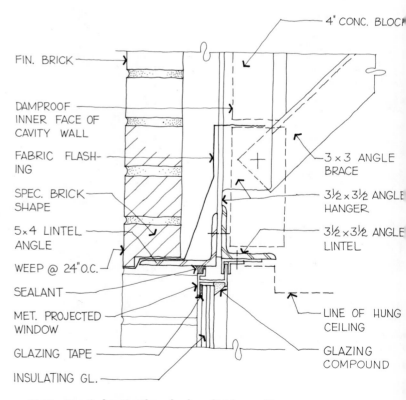

Fig. 3   A vertical section through a hung lintel assembly.

Acknowledgments

Many people have contributed information and time to the preparation of this volume, and I would like to thank them.

My wife, Phyllis Sperling, an architect, has acted as consultant and adviser on this project from its inception. I cannot imagine how this book could have been completed without her constructive criticism and encouragement.

I am grateful to President Ursula Schwerin, of the New York City Technical College of the City University of New York, whose understanding and support allowed me to take a "fellowship leave" that made the timely conclusion of this book possible.

Thanks to the staff of the McGraw-Hill Book Company, in particular, Jeremy Robinson, whose initial encouragement moved me forward on this project, Joan Zseleczky, sponsoring editor, and Olive Collen, the book's editing supervisor, whose patience and recommendations were most helpful to me.

The photographs shown in Chapters 8 and 10 were provided by the generosity of Gil Amiaga, architectural photographer.

The information contained within the separate chapters of this book was made possible by contributing architectural firms, building contractors, and the individuals within these firms who made the pertinent information available to me, sometimes at a considerable expenditure of their own time:

CHRISTOPHER SEDDON *Director, Foster Associates, Hong Kong*

PHILIP G. BONZON *Design Manager and* GENE PACE *Engineering Supervisor, Cupples Products Division of H. H. Robertson Company*

JANE COHN *Director of Communications, Haines Lundberg Waehler*

ANTHONY LOUVIS *Partner,* GEORGE REHL *Associate,* RICHARD BEAUMONT *Project Architect, Davis, Brody & Associates*

DONALD E. GROSSMAN *Vice President, Shreve Lamb & Harmon Associates, PC*

EDMUND H. H. CADDY *Partner, Raymond, Rado, Caddy & Bonnington Architects/Planners*

A. PRESTON MOORE *Associate Partner, I. M. Pei and Partners*

BRUCE THOMPSON *Mitchell/Giurgola Architects*

Herman Sands

Wall Systems

1 Introduction

The following chapters of this book deal with the technical aspects of detailing and construction assemblies and with related information that explores cladding systems in general and their relation to building structure. However, this material requires some kind of framework so that the reader may gain an enhanced understanding of its significance. In a larger sense, the drawings and details indicate where we are in relation to the building industry today and where we may be heading in the future. We are not, after all, the end of history but a point on its path.

Construction details, drawings, and the technical information contained within them are the driving force of a building project. We refer to them during all phases of construction, review them during a dispute, and fall back on them during litigation or arbitration. They collectively represent the construction wisdom—or lack thereof—that the architect brings to a project. It is this material, when accurately followed by contractors, that results in the final product. The details are no less concrete than the construction itself. They function in much the same way that genes and genetic coding relate to the development of all living things. The details and drawings control the development of a building.

Since architecture is not merely an art form but also a profession and a business—in that descending order, one hopes—economy of expression in graphic and verbal material is essential to the successful and profitable management of a project. What we draw and how we write is crucial. Shop drawings are often considered the construction alter ego of the architect's working drawings. They contain information that strongly affects the fulfillment of the details and the development of a project. The architect often views the submission of shop drawings by the contractor as a threat to the integrity of the project. The contractor, on the other hand, views the shop drawings as the practical salvation of a detail or assembly.

Legal considerations govern all actions in the construction industry. As architects, we must protect ourselves, the client, and even the contractor. Misunderstandings that lead to litigation, and errors that result in negligence, must be avoided at all costs.

The following material represents the author's desire to present a philosophical and historical framework for the many buildings, details, and construction assemblies included in this book. The ten building examples described here reflect high standards of design. They are honest, handsome in the main, and spectacular in several instances. They were chosen because they present an overview of major cladding systems and their relation to building structure. They are also representative of the modern architectural movement that forms a strong link with the past and points positively to the potential of our future.

A HISTORICAL PERSPECTIVE

The way we see ourselves and who we really are is an absorbing philosophical subject that engages our interest over a broad range of concerns, such as economics, politics, and sociology, and that should be extended to architecture and the way it is practiced today. Do our aesthetic ideals jibe with reality? And, for that matter, what *are* our ideals? Do we practice contemporary architecture by virtue of the fact that we live in the present? Or is there some discipline that we subscribe to as professionals that binds us to the goals of society and the "general good"? Do our architectural designs originate from a point at which technology, planning, and aesthetics coalesce? Or do we operate out of personal whimsy, picking and choosing from various design menus that may be stylish at this time?

The education of construction professionals generally reflects meager requirements for courses in aesthetics and history. This lack of background tends to leave us unable to discern the interaction between the past, current technology, and design in general. We may sense that we are the inheritors of a historical tradition, but we may lack the wherewithal to interpret that tradition.

On the one hand, contemporary architecture seems to have failed to provide the emotional element that we want and need, and we therefore search for a new vernacular—one that invariably (and ironically) returns to an imagined past. (A broken pediment on the entry to a classical building or the top of a piece of Georgian furniture is visually pleasing, but the use of such decorative elements as motifs on high-rise structures is inappropriate, to say the least.)

On the other hand, under the influence of contemporary industrial design and manufacture, we have come to assume that the quintessential product is one that not only functions well but *looks* as if it should function well. Thus our aerodynamically styled automobiles travel no faster than traffic laws allow. Redundant styling, in both industry and architecture, very often follows the dictates of fashion, rather than of logic. Because fashion makes money and logic is less ''marketable,'' it is easy to understand the lapse of discipline.

It is easy, too, to understand the conflict evident in architecture today: our heritage versus technological developments that continue to revolutionize construction methods and materials.

The late nineteenth century saw the demise of the Chicago school and, then, the rise of unfettered eclecticism in our architecture. Skyscrapers raised everything—from French châteaux to Egyptian pyramids, with a host of attendant decorative gimcracks—thirty to forty stories above the street. Moldings, pilasters, and pediments were pasted all over the scene in order to ensure ''design consistency'' (if not aesthetic honesty).

This eclecticism peaked during the time between the two world wars. It was buttressed by an impressive technology that seemed to have no practical limitations. For example, the curtain wall of the past, whether it reflected the Chicago school or was extracted from the Beaux Arts, was composed of a masonry facing material with a brick backup wall and an interior plaster finish. Windows were set into these walls, with overhead iron lintels supporting the limited weight of the masonry. Ornamentation took the form of cast terra-cotta moldings; for instance, the Chicago school used floral and geometric motifs. Neorenaissance decorative elements, however, were composed of Greek waves, eggs and darts, triglyphs and metopes, dentils, attached pilasters in the classical orders, and a host of triangular and arched pediments over windows and doors. The Romans may have won their last great victory fifteen centuries after their fall.

The early-twentieth-century curtain wall was made possible by the development of a skeleton frame composed of steel girders and columns fabricated originally of plates and refined by the rolling process into the shapes we are familiar with today.

About the same time—the period between the two wars—the Bauhaus arose. The movement was instrumental in illuminating a trail to more effective production based upon well-designed products that were industrially practical. This approach had great appeal for architects who saw a continuum of society, industry, and design. The beginning of World War II saw such influential teachers and architects as Walter Gropius, Mies van der Rohe, and Marcel Breuer arrive in the United States and exercise enormous influence over the development of the design movement that followed the war. We turned our backs on the past and marched into what we conceived of as being a ''brave new world.'' The past, however, has a persistence that is both powerful and demanding and, should we choose to explore it, a utility that can be applied to the present.

In the early decades of the twentieth century, marvels of technology—structural steel, large sheets of glass, elevators, electric motors, and generators for light and power—beckoned invitingly to the future. In the transportation industry the past exercised only a minor influence on the design of steam locomotives, ocean liners, airplanes, and dirigibles; the imperatives of technology were generally recognized and accommodated. However, building construction, anchored as it was to the past, did not adapt to, and grow with, the new technology, except in the hands of certain architects and designers in the United States and abroad. It became clear early on that *any* style of architecture could be incorporated into the contemporary technological idiom. Architecture became a kind of eclectic stage set where the history of previous human technological triumphs could be paraded literally over the heads of the masses unhindered by the traditions, social constraints, and technology that had existed in the past. Today we are in a position to do exactly the same as was done earlier this century. Precast concrete, stamped metal panels, vacuum-formed plastics, and other lightweight materials provided by powerful industries driven by little more than market values can and do provide virtually any shape or finish for a material. Industrial processes permit the manufacture of materials that, visually, may run the design gamut from neoclassical to ''fractured modern.'' We can literally hang anything from our structures and get away with it—technically, if not morally.

Curtain wall technology as developed after World War II relies upon a combination of opaque and clear glass panels held in place by vertical and horizontal metal extrusions that bridge the distance between floor slabs and spandrel assemblies. These linear elements actually form the secondary structure that reinforces the panel skin of the cladding. Since the adoption of this technology, purists among us have explored ways to simplify the relation of skin and structure. Glass technology has obliged us with the development of tough new glass and glazing assemblies using high-strength adhesives and composite glass products. Chapters 2 and 4 deal with buildings in which this new technology has been explored. Glass itself can now be used to span and enclose the interiors of buildings.

It appears that we should now be able to dip into the past and exercise our affection for historical styles more effectively. But what part of history should we tap for contemporary reinterpretation? Should we throw all the styles together as in a Victorian potpourri, or should we focus on a phase of the past that is particularly seductive for us? We might, like Antonio Gaudí, choose to bring the gothic age to a further degree of fulfillment. We could reawaken the ogive, the lancet window, the flying buttress, and so forth. But what would we accomplish by this kind of exercise? It could be done, but our technology would have to go through contortions to satisfy such demands.

For example, the Cathedral of St. John the Divine in New York City has embarked upon a construction program for the completion of its west wall towers. An English stonemason familiar with gothic detailing was invited to the United States to train a group of apprentice stonecutters and stonemasons to work on the project. Our own labor pool was apparently unable to supply the required talent and expertise.

A knowledge of history is certainly invaluable; it educates us with respect to the life cycle of a style or school of design. But the fact that the technology exists to reproduce a historical style does not mean that this is how our technology should be used.

Architectural design development requires the existence of a technology of sufficient force to drive the movement's concepts forward. The beginnings of a new architecture are, paradoxically, hesitant and revolutionary at the same time. The skill and assurance gained in the past serve to buttress innovative efforts in much the same way that Romanesque architecture served as a midwife to the birth of the gothic age. The successful design movement progresses next into a mature stage of development in which rough edges are polished and strength becomes beauty. The later stages are very often associated with decay and a weakening vitality of, and lessening of commitment to, the style. We seem to have attempted to abort the development of our own contemporary architectural movement, a school of thought that has not even had an adequate chance to mature. We appear to be willing to enter the rococo age of another time frame and to decay there rather than to explore the vitality of the present, with its powerful technology and industrial base.

ECONOMY OF EXPRESSION

Economy of expression is a vital concern for architects, given the complexity of our industry and the specter of computer-aided design and drafting (CADD) looming before us. In many areas of our industry, CADD has already become a reality that must be dealt with. Logic and incisiveness are qualities required for the successful use of computers in architecture, but these virtues are not limited to the use of computers. Even if we do not use CADD in the office, we should use more logical thought as we develop details, drawings, and specifications and coordinate these aspects of our work.

In order to understand the technical underpinning of the profession, we must differentiate between words and pictures. We deal in these two major languages even though one is a semantic conveyance and the other is an abstraction of a three-dimensional quantity. Working drawings are generally explanatory diagrams that represent the design realization of the architect translated into two dimensions. These diagrams come to us in the form of plans, elevations, details, and sections. All drawings require accompanying text for the sake of clarity and understanding. We therefore combine words with pictures, and it is imperative that we understand the importance of brevity in the use of those words. The verbal part of the architect's professional language includes the development of specifications. The specs have no pictures, and the words must be carefully chosen for understanding and legal import.

When we label an object in a working drawing, we want that label to be as comprehensive and direct as possible. It might look nice to have extensive notes on a drawing, but not when they are going to confuse the contractor or possibly provoke a lawsuit that will damage the reputation of the architect. For example, when we label a piece of aluminum trim on a window or a storefront, we might say that it is metal or aluminum and indicate its use on the drawing if it is not self-evident. We would not note its finish, alloy, or color or dwell extensively on tests, schedules, or shop drawings. These considerations are always addressed more appropriately in the text of the specifications. If there is a conflict over interpretation of the text in the drawings and specifications, the text in the specifications will always take legal precedence. Moreover, drawings that are as simple and direct as possible are easier to understand. But by all means let that picture mean a thousand words.

Writing the specifications, on the other hand, is not necessarily a creative activity. Most governmental projects require that we follow a standard format such as the one developed by the Construction Specifications Institute (CSI) and adopted by the American Institute of Architects (AIA) and *Sweet's Catalogue for Material Listing*. Economy of expression is required in specifications as well as in drawings. We are expected to describe the scope of the work and the way a given material is to be applied, or an assembly used, on a job. Next, we include a list of general requirements, samples to be submitted, schedules, shop drawings, and various other requirements of the project. This process is repeated until all major materials and assemblies are explained in writing. It is clear that a great deal of written material on a drawing would be redundant.

There are specification variations that provide different types of information. Instead of prescribing a specific material or method, the specifier may wish to rely on the expertise of the manufacturer or subcontractor for the selection of a material or a method of installation. The "performance" of the assembly is of paramount concern for the specifier, who writes the specifications so that only the final results are called for, and the contractor is then responsible for making the system work. The architect cannot shed legal responsibility during this procedure, and the resultant submission by the manufacturer or "sub" should be checked by the architect and consulting engineers for conformance to technical standards and safety requirements. Specs and drawings have clear and separate areas of concern, and it requires a sense of professional discipline to maintain the optimum performance of each of these components of the contract document. The Gilbane Building in New Haven, Connecticut, and the Tower Building in Philadelphia, Pennsylvania, described in Chapters 6 and 11, respectively, are examples of buildings in which the architects requested that the subcontractor provide "performance specifications" for certain major building assemblies.

Working drawings should be given a clear and consistent format, and uniform guidelines for the progress of the job should be provided. The fact that *every* material used in a project is carefully described in the specifications means that all notes or labels used in the drawings must be incisive. In a sense the parts of an assembly should be "tagged" so that they are identified and their relation to adjacent construction clearly delineated. To this end we use abbreviations in order to speed the drafting process. It is important to standardize the abbreviations so that there is no question about the meaning of the drawings; abbreviations used in specifications should be treated the same way. Texture or graphic material designations are visual explanatory tools that should be used for identification or to enhance the readability of the drawings. The embellishment of a detail or a drawing for aesthetic reasons is redundant. Texture is a form of labeling that should be used uniformly and sparingly in order to highlight the information transmitted on the drawings. The AIA has developed guidelines for the use of abbreviations and material designations or texture; these guidelines should be followed.

Individual expression is a principle that is precious to me in general—but not in the drafting room. We should attempt to avoid individual peculiarities that confuse the person who ultimately uses the drawings. Lettering style is valid only when it can be easily read, it is important to standardize symbols and the graphic presentation so that the rules are clear to all participants in the development of the contract document. It is frustrating and counterproductive to stumble over someone's individual lettering style. An office with which I was formerly associated once issued a set of contract drawings that included plans and details for a school playground. The basketball backboard was positioned on the basis of an incorrect dimension because the drafter confused the contractor with poor

lettering. The foundation for the backboard post and the installation of the post proceeded on the basis of this error, and the problem was not discovered until the paving was installed and the court lines were drawn. This problem could have been avoided if everyone in the office had used a consistent lettering style.

FREEHAND DETAILING

Conventional wisdom has it that the principal of a firm is ranked highest on the status rungs of an office, but for those of us who have been there, the acknowledged monarch of the drafting room is the detailer. It is the detailer who ultimately shapes the form of the final product—the building itself. The traditional procedure for detailing a design follows a rather tortuous trail from the designer to the project architect and back again for modifications and finally to the job captain or production chief, who then assigns the development of the details to one of the reigning nobility free to handle the project. The designer understands, in this process, that he or she must coordinate the work in order to maintain control over the final appearance of the project. If the schedule allows, the designer will attempt to do precisely this; if, on the other hand, the designer is involved with other projects, the realization of the design will fall into the hands of a detailer, who more often than not is a senior drafter who has earned the employer's trust and can be counted upon to implement office standards wherever possible. This system sometimes does not produce the results expected by the designers or the firm's principals, and the work is fine-tuned until it satisfies the parties involved or is cleared to proceed by default. The single most problematic area in the development of working drawings is usually quality control of coordination of design and final detailing.

Ideally, design detailing should be viewed as a continuum that begins with the preliminary phases of a project and ends only after construction has been completed. The compartmentalization of disciplines should not be permitted to interrupt the orderly development of ideas when the architect deals with a project in the office and at the job site. Moreover, there should be no second or third string of quality for detailing a building. If it is important to have a consistent aesthetic statement for a project, that requirement should be applied throughout the building by a person who is knowledgeable and experienced with its design and technical requirements.

A method of ensuring the consistent development of details can be found by examining one way in which freehand detailing can be used in the development of working drawings. Here the designer can and should lead the team in solving problems of systems development and assembly refinement. In the system that is usually used, the designer develops a series of tentative vertical and horizontal wall sections that are part of the preliminary design phase. These are generally turned over to the production department of an office or are used by the project team to develop the details for the contract documents. The sketches are generally freehand and for the sake of clarity are redrawn on standard office sheets for reproduction and issue. The inefficiency of the system becomes apparent when the designer must sit down with the drafter and explain the system thoroughly and must be available for periodic consultation and review of the material being developed.

A more efficient method is simply to reproduce the designer's freehand sketches. Freehand detail sketches that are reduced during reproduction are crisp, and the softness of line evident in the original is replaced with what appears to be hard-line copy that is quite readable and presentable. Original freehand sketches are usually drawn at 3 inches = 1 foot and then reduced by one-half. Lettering on the original sketch is drawn twice the size required so that it will appear to be of normal size when reduced. The reduced sketches are then mounted on a standard-sized board and photographed in order to generate a reproducible transparency. When the tape marks are eradicated, it is very difficult to spot the difference between a freehand working drawing generated by the designer and its equivalent hard-line copy generated by the drafter under the supervision of the designer. However, there is an enormous change in emphasis. The project designer is assured of ongoing continuity during the transition to the working drawing phase. Since only the designer is generating this information, it is possible for the designer to have complete control over its coordination and development. The majority of details and sections shown in this book were developed by the author using a freehand line technique and can be studied as examples of this type of drawing. The designer, it is true, is required to work a little more neatly than he or she might care to, but the advantages of this system are enormous and avoid the invariable misunderstandings that develop when the drafter translates the designer's work into hard-line drawings. The cost of the photocopies and required retouching are negligible in comparison with the time saved during refinement and detail development.

SHOP DRAWINGS

Shop drawings are called for by the architect during the construction management phase of a project. Specific subcontractors are required to submit drawings based upon their interpretation of the contract material provided by the architect. The architect and the engineer often make general reference to certain assemblies that can be clarified by the responsible subcontractor (elevators, kitchen equipment, hardware, and so forth). Sometimes several methods of executing a specific detail are acceptable to the architect. In short, the subcontractor redraws the assembly that his or her firm is responsible for and submits it to the architect for approval, modification, or rejection. The architect generally requires this type of clarification for assemblies such as structure, architectural metal, windows, cabinetwork, ductwork, and miscellaneous iron.

The submission of shop drawings provides a valuable tool with which the architect can review the intent of the contractor with respect to certain key areas of construction. It allows the architect to check the coordination of these areas with adjacent construction and systems. Shop drawings at best are cumbersome and introduce a host of problems with respect to responsibility and control. In principle, the architect's review of the shop drawings results in only conditional approval or rejection. This should not make the architect liable for the future commission of errors by the contractor of the assembly in question. Nor should it relieve the contractor of responsibility for the workmanship of the installation.

In fact, the architect may have considerably more responsibilty for the review than bargained for. As a member of the American Arbitration Association, I have attended seminars and participated in discussions that explored ways of minimizing the architect's exposure to liability during construction. One problem area that seemed to surface consistently was the architect's treatment of shop drawings. A very simple word like "approved" takes on a host of frightening semantic possibilities. What has the architect approved? Is the approval qualified? Or are errors that the contractor introduced into the submission construed to be part of this approval? It became apparent to the profession that "approved" was a treacherous word that required modification in order to protect the user. "Approved for design only" has now replaced "approved" on almost all rubber stamps used in offices today, but the problem persists. Even "rejected", a normally nondebatable word, can provoke litigation, and the interpretations of "approved as noted" have become positively convoluted.

The current structure of the architectural profession developed during the nineteeth century, when architects were "gentlemen" and inflation was almost nonexistent. The profession, the trades, and the construction process proceeded in a leisurely manner, and much of our current system reflects the pace of this earlier time. Unfortunately, today's demands are forcing a reevaluation of our procedures and priorities. The 1970s were years during which the United States sustained double-digit inflation that was responsible for building costs much higher than initial estimates. In many cases the year or two it took to actually construct a building were directly responsible for an alarming cost escalation. New contract forms have been established that are designed to streamline the process of building and minimize the delays during design and construction in order to avoid inflated material costs and compounded union wage demands.

Several building examples included in this book suggest different ways of enfranchising the contractor to perform a more integral function in the development and refinement of assemblies for construction. Chapters 2, 6, and 11 deal with buildings that were designed and built with a high degree of contractor involvement. In these instances the contractor submitted a proposal against performance and design requirements. The curtain wall assemblies in these three buildings were extremely complex and required pragmatic expertise that the architects believed was more appropriately a function of the subcontractors' experience. The contractors who were finally selected for these projects developed their own proposals against the architects' designs and performance specifications. The contractors were selected on the basis of experience, cost, and reputation, and their proposals were subject to architectural and engineering review. It is not uncommon for an architect to feel unqualified to act as an expert on a specific system or method of construction and to believe with some degree of assurance that the producer of a product who is a specialist will be able to fabricate an assembly successfully. In the building examples cited, this procedure resulted in a saving of time for owners, architects, and contractors. It avoided the problems that might have developed if the architects had used more traditional forms of contract development that required an expertise that was simply not there and a costly, time-consuming process of shop drawing submissions and review.

Another method of streamlining the development of contract documents is "fast tracking", a team effort in which the architect and the builder enter into a contract with the owner in order to provide a full range of professional services geared to carrying out the construction process as quickly as possible. For example, the architect, after having designed the project in consultation with the contractor who is providing technical background and cost-control information, embarks on working drawings for the building foundation. The contractor does not have to wait for the entire set of drawings to be completed but is able to start work immediately on excavation and foundation construction. While this is going on, the structure is designed and fabricated, ready for assembly. Other materials are ordered, and the subcontractors are prepared to begin their work when required by the contract or *critical path* analysis for the project. A host of other assemblies can be fabricated as the architect develops the balance of the drawings and specifications. It is evident that this type of procedure requires the closest degree of cooperation and professionalism on the part of all concerned.

The Hong Kong and Shanghai Bank Building discussed in Chapter 2 is an example of this type of construction approach. It is an extremely complex project that was completed in record time as a result of fast tracking. This type of construction is becoming extremely popular, and many additional examples are now being built or have been completed.

LEGAL AND PRACTICAL CONSIDERATIONS

Architects find themselves in a curious position during their careers. They are expected to execute their multiple responsibilities in accordance with the highest professional standards. This is not an ideal put forward for the purpose of general discussion but a fact that requires some attention. If architects do not perform well professionally, the outcome of their lack of

expertise, whether it is due to ignorance or misjudgment, can be painful at best and downright disastrous at worst. Living under the shadow of unlimited liability without a statute of limitations may be the closest an architect comes to purgatory while still alive. The state of New York, for instance, does not have a time limit for professional liability, and an architect's estate may be held liable for damages resulting from legal action.

An architect, whether principal, associate, or employee, must be a *defensive practitioner* and must behave as if every move taken on a project will be subject to legal scrutiny and possible litigation. Not being expert in all areas of our industry is certainly not a mortal sin, especially since expert advice may be obtained from professional consultants. For example, cost estimating is very often called for by an owner as part of a contract with an architect. It is not uncommon to find a requirement that the architect's initial cost estimate and the final bid be no more than 10 percent apart. Many governmental projects require no more than a 5 percent discrepancy between the architect's estimates and the final bid. If the construction bids are in excess of the amounts specified in the architect's contract, the architect will probably have to redesign the project at his or her own expense in order to conform to the original estimates. Reflect for a moment that even before being deeply involved with a project, the architect must begin to submit accurate cost estimates that may establish liability in the future. Retaining a cost consultant at the earliest stages of contract preparation becomes imperative under these circumstances.

The development of an architectural assignment is very much like running a long obstacle course with hurdles to jump, pits to cross, walls to climb. You may believe that you have finished the course successfully only to find that you are disqualified because you missed some of the obstacles. Instead of attempting to perform single-handedly in areas in which you have not established competence, it is much better to view the endeavor as a team effort. Sometimes misplaced self-confidence causes problems. One of my earliest assignments in practice was a penthouse renovation that required new steel framing. My firm used a consultant engineer for this purpose, and all the steel was designed in one piece with the expectation that the material would be hoisted into place. The contractor, on the other hand, requested that the steel be cut and reconnected after transport from the street to the upper floor in the building elevator. We agreed with the general contractor because city approval would be time-consuming, and for such a small amount of steel hoisting, the process would be expensive. The contractor submitted shop drawings, which I reviewed and approved. The detail of the steel cut and reconnection appeared sound, and I assumed that the beams would be cut at the third points so as not to overstress their midpoint loading. I approved the shop drawings without checking with the engineer, and the project proceeded. Several weeks later I received an emergency call from the contractor saying that one main beam had deflected excessively and was failing. I requested that he immediately shore the area and do nothing more to load the structure until I could get there with the engineer. Upon inspection, I saw to my dismay that my earlier assumption had been false; the beam had been cut at the midpoint. The contractor was also shaken. Fortunately the engineer had a solution that allowed us to salvage the installation. The contractor was so pleased that he acknowledged that the structural working drawings might have been confusing and agreed to make the change with little or no additional cost. The engineer leaned toward me and whispered, "If you want to fly solo, first learn how to fly." I was much more careful in the future and learned that caution is not necessarily a reactionary trait.

There is no shortage of problems that people can create for themselves. However, architects have much more to consider than their own concerns with respect to the way they perform professionally. Their clients, staff, and consultants expect them to lead effectively and make measured judgments for the progress and benefit of a job. Research, consultation, and an open mind can pave the way to orderly project development. Don't assume anything, and try not to make mistakes in the beginning of a project that will haunt you at its conclusion. If you have a constitutional inability to read fine print, buy a magnifying glass. Zoning, building codes, costs, engineering, and specifications demand expertise; be prepared to learn the required skills or obtain them professionally. It is not possible to avoid mistakes, but we must all learn how to minimize them.

Design detailing requires experience and research into systems and materials. You will find that the examples presented in this book are the product of extensive effort by the architects who designed the buildings and the contractors who built them. In these structures, as in the development of any system or detail, there is a hierarchy of concerns, with safety standing at the top of the list. Inasmuch as an architect may make a contractor legally responsible for the correctness of an assembly, the safety of that construction falls squarely on the shoulders of the architect (or architect-engineer). If the system fails, the architect will be held liable for civil and possibly criminal charges. A study of the Kansas City disaster of July 19, 1981, indicated that the engineers for the structure were responsible for the collapse of the suspended walkways. The elegant suspension system for the interior pedestrian bridges was unfortunately totally inadequate, and major loss of life resulted from its collapse. Structural and architectural detailing of a building design must be viewed as a total discipline that reflects aesthetics and, no less importantly, sound engineering and building know-how. Of all criteria, developing safety must rank highest in the agenda of the architect.

Close on the heels of this consideration is the structural integrity of a system, which must be viewed as worthy of careful research and product development. It is in this area that the architect and the contractor may be able to make the most significant contribution to a project. Regardless of who on this team makes the system work, it remains the responsibility of the architect to see that it is done. Leaks, creaks, and cracks are the bane of architecture. Although they may not be evident initially, flaws in the design and defects in the construction make an otherwise good building age into a potential wreck that can do nothing for the reputation of its designers or builders. A building must remain watertight, stable, and free of recurrent problems that are the afterbirth of sloppy design. A client who is being dripped upon can be assuredly disposed to withhold references and may even pursue the responsible parties legally.

After all the preceding exhortations toward caution, I should point out that there is a joy attached to the process of design and detailing that can be totally self-satisfying. In many ways the development of a building is like the growth of a child. It is conceived in creative joy and must be protected and nurtured during the process of development. Its initial steps are tentative, but it develops and grows until it takes on an identity of its own.

I have enjoyed the preparation of this book enormously and have learned through it to appreciate some of the really fine planning that went into the development of the buildings shown as examples. Analyzing the interaction of the cladding system and structure of the buildings in isometric sketches and section studies allowed me to gain an insight that I would like to share with the reader respecting some of the motivating factors that the building designers and contractors had to deal with in order to make these projects successful.

2 The Hong Kong and Shanghai Bank Building

Hong Kong   ARCHITECTS: Foster Associates Hong Kong; Ove Arup and Partners

Fig. 1   Model representing the Hong Kong and Shanghai Bank Building as it might be seen from Kowloon across the harbor.

State of the art is an expression that is bandied about all too frequently. We hear it in discussions about cars, computers, medicine, and building products. It is unusual and exciting when one encounters it in an entire building such as the Hong Kong and Shanghai Bank Building designed by Foster Associates Hong Kong and Ove Arup and Partners, structural engineers.

This project would be considered extraordinary if one considered only its technical innovations. When seen as a totality, the building becomes a lyric design statement, a direct heir of the modern architectural movement. Figure 1 is a view of of an excellent model that represents the building as it might be seen from across the harbor in Kowloon. It is, incidentally, this model that has been on display in various museums throughout the United States. The tower is forty-six stories high with four subcellars and rises to a height of 590 feet. A close examination of its structural and cladding system reveals a design both logical and brilliant in its conception. Eight structural masts support the trusses from which the floors and service modules are suspended. Two rows of masts running in a north-south orientation are apparent in Figure 1. One can see the articulated tensile and compressive elements of the structure in this view. The building is divided into several vertical office zones, each four to seven stories high. Each floor is supported by the masts and vertical steel hangers suspended from the truss elements above. This structural system allows for office space that is unencumbered by columns and other structural elements. The service elements, such as mechanical equipment, elevators, stairs, and toilets, were delivered to the site as prefabricated modules manufactured by various firms throughout the world. For example, the service modules containing the lavatories were imported from Japan and lifted by crane into slots provided for them adjacent to the structural masts, thus accelerating the rate of construction of this project.

Norman Foster likened the spatial organization of this building to a series of vertical "villages" separated by two-story staging areas that are reached by high-speed express elevators from the street-level lobby. The local building codes require areas of refuge, accessible to the outdoors, in case of fire. These staging areas have been planned as landscaped terraces and are used for nonoffice functions such as public circulation, dining, and conferences. The trusses that

Fig. 2 Architect's model showing the masts, service cores, and glass-lined stair towers.

carry the suspended office zones below are visually expressed at these levels and form a powerful backdrop to the activities taking place there. Vertical circulation between the various levels of each "village" is achieved through the use of escalators.

Figure 2 is a view of the architect's model showing the masts, service cores, and glass-lined stair towers. Note the cross bracing apparent in this elevation, as it is typical and reinforces the building masts against strong winds and other lateral movement. As one moves closer to the building, another important aspect of the design becomes apparent, namely, the cladding system. The structural elements both inside and outside the building as well as the exterior walls are covered with aluminum and/or tempered glass vision panels. This aluminum-and-glass system was designed to withstand the very severe typhoon forces generated in this area of the world.

The contractor chosen to develop the cladding system of the structure and walls was Cupples Products Division, part of the H. H. Robertson Company, located in St. Louis, Missouri. This company also developed the Tower Building cladding system for Mitchell/Giurgola Architects that is described in Chapter 11. The Hong Kong and Shanghai Bank Building, scheduled for completion in 1985, is being constructed using the fast-track system (i.e., the building is being constructed as the working drawings are completed).

In order to facilitate the production of the more than 1 million square feet of cladding required by this project, Cupples Products was required to begin fabrication as soon as possible. A team led by Philip Bonzon, design manager for Cupples Products, was dispatched to Foster Associates' main office in London in order to confer on the design and detailing of the cladding system. Thousands of freehand sketches were executed by the architects and the manufacturer before they arrived at a final approach. After several weeks of brainstorming, the team fixed the design of the cladding system as a contractual item, and the Cupples Products team returned to the United States to develop shop drawings and production models and to test the system for structural integrity and weathertightness. The following is a small sampling of visual material that illustrates the enormous energy expended in this endeavor. Figure 3 is a preliminary drawing analyzing a corner of the supporting mast and column. Shown here are the shape and size of the cladding elements with respect to the slab to slab height of 3.9 meters (12

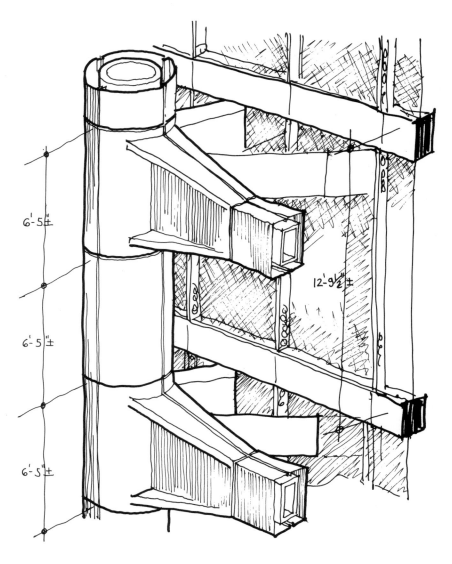

Fig. 3   Preliminary drawing analyzing a corner of the supporting mast and column.

feet 8 inches). Figure 4 is a horizontal section through the column portion of the mast and indicates the structural differences between the columns of the lower and the upper floors. Also shown here is a plan view of the integral catwalks and sunshades. An enlarged section view of the mullion is shown in Figure 5, and the interaction of a column cover panel and the structure is developed in Figure 6. These elements will be discussed again in further detail. It is important to understand how closely interwoven the activities of the architect and contractor were with respect to achieving a successful curtain wall and cladding system for the structure.

A basic module of 1200 millimeters (approximately 4 feet) was used throughout the building. It was decided that all structural connections were to take place through the glass, 600 millimeters (about 2 feet) off the module, in order to avoid a conflict between the primary structure and the cladding elements. A clearance of 150 millimeters (approximately 6 inches) was established as the interval between various structural members, such as the mast and the horizontal diagonal bracing, and their respective cladding elements. These decisions allowed the fabrication of the cladding system to proceed with the assurance that the skin and the structure of the building would be easily joined. The manufacturer used additional production equipment that was put on line in order to develop the very complex components called for by the project. Robotic welding and computer-controlled milling devices figured prominently in the development of the supplier's production system for this project.

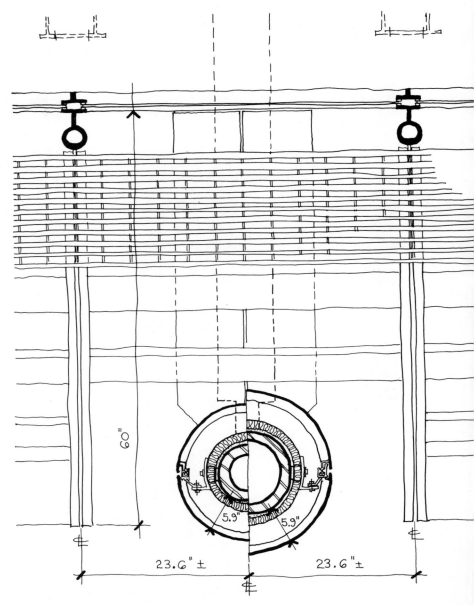

Fig. 4 Horizontal section through column portion of the mast showing structural differences between the columns of the lower and upper floors.

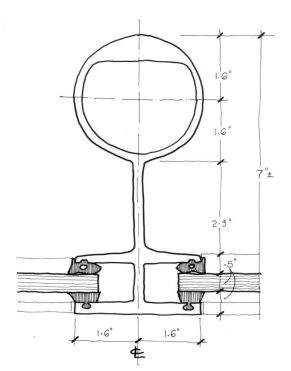

Fig. 5   Enlarged section view of the mullion.

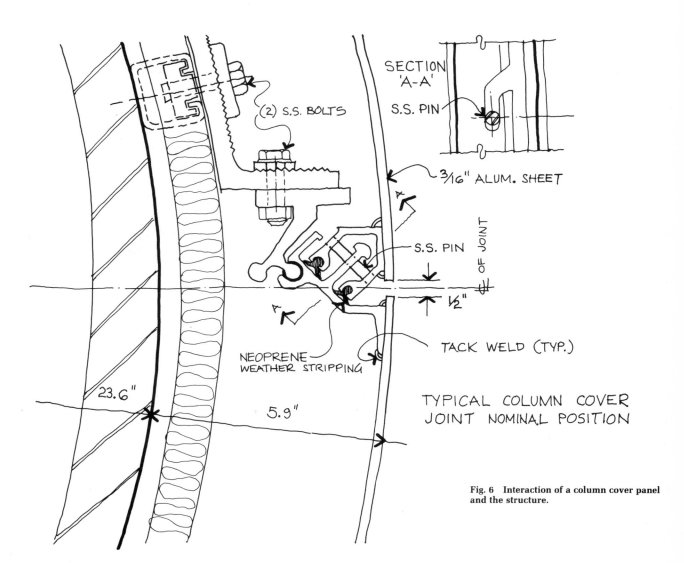

(2) S.S. BOLTS

SECTION 'A-A'

S.S. PIN

3/16" ALUM. SHEET

S.S. PIN

₵ OF JOINT

½"

TACK WELD (TYP.)

NEOPRENE WEATHER STRIPPING

23.6"

5.9"

TYPICAL COLUMN COVER JOINT NOMINAL POSITION

Fig. 6   Interaction of a column cover panel and the structure.

Figure 7 is a view of a one-story mock-up that was exhibited at the Royal Academy of Art in London. This close-up shows the exceptional quality of craftsmanship achieved as evidenced by the uniform smoothness of finish, the precision of the assembly, and the plumb alignment of the fluoropolymer-coated aluminum panels to each other, the curtain wall, and the sun louvers. Also apparent is the full-access raised aluminum floor shown on the lower left of the photograph.

A full-scale three-story mock-up of the cladding system was constructed in the Cupples Products plant in St. Louis in order to test the system for watertightness and to develop methods of fabrication for the components. The mock-up was statically and dynamically tested for water penetration and used extensively to troubleshoot the cladding system. The photographs in this chapter that show the fabrication of this system are derived from actual experience with the mock-up. The modules were erected and disassembled several times, and construction supervisors from Hong Kong were trained so that they could teach other workers the construction methods that would be used for the fabrication of the actual building. The mock-up was shipped to Hong Kong for further training exercises when the contractor exhausted all the tests used to analyze the performance of the system.

Since severe typhoons are not uncommon in Hong Kong, the structure and the cladding of the tower were subjected to rigorous testing and quality-control procedures. The tower's almost revolutionary suspension system was designed to accommodate building movement, but this aspect of the structure presented significant waterproofing problems. Cupples Products, having already developed a system called *pressure equalization (PE)* for the World Trade Center Towers and the Sears Tower, had a good deal of experience with this matter. According to the manufacturer:

Three conditions must exist simultaneously before water penetrates a wall system: 1. An opening 2. Water at the opening 3. Force to drive the water through the opening. If you can eliminate one of these elements, you can eliminate water leakage. Since water cannot be eliminated from the exterior, and it is not practical to assume that an opening will never exist, the pressure differential between the glazing pocket and the exterior must be eliminated. Once this happens, there will be no longer a force to carry water through any opening.

Pressure equalization is achieved by the use of a series of baffled openings in the cladding that allow wind to penetrate the system through special gaskets that permit the flow of air but prevent the passage of water. The wind that passes through the gaskets and baffled openings equalizes the pressure differential between the interior of the curtain wall and the outside. All components were tested for a static design

Fig. 7 A one-story mock-up.

load that was equivalent to wind speeds in excess of 245 miles per hour. The dynamic water-penetration test was performed using an 1800-horsepower Navy carrier plane that threw water at the facade at a rate equivalent to an 8-inch-per-hour rainfall. The duration of the tests generally was for periods of eight hours under continuous observation. The system passed all its tests.

The management of the bank requested that this structure "be the finest building ever built by mankind." It is apparent from an exhaustive analysis of the curtain wall and cladding system that this building indeed encompasses some extraordinary design concepts and original technological

developments. Figure 8 is an isometric sketch of a typical wall section. Shown here are all the basic components that make up this sophisticated assembly and the relation of the assembly to the structure. The sunshades and the integral catwalk used for window cleaning are conspicuous elements that take their form from a carefully analyzed requirement for shading and building maintenance. What is not clearly evident is the rationale for the angles of the sunshade louvers, each of which is set at a slightly different angle. Beyond practical considerations, the configuration of the sunshades was the result of a request by the director of the bank that he be able to look

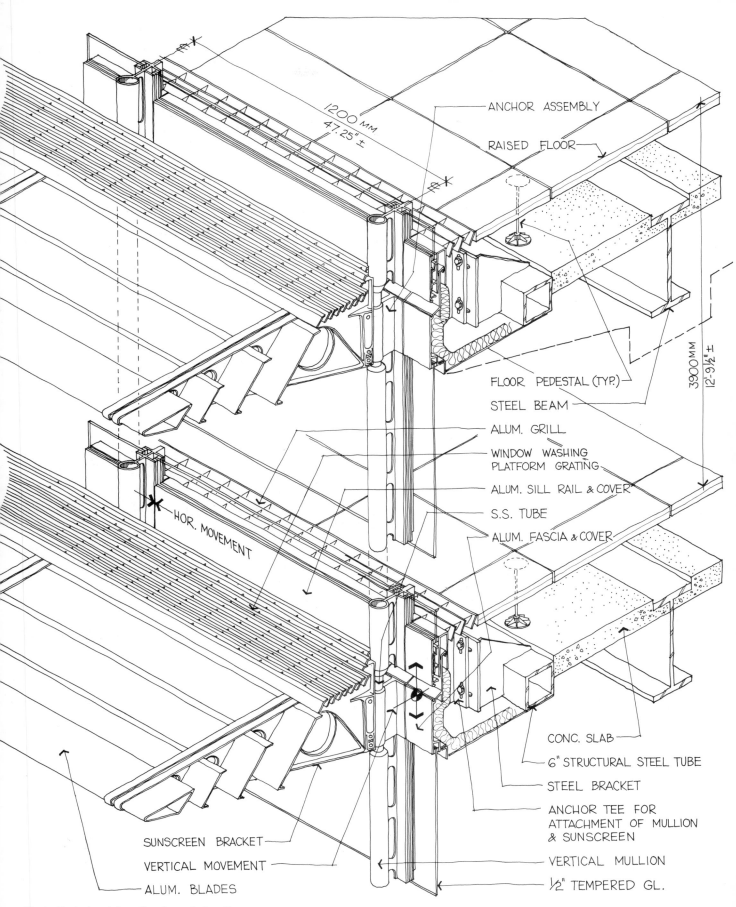

ANCHOR ASSEMBLY

RAISED FLOOR

1200 MM
47.25" ±

FLOOR PEDESTAL (TYP.)

STEEL BEAM

ALUM. GRILL

WINDOW WASHING
PLATFORM GRATING

ALUM. SILL RAIL & COVER

S.S. TUBE

ALUM. FASCIA & COVER

HOR. MOVEMENT

3900MM
12'-9½" ±

CONC. SLAB

6" STRUCTURAL STEEL TUBE

STEEL BRACKET

ANCHOR TEE FOR
ATTACHMENT OF MULLION
& SUNSCREEN

VERTICAL MULLION

½" TEMPERED GL.

SUNSCREEN BRACKET

VERTICAL MOVEMENT

ALUM. BLADES

Fig. 8 Typical curtain wall and spandrel section.

down on a statue of the founder in the square below. The angles selected for the louvers allow the director to do so, without compromising the function of the sunshades in the least. Thus in this case the human element is truly the most important part of the building.

The basic elements of the curtain wall are shown in Figure 9, which supplements the view of the system shown in Figure 8. The mechanic in the photograph is working on part of the catwalk. The bracket that is shown holds the louver; and the bracket's attachment to the aluminum anchor assembly is shown penetrating the fascia. The worker's legs are straddling the anchor T and steel bracket assembly. An exploded view of these components independent of the structure is shown in Figure 10. Here one can study the central element of this system—the aluminum anchor assembly, which is made up of an extrusion that receives the stainless steel mullion tube. The rear portion of the anchor is fabricated

of cast aluminum and is designed to secure the curtain wall to the structure. The vertical mullion is engaged by the stainless steel tube and is further strengthened by an integral aluminum casting at the point of connection. The fascia and the sunshade bracket are secured to the anchor, completing this typical assembly.

The following paragraph is the manufacturer's description of its technical approach to curtain wall fabrication and performance and is taken from a pamphlet called *World Wall*, published in 1983:

Construction tolerances between the curtain wall and the building structure are accommodated by adjustable mullion anchors. To transmit wind and dead loads to the building structure, vertical mullions are anchored to inserts at each floor and horizontal framing members are joined to vertical members with cast aluminum splines. The wall system must allow for vertical and horizontal building movements. Vertical wall and building movements such as thermal

expansion, liveload deflection of floor slabs and differential floor movements are accommodated in the interlocking sill rails. Horizontal thermal expansion is accepted in the joints between the horizontal rails and the vertical mullions. Because this movement is accommodated within each module and is not accumulative, the joints can be relatively small. Each horizontal head rail and interlocking sill rail form continuous gutters to weep any water penetration to the exterior through a baffled weep system.

Heavy arrows indicate the horizontal and vertical movement of the curtain wall shown in Figure 8. The vertical aluminum mullions are secured to the anchor assembly by stainless steel tubes that allow for the considerable degree of vertical movement necessitated by this structure. An aluminum grill separates the raised floor from the glass itself and is designed to deliver air from the various mechanical equipment modules of the building. The raised floor, another Cupples Products fabrication that was designed for this building, is extremely flexible and strong. The panel itself is composed of an aluminum honeycomb core weighing only 20.4 kilograms (45 pounds) per panel. The panel is designed to receive a uniform load of 45.4 kilograms (100 pounds), or a point load of 500 kilograms (1100 pounds). This approximately 1200-millimeter-square (4-foot-square) panel is supported at each corner by an adjustable pedestal that is leveled by a laser-beam survey method. This floor system allows all heating, ventilating, and air conditioning (HVAC), telephone, power, and plumbing lines to be completely accessible and creates between the finished floor and the concrete slab a plenum that permits each floor of this building to be serviced without interfering with the floor below, as might be the case with a conventional mechanical delivery system located in the ceiling.

Fig. 9 Basic elements of curtain wall.

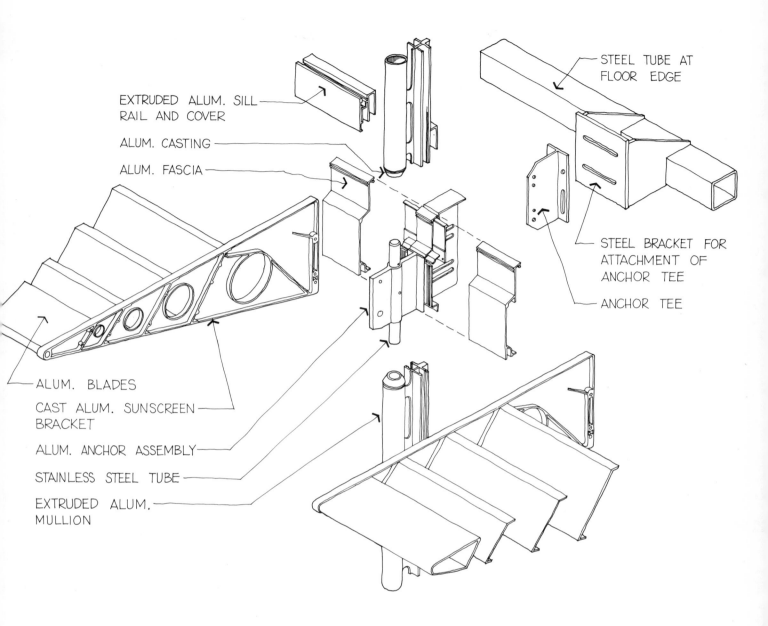

EXTRUDED ALUM. SILL
RAIL AND COVER

ALUM. CASTING

ALUM. FASCIA

STEEL TUBE AT
FLOOR EDGE

STEEL BRACKET FOR
ATTACHMENT OF
ANCHOR TEE

ANCHOR TEE

ALUM. BLADES

CAST ALUM. SUNSCREEN
BRACKET

ALUM. ANCHOR ASSEMBLY

STAINLESS STEEL TUBE

EXTRUDED ALUM.
MULLION

Fig. 10 Exploded view of anchor assembly.

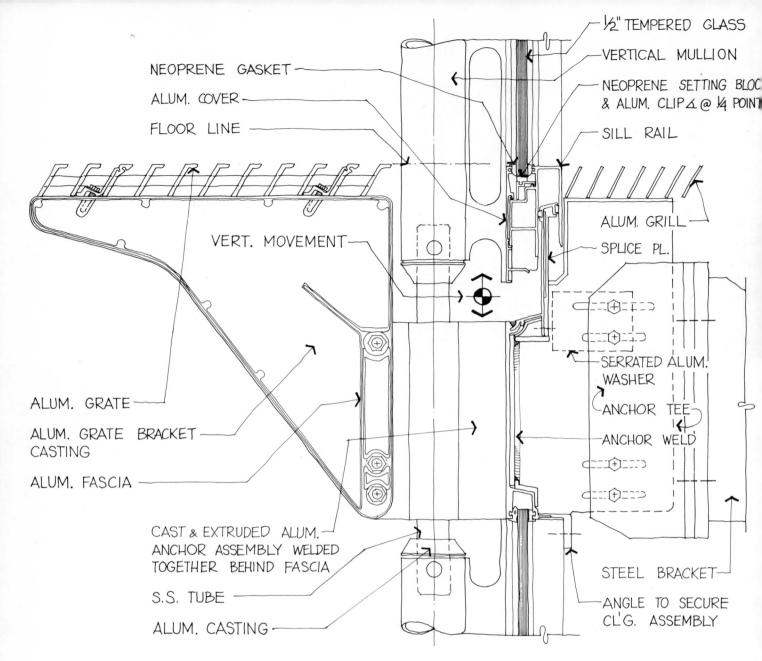

NEOPRENE GASKET

ALUM. COVER

FLOOR LINE

VERT. MOVEMENT

ALUM. GRATE

ALUM. GRATE BRACKET CASTING

ALUM. FASCIA

CAST & EXTRUDED ALUM. ANCHOR ASSEMBLY WELDED TOGETHER BEHIND FASCIA

S.S. TUBE

ALUM. CASTING

½" TEMPERED GLASS

VERTICAL MULLION

NEOPRENE SETTING BLOC & ALUM. CLIP △ @ ¼ POINT

SILL RAIL

ALUM. GRILL

SPLICE PL.

SERRATED ALUM. WASHER

ANCHOR TEE

ANCHOR WELD

STEEL BRACKET

ANGLE TO SECURE CL'G. ASSEMBLY

Fig. 11 Vertical section through the window-cleaning catwalk.

Figure 11 is a vertical section that indicates a variation of the catwalk support bracket that is used where the shading devices are not required. The vertical clearance between the sill rail cover and the fascia is noted. It is here that the anchor assembly is shown penetrating the fascia and attaching itself to the anchor T. The vertical mullions with their top and bottom aluminum castings engage the stainless steel tubes that secure, and allow for expansion of, these members through the anchor assembly. Figure 12 shows this bracket and its attachment to the anchor assembly.

Figure 13 is a horizontal section through the anchor assembly, and it is at this point that we can see the two parts of this component. The exterior portion is a heavy 12.7-millimeter (½-inch) extrusion that is welded to an aluminum anchor casting. This assembly is bolted to the steel anchor T and is secured to the structure through a

Fig. 12 Catwalk support bracket and its attachment to anchor assembly.

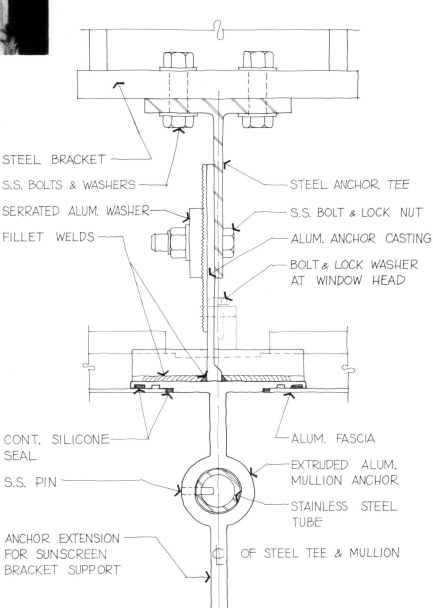

STEEL BRACKET

S.S. BOLTS & WASHERS

SERRATED ALUM. WASHER

FILLET WELDS

STEEL ANCHOR TEE

S.S. BOLT & LOCK NUT

ALUM. ANCHOR CASTING

BOLT & LOCK WASHER AT WINDOW HEAD

CONT. SILICONE SEAL

S.S. PIN

ALUM. FASCIA

EXTRUDED ALUM. MULLION ANCHOR

STAINLESS STEEL TUBE

ANCHOR EXTENSION FOR SUNSCREEN BRACKET SUPPORT

OF STEEL TEE & MULLION

Fig. 13 Horizontal section through a typical anchor assembly.

steel bracket. Figure 14 shows how this assembly picks up the fascia and the sill rail. Figure 15 is a horizontal section through a typical vertical mullion; the tempered glass and the top of the sill rail joined by a splice plate, shown in dotted lines, can be seen. The detail is elegant in its simplicity and retains the initial concept of the preliminary design shown in Figure 5.

Adding to the usual problems of curtain wall design is the problem of dealing with a structure that literally weaves itself through the mass of the building. Figure 16 is an isometric sketch of the upper portion of the tower. The mast assembly is shown here at the face of the building and again along the top of the paneled roof. To the left may be seen the service modules and the staircases. The successful interaction of wall module, mast, and truss is the central technical issue of this cladding system, and it is here that the completed building will succeed or fail as a pragmatic exercise.

Fig. 14 Anchor assembly, fascia, and sill rail.

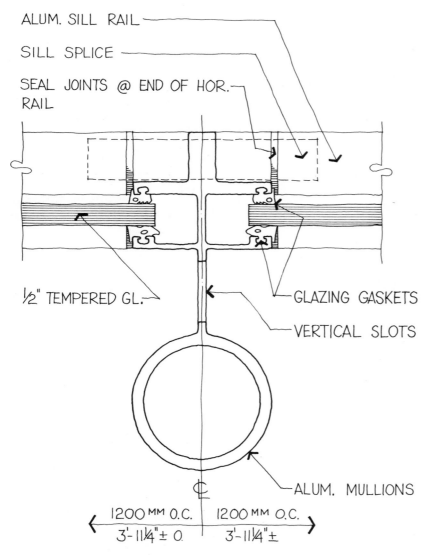

ALUM. SILL RAIL

SILL SPLICE

SEAL JOINTS @ END OF HOR. RAIL

½" TEMPERED GL.

GLAZING GASKETS

VERTICAL SLOTS

ALUM. MULLIONS

1200 MM O.C.
3'-11¼"± 0.

1200 MM O.C.
3'-11¼"±

Fig. 15 Plan section through a typical vertical mullion.

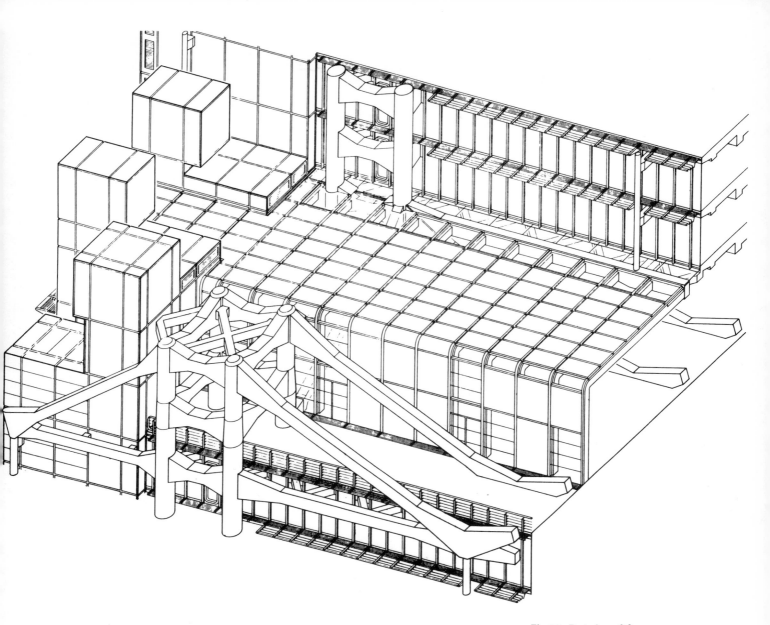

Fig. 16   Part view of the upper
tower, mast, and truss.

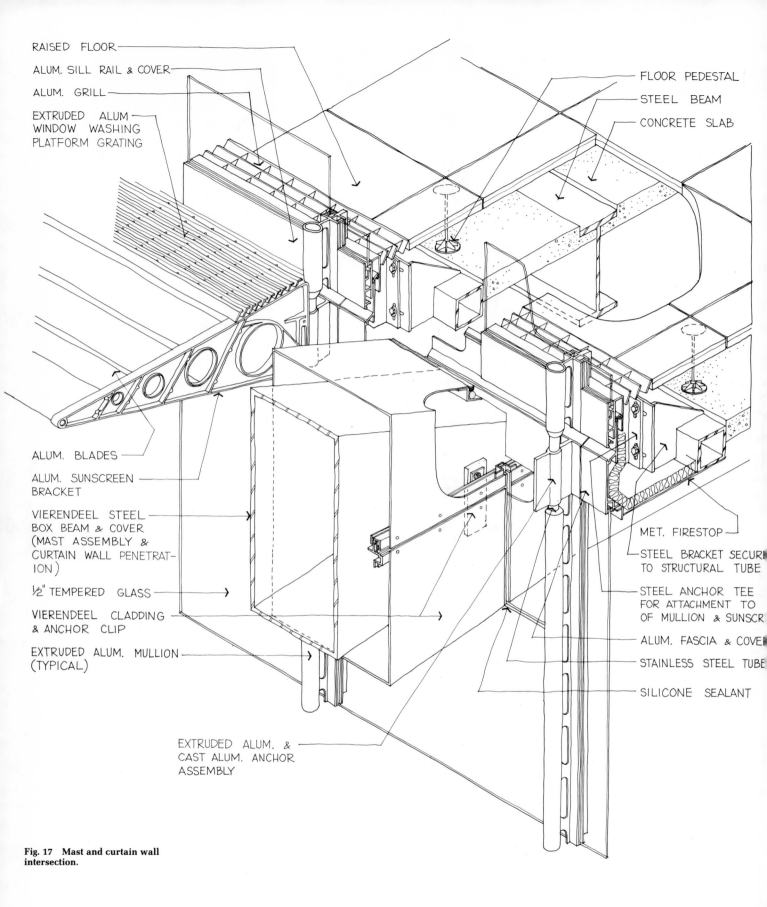

RAISED FLOOR

ALUM. SILL RAIL & COVER

ALUM. GRILL

EXTRUDED ALUM
WINDOW WASHING
PLATFORM GRATING

FLOOR PEDESTAL

STEEL BEAM

CONCRETE SLAB

ALUM. BLADES

ALUM. SUNSCREEN
BRACKET

VIERENDEEL STEEL
BOX BEAM & COVER
(MAST ASSEMBLY &
CURTAIN WALL PENETRAT-
ION)

½" TEMPERED GLASS

VIERENDEEL CLADDING
& ANCHOR CLIP

EXTRUDED ALUM. MULLION
(TYPICAL)

MET. FIRESTOP

STEEL BRACKET SECUR
TO STRUCTURAL TUBE

STEEL ANCHOR TEE
FOR ATTACHMENT TO
OF MULLION & SUNSCR

ALUM. FASCIA & COVE

STAINLESS STEEL TUBE

SILICONE SEALANT

EXTRUDED ALUM. &
CAST ALUM. ANCHOR
ASSEMBLY

**Fig. 17 Mast and curtain wall
intersection.**

The transition between the curtain wall and the structural cladding can be studied in Figure 17. The Vierendeel steel box beam of the mast assembly penetrates the glass curtain wall and the fascia cover as it moves toward the heavier structural elements contained more deeply within the building. The cladding of this beam becomes critical in that it must be made weathertight. Figure 18 is a view from the inside of the mock-up looking toward the corner column of the mast and shows the cross bracing and a part view of the box beam analyzed in Figure 17. The exterior and interior cladding is separated at the glass line in order to accommodate the various vision panels that enclose this assembly. Positive gaskets and synthetic sealants are used extensively to make this system work. Figure 19 is a vertical section that illustrates the method by which the cladding is secured to the box beam. The

Fig. 18   Cross bracing and part view of box beam analyzed in Figure 17.

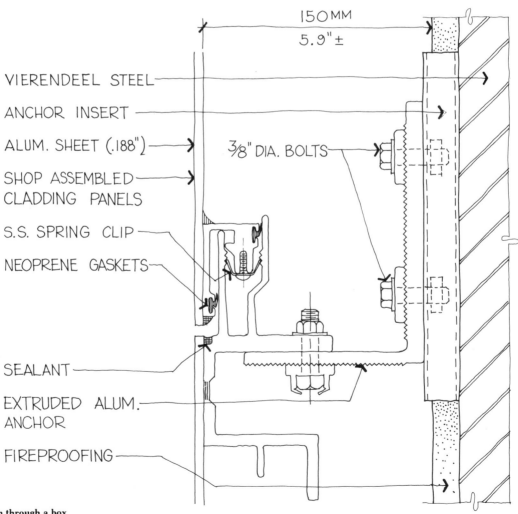

Fig. 19   Vertical section through a box beam and cladding.

system is further delineated in Figure 20, which allows us to study this connection in an isometric sketch. The lower cladding element is secured to an extruded and serrated anchor clip that is attached to an insert welded to the structural steel. Figure 19 indicates the cladding panels and their attachment to the box beam. Note the gaskets that allow air to penetrate the system while water is prevented from doing so, thus providing the pressure equalization described earlier. A simple stainless steel spring clip secures the upper cladding to the lower section of this assembly.

The relation of the cladding to the structural mast can be studied more carefully in Figure 21, in which a two-story section of a typical mast is viewed from below in an isometric projection. The shaded portion of the mast cladding represents the exterior elements of this system. Here can be seen the separation of the cladding elements that are designed to receive the glass curtain wall assembly. The upper portion of Figure 21 exposes the structure to show the many anchor inserts provided to receive the cladding elements. These anchor inserts are similar to the one shown in Figure 20.

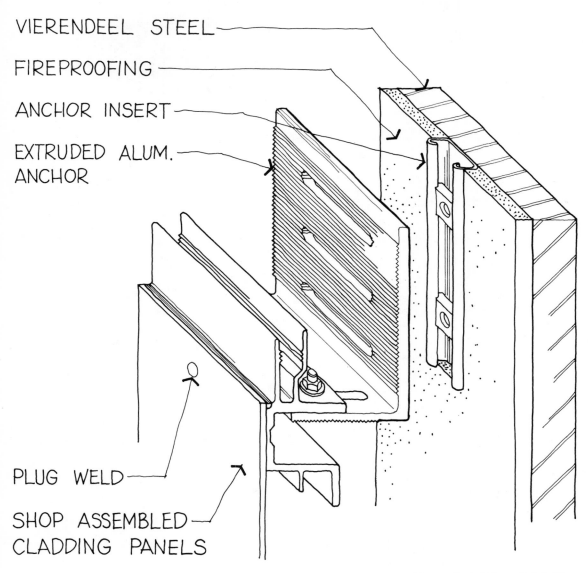

VIERENDEEL STEEL

FIREPROOFING

ANCHOR INSERT

EXTRUDED ALUM. ANCHOR

PLUG WELD

SHOP ASSEMBLED CLADDING PANELS

Fig. 20   Typical Vierendeel cladding anchor.

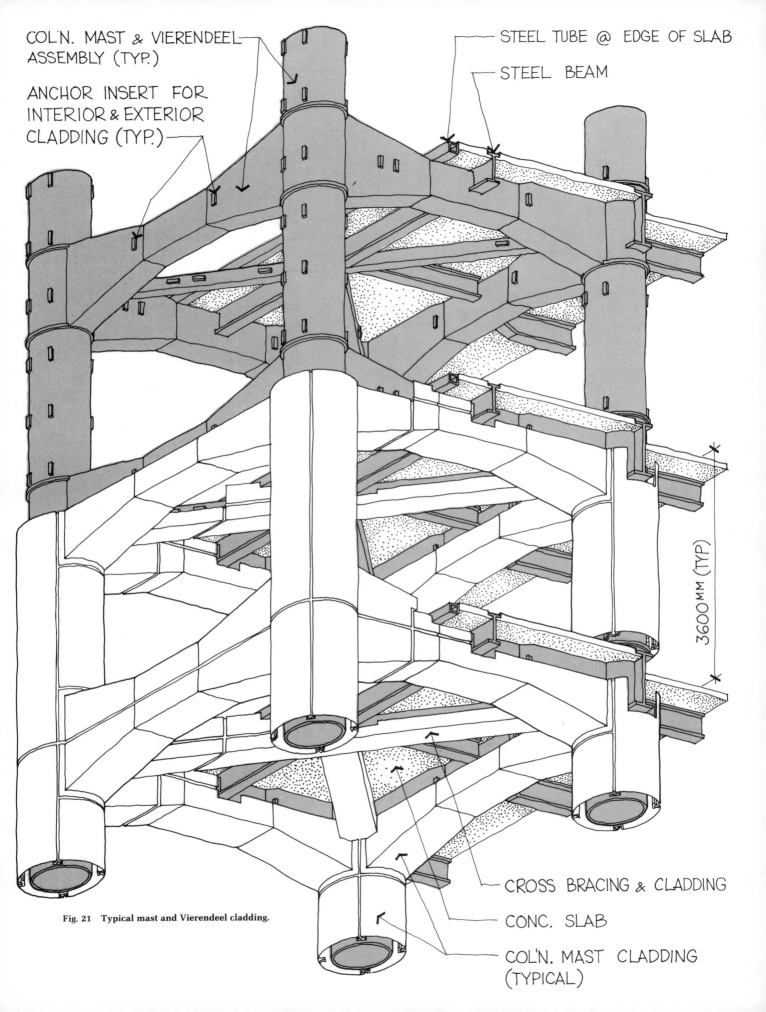

COL'N. MAST & VIERENDEEL ASSEMBLY (TYP.)

ANCHOR INSERT FOR INTERIOR & EXTERIOR CLADDING (TYP.)

STEEL TUBE @ EDGE OF SLAB

STEEL BEAM

3600 MM (TYP)

CROSS BRACING & CLADDING

CONC. SLAB

COL'N. MAST CLADDING (TYPICAL)

Fig. 21 Typical mast and Vierendeel cladding.

The cladding for the outer truss is illustrated isometrically in Figure 22. Also shown is a portion of the mast as seen looking down upon this assembly. The rear truss is shown with the cladding elements removed, revealing the tensile and compressive elements of the structure. In addition, the drawing shows the beam that is horizontal and perpendicular to the mast that supports the interior slab at that point.

Fig. 22   Cladding at the outer truss assembly.

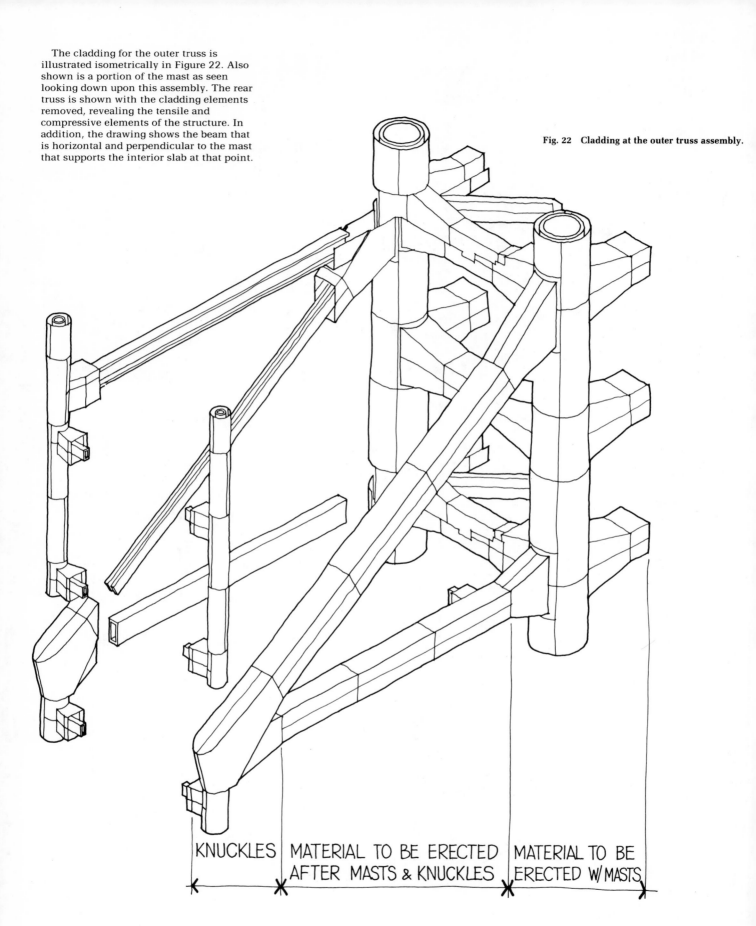

KNUCKLES | MATERIAL TO BE ERECTED AFTER MASTS & KNUCKLES | MATERIAL TO BE ERECTED W/MASTS

Figure 23, a photograph taken of a large-scale model, shows the outer truss assembly and its relation to a typical refuge floor, or staging area. Also shown are curtain wall assemblies for this area. The drawing of the knuckles at the outer portion of the truss illustrates how the floor hangers are suspended from this structure. A study of this area is shown in Figure 24. Here, in preliminary form, is shown the basic assembly for the vertical hanger at the "knuckle" ends of the truss. It is astonishing that so many issues were competently resolved at such an early state of design development and that subsequent revision: or redesign of building systems was unnecessary.

Fig. 23   Large-scale model showing outer truss assembly and its relation to typical refuge floor, or staging area.

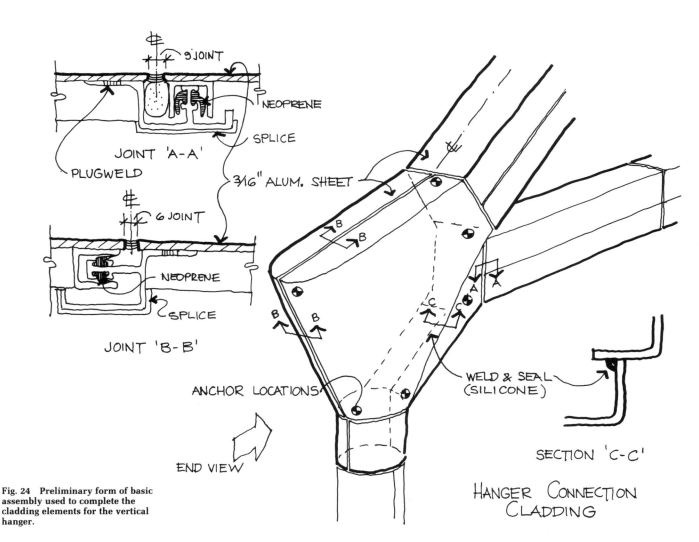

Fig. 24   Preliminary form of basic assembly used to complete the cladding elements for the vertical hanger.

Figure 25 is a plan section that illustrates the relation of the curved exterior cladding to the column structure. The interval between the cladding and the column is 150 millimeters (6.0 inches). This clearance is maintained with a high degree of tolerance throughout the column and mast assemblies. It is interesting to note that the curved panels that form the column cladding are the product of some very advanced metal-forming processes. Instead of attempting to form a curved panel in one piece, the manufacturer incrementally stamped the panels so that the stamped portion reflected a small segment of the final curve. The stamping process was accurate enough to form a curved panel with no evidence of the multiple steps taken to form the required curve. Figure 25 can be better understood when studied together with Figure 26, an isometric view of the components, anchor, and inserts that receive the cladding assembly. The column cladding is complex, and since all connections for this assembly are concealed, it might be illuminating to review the various steps taken to clad the column, as shown in Figures 27 through 31.

Fig. 25   Plan section through the column cladding.

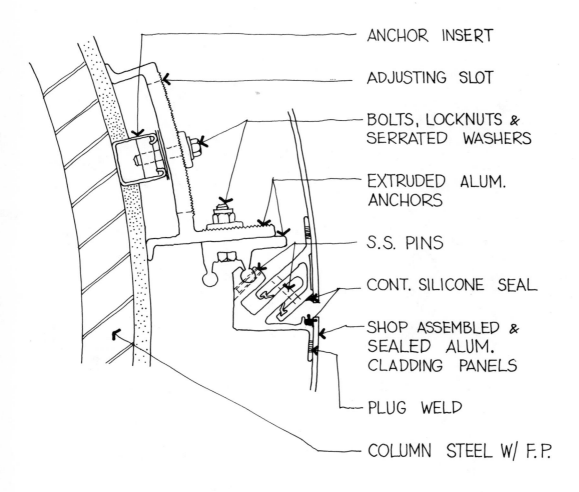

ANCHOR INSERT

ADJUSTING SLOT

BOLTS, LOCKNUTS & SERRATED WASHERS

EXTRUDED ALUM. ANCHORS

S.S. PINS

CONT. SILICONE SEAL

SHOP ASSEMBLED & SEALED ALUM. CLADDING PANELS

PLUG WELD

COLUMN STEEL W/ F.P.

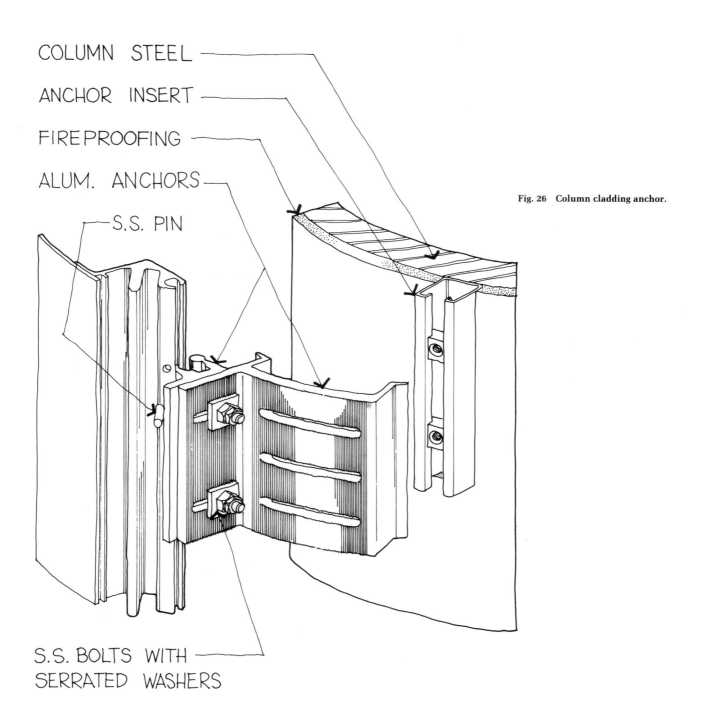

COLUMN STEEL

ANCHOR INSERT

FIREPROOFING

ALUM. ANCHORS

S.S. PIN

S.S. BOLTS WITH
SERRATED WASHERS

Fig. 26   Column cladding anchor.

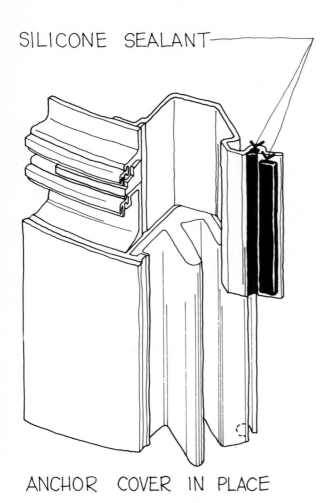

SILICONE SEALANT

Fig. 27   Column cladding (four-way joint).

ANCHOR COVER IN PLACE

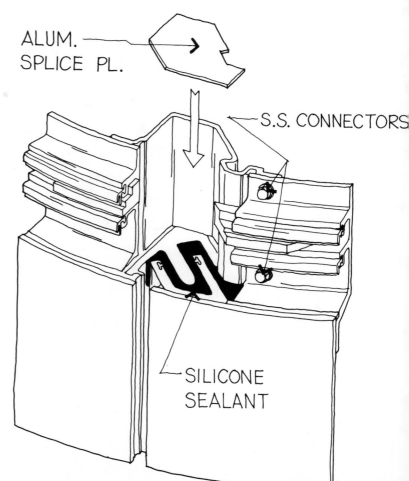

ALUM. SPLICE PL.

S.S. CONNECTORS

SILICONE SEALANT

Fig. 28   Clip-on cover for column in place.

Figure 27 shows a curved exterior panel secured to its mounting clips. This assembly is called the anchor cover. The upper-right portion of the diagram shows the installation of sealant, required before the next step in the assembly can take place. The clip-on cover is secured to the anchor in Figure 28. Stainless steel connectors secure the anchorage for the next assembly step. An aluminum splice plate, shown in exploded view, is then inserted into this assembly. The upper anchor cover is shown about to be installed in the lower assembly in Figure 29. Note the application of the sealant and the rear

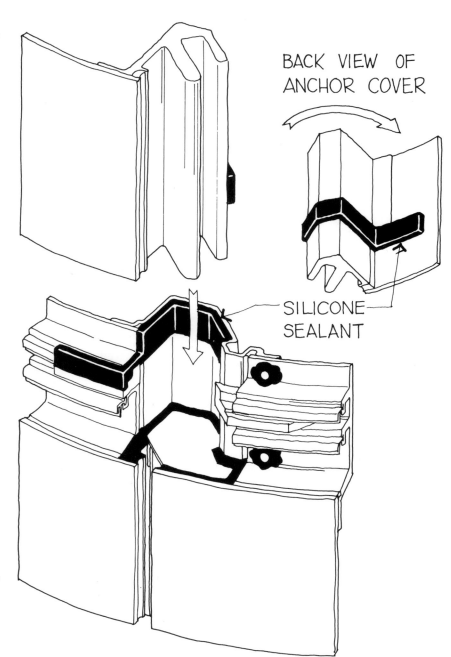

BACK VIEW OF ANCHOR COVER

SILICONE SEALANT

Fig. 29   Jamb interlock and splice plate.

JAMB INTERLOCK & SPLICE PLATE SEALED – BACK OF ANCHOR COVER JAMB SEALED PRIOR TO SETTING COVER IN PLACE

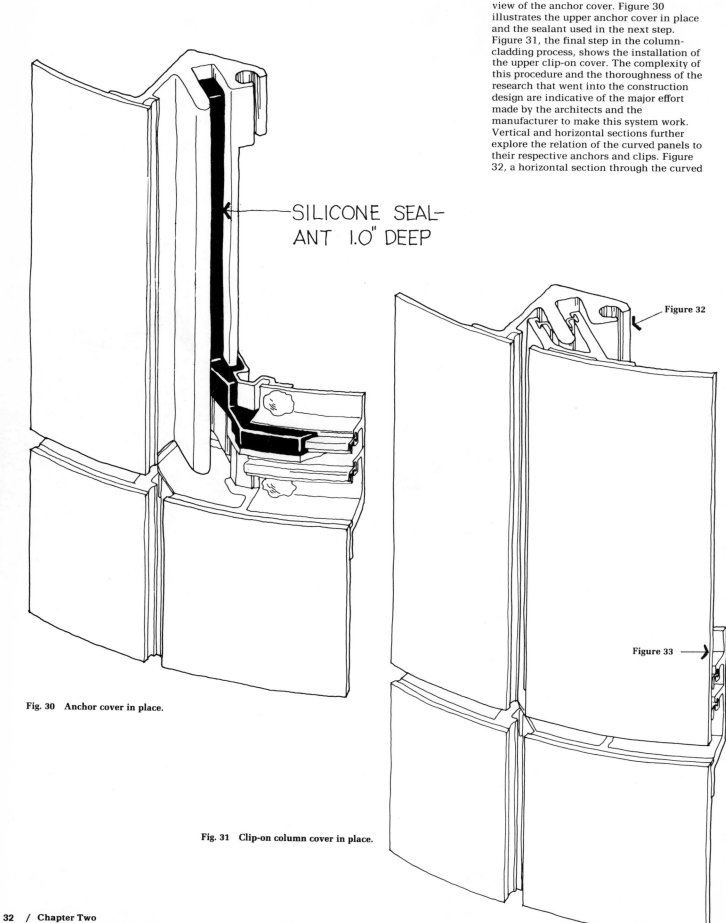

view of the anchor cover. Figure 30
illustrates the upper anchor cover in place
and the sealant used in the next step.
Figure 31, the final step in the column-
cladding process, shows the installation of
the upper clip-on cover. The complexity of
this procedure and the thoroughness of the
research that went into the construction
design are indicative of the major effort
made by the architects and the
manufacturer to make this system work.
Vertical and horizontal sections further
explore the relation of the curved panels to
their respective anchors and clips. Figure
32, a horizontal section through the curved

SILICONE SEAL-
ANT 1.0" DEEP

Figure 32

Figure 33

Fig. 30   Anchor cover in place.

Fig. 31   Clip-on column cover in place.

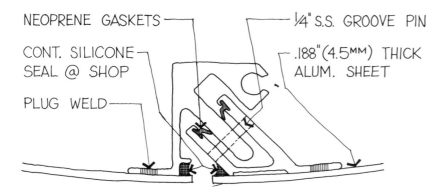

NEOPRENE GASKETS

CONT. SILICONE
SEAL @ SHOP

PLUG WELD

¼" S.S. GROOVE PIN

.188"(4.5MM) THICK
ALUM. SHEET

**Fig. 32 Horizontal section through
column cladding and jamb interlock.**

panels, shows the plug welds used to secure
the anchor and clip assembly. The gaskets
that allow the equalization of pressure in
this system are indicated, as are the shop-
applied panel sealants. Figure 33 is a
vertical cut through the panel intersection
and shows the extruded head that receives
gaskets for the upper clip-on panel and a
turnbuckle connection that helps reinforce
the curve of the column panel. Figure 34
shows workers assembling the column-
cladding components on the mock-up. This
photograph, like Figure 30, shows the
bayonet receiver designed to accept the
clip-on cover.

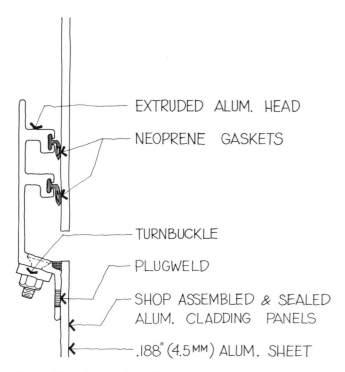

EXTRUDED ALUM. HEAD

NEOPRENE GASKETS

TURNBUCKLE

PLUGWELD

SHOP ASSEMBLED & SEALED
ALUM. CLADDING PANELS

.188" (4.5MM) ALUM. SHEET

**Fig. 33 Vertical section through the
column head rail and the centerline of
the Vierendeel truss.**

**Fig. 34 Workers assembling
column-cladding components.**

3 Family Court Building of the City of New York

New York, New York   ARCHITECTS: Haines Lundberg Waehler

Fig. 1   The intricate bas-relief of the facade.

The Family Court Building of the City of New York, located in the Civic Center area of lower Manhattan, was designed by the architectural firm of Haines Lundberg Waehler. This building uses much of the current working vocabulary of stone and glass curtain wall technology. The courthouse has a sculptural quality; the viewer feels that it was carved from a solid block of black granite. A student of construction can derive an effective lesson in material application by an analysis of the ways in which granite veneer was used in this building to make the veneer conform to the underlying structure. In studying the assemblies detailed in this chapter, the reader should note the care taken to provide for the proper installation and adequate support of the granite. The stone panels are attached to the structure with anchors, clips, angle supports, clamps, and other hardware. Care was required in the selection of these elements since such hardware is often subject to corrosion and failure. It is not uncommon in New York City to see whole segments of masonry facades being removed and replaced as a result of anchor and lintel failure.

The color of the granite selected by the architects for the curtain walls is black, placing the building in stark contrast to its neighbors. As seen in Figure 1, the courthouse's facade is an intricate bas-relief containing angled setbacks, loggias, bridges, and other articulated sections sculpted from the building's mass. The structure of the building is primarily reinforced concrete. Special elevation details are formed by a secondary steel structure composed of miscellaneous sections. The granite panels covering the vertical planes of the facade are highly polished and reflective in contrast to the mat "flame" finish panels, which appear to absorb light, covering setbacks and soffits. The contrasting finishes are used to good effect visually and develop a strong play of light and texture.

Figure 2 is a part view of the area slated for detailed analysis in this chapter. Note the three-dimensional relation of the sculptural elements on the upper portion of the facade. Figure 3 is an isometric view of part of the tenth, eleventh, and twelfth floors, indicating a projected granite "eyebrow", or three-dimensional T, providing a shade structure for the glass of the tenth and eleventh floors. A terrace is located on the tenth floor, and the similarities of terrace and roof construction are compared in subsequent illustrations.

Fig. 2 Part view of the eighth and ninth floor loggia.

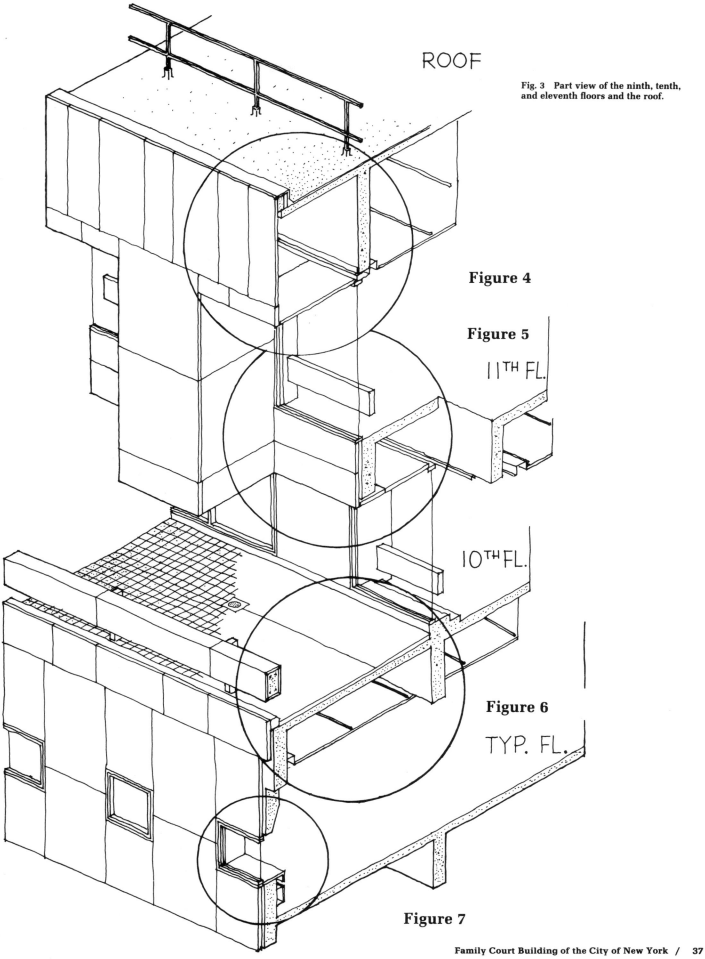

ROOF

Fig. 3 Part view of the ninth, tenth, and eleventh floors and the roof.

Figure 4

Figure 5

11TH FL.

10TH FL.

Figure 6

TYP. FL.

Figure 7

Four assemblies have been developed into isometric diagrams as follows. Figure 4 shows the twelfth-floor (roof) spandrel and first soffit setback. Figure 5 shows the eleventh-floor spandrel and the second setback. Figure 6 shows the tenth-floor setback, balcony, and railing; and Figure 7 shows a typical window.

Figure 4 illustrates the cantilevered roof slab and spandrel beam in relation to the projected secondary steel structure supporting the stone veneer. The granite facing panels are supported by continuous vertical and horizontal steel angles secured to the concrete structure with various inserts. Additional corrosion-resistant 4- by 4-inch bracing angles provide structural rigidity. This diagram reveals the use of concrete fill and roofing insulation on the slab to provide the proper pitch and watertight construction for the floor below. In practice, the lightweight concrete fill has a minimum depth of 1½ inches, and additional fill is used to give a positive pitch to the roof drain. Special care must be taken when an object such as the 2-inch-square tubing that supports the railing assembly penetrates the roofing membrane. As can be seen in this drawing, the flashing is incorporated into the built-up roofing. Incidentally, the small space between the flashing and the railing tube is sealed with lead.

The window frame, the drapery pocket, and the suspended plaster ceiling are seen in the lower right portion of this drawing, and their attachment to the structure is noted. The suspended plaster ceiling is secured to galvanized expanded wire lath attached to ¾-inch channels. These in turn are supported by 1½-inch channel runners spaced at 4 feet on center. The runners are secured to the slab above with either 1-inch metal straps or ¼-inch steel rods that are positively attached to the slab with approved anchoring devices. This assembly and its variations are approved by the New York City building code. (Care must be exercised at all times with respect to code conformance for all materials and assemblies used on a project.) The ¾-inch glass is set in a gasket which is clamped in place and secured to the tubular aluminum window frame. This detail could be modified to contain an insulated glass panel, which would be more energy efficient than the single thickness of glass called for in the contract.

The bulk of the vertical granite facing used in this building is 1¾ inches thick. The exception occurs at shelf angle supports, where the granite is 2¼ inches thick in order to absorb the additional compressive stress developed by this assembly. This relation may be studied in Figure 8, a vertical section through a typical stone soffit. Here the fascia makes a transition to a soffit composed of 2-inch-thick granite. All exposed metal in this detail as well as in other parts of the building is painted black to match the granite. Anchoring, doweling, and clamping of the granite are all accomplished by the use of stainless steel accessories, and are in accordance with current standards of approved stone veneer construction.

The anchorage specifications were delineated by the architect as follows:

Veneer stone shall have anchors and dowels as indicated on drawings, complying with requirements of local authorities having jurisdiction but shall have not less than 4 anchors per stone.

All vertical granite sheets have top, bottom, and suitably placed side anchors. At least one anchor for every 400 square inches of surface area was installed. The joints at the intersections of stone panels are no more than ¼ inch wide and are protected from the weather by sealants and butyl rod backups. These are interrupted at regular intervals by weep holes at the horizontal courses. In Figure 8, a 2- by 4-inch aluminum strap is welded to a bent aluminum plate, forming a continuous bracket seating the granite soffit. The bracket is treated as a shallow reveal and is painted to match the color and finish of the stone. We catch a glimpse of this system in Figure 2, in which an extensive soffit area reflects the detail shown. The vertical stone facing is secured to the shelf angle with a simple ¾-inch welded steel rod. Both the facing and the lower stones are secured to each other with a dowel and eyebolt tied back to the vertical angle.

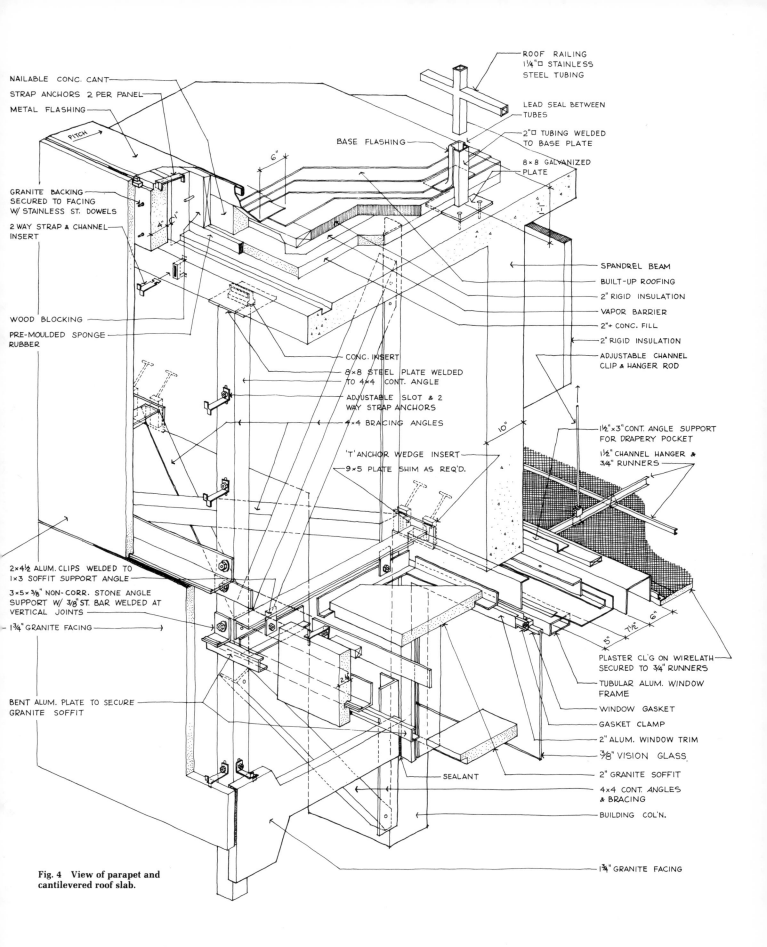

NAILABLE CONC. CANT.
STRAP ANCHORS 2 PER PANEL
METAL FLASHING

PITCH

GRANITE BACKING
SECURED TO FACING
W/ STAINLESS ST. DOWELS

2 WAY STRAP & CHANNEL
INSERT

4" C

WOOD BLOCKING
PRE-MOULDED SPONGE
RUBBER

2×4½ ALUM. CLIPS WELDED TO
1×3 SOFFIT SUPPORT ANGLE
3×5×⅜" NON-CORR. STONE ANGLE
SUPPORT W/ ⅜" ST. BAR WELDED AT
VERTICAL JOINTS
1¾" GRANITE FACING

BENT ALUM. PLATE TO SECURE
GRANITE SOFFIT

Fig. 4   View of parapet and
cantilevered roof slab.

ROOF RAILING
1¼"□ STAINLESS
STEEL TUBING

LEAD SEAL BETWEEN
TUBES

BASE FLASHING

2"□ TUBING WELDED
TO BASE PLATE

8×8 GALVANIZED
PLATE

6"

CONC. INSERT
8×8 STEEL PLATE WELDED
TO 4×4 CONT. ANGLE
ADJUSTABLE SLOT & 2
WAY STRAP ANCHORS
4×4 BRACING ANGLES

'T' ANCHOR WEDGE INSERT
9×5 PLATE SHIM AS REQ'D.

10"

10"

2½"

SEALANT

SPANDREL BEAM
BUILT-UP ROOFING
2" RIGID INSULATION
VAPOR BARRIER
2"+ CONC. FILL
2" RIGID INSULATION
ADJUSTABLE CHANNEL
CLIP & HANGER ROD

1½"×3" CONT. ANGLE SUPPORT
FOR DRAPERY POCKET
1½" CHANNEL HANGER &
¾" RUNNERS

6"
1½"
5"

PLASTER CL'G ON WIRELATH
SECURED TO ¾" RUNNERS
TUBULAR ALUM. WINDOW
FRAME
WINDOW GASKET
GASKET CLAMP
2" ALUM. WINDOW TRIM
⅜" VISION GLASS
2" GRANITE SOFFIT
4×4 CONT. ANGLES
& BRACING
BUILDING COL'N.

1¾" GRANITE FACING

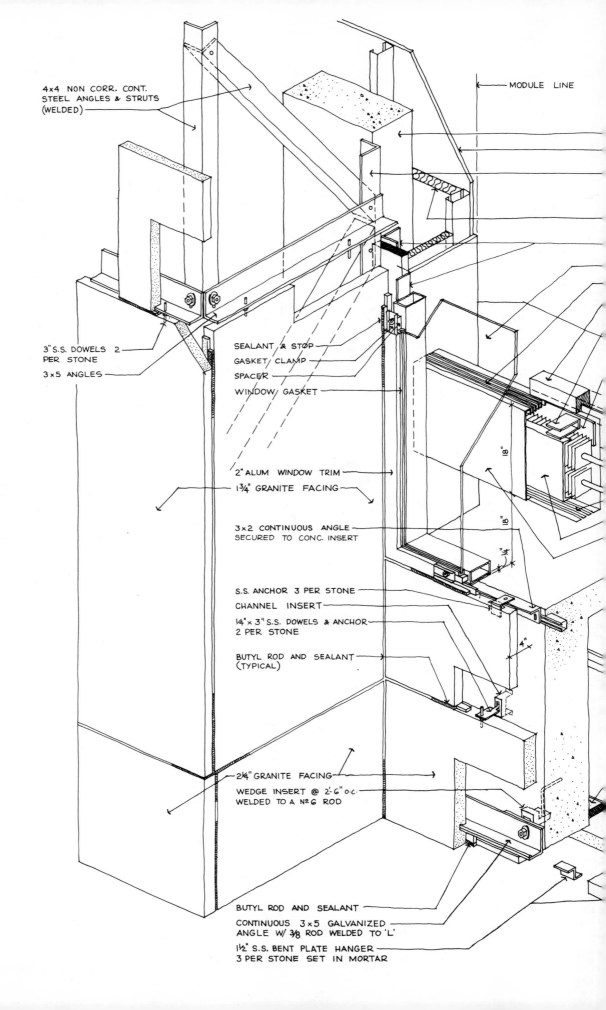

4x4 NON CORR. CONT.
STEEL ANGLES & STRUTS
(WELDED)

MODULE LINE

3" S.S. DOWELS 2
PER STONE

3 x 5 ANGLES

SEALANT & STOP
GASKET CLAMP
SPACER
WINDOW GASKET

2" ALUM WINDOW TRIM

1¾" GRANITE FACING

3 x 2 CONTINUOUS ANGLE
SECURED TO CONC. INSERT

18"

18"

¼"

4"

S.S. ANCHOR 3 PER STONE

CHANNEL INSERT

¼" x 3" S.S. DOWELS & ANCHOR
2 PER STONE

BUTYL ROD AND SEALANT
(TYPICAL)

2¼" GRANITE FACING

WEDGE INSERT @ 2'-6" O.C.
WELDED TO A № 6 ROD

BUTYL ROD AND SEALANT

CONTINUOUS 3 x 5 GALVANIZED
ANGLE W/ ⅜ ROD WELDED TO 'L'

1½" S.S. BENT PLATE HANGER
3 PER STONE SET IN MORTAR

NCRETE BLD'G. COLUMN

GYPSUM BOARD ON
TAL STUDS

4 VERTICAL ANGLES SECURED
WALLS TO TOP & BOT SPANDRELS

BLANKET INSULATION
CLOSURE ANGLES
GID INSULATION

POLISHED PLATE GL.
RUDED ALUM. GRILL
HARDWOOD RAILING
AP ANCHOR
T. STEEL PLATE

STER CEILING ON WIRELATH
URED TO CHANNEL RUNNERS
PERY POCKET & BRACKET
PORT
TUBE CONVECTOR
MPED GRILL
HANNEL SECURED
MULLIONS
VECTOR ENCLOSURE

STABLE LOOP INSERT
URED TO REINFORCING

T. 8" PLATE SECURED TO
W/ ADJ. CONC. INSERT
M

NSULATION

T. BENT ALUM. PLATE
ANGLE SECURED TO
ATE
UM. WINDOW TRIM

OW GASKET &
P

LAR ALUM. WINDOW FRAME
IDING DOOR TRACK

NG TILE INSERT

ANITE SOFFIT

ALUM. "T"

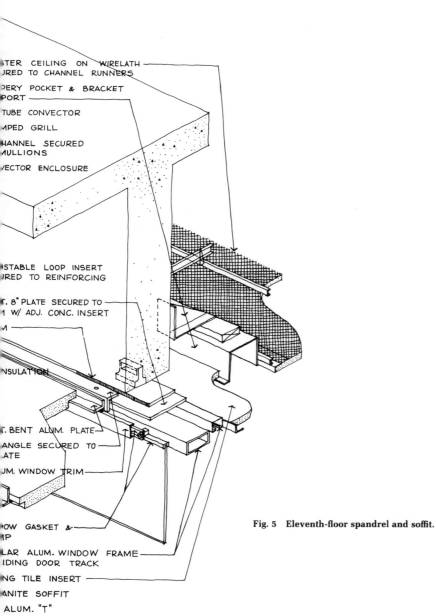

Fig. 5 Eleventh-floor spandrel and soffit.

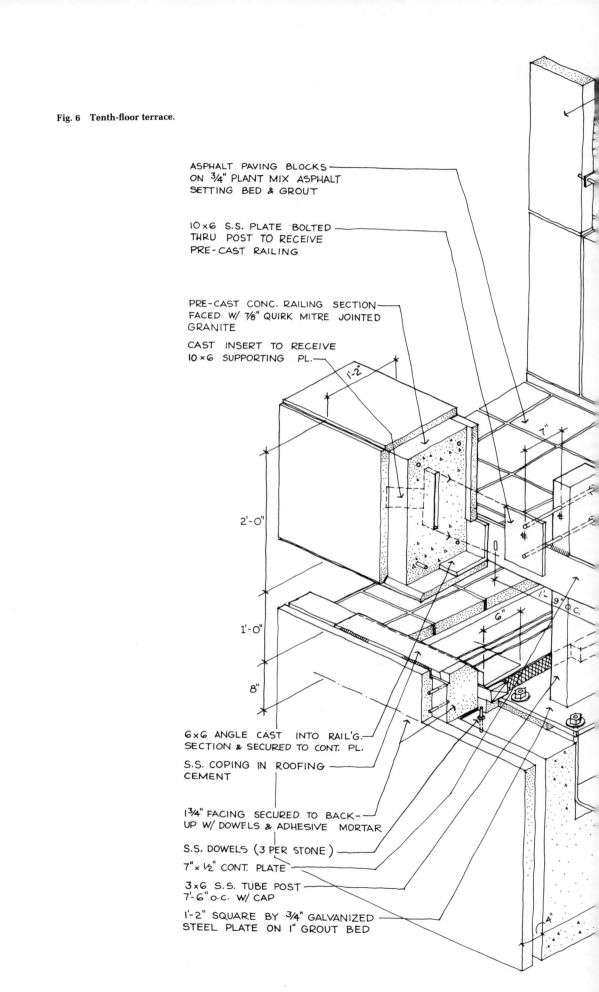

Fig. 6   Tenth-floor terrace.

ASPHALT PAVING BLOCKS
ON ¾" PLANT MIX ASPHALT
SETTING BED & GROUT

10×6 S.S. PLATE BOLTED
THRU POST TO RECEIVE
PRE-CAST RAILING

PRE-CAST CONC. RAILING SECTION
FACED W/ ⅞" QUIRK MITRE JOINTED
GRANITE

CAST INSERT TO RECEIVE
10×6 SUPPORTING PL.

1-2

7"

2'-0"

1'-0"

1'-9" O.C.

6"

8"

6×6 ANGLE CAST INTO RAIL'G.
SECTION & SECURED TO CONT. PL.

S.S. COPING IN ROOFING
CEMENT

1¾" FACING SECURED TO BACK-
UP W/ DOWELS & ADHESIVE MORTAR

S.S. DOWELS (3 PER STONE)

7"×½" CONT. PLATE

3×6 S.S. TUBE POST
7'-6" O.C. W/ CAP

1'-2" SQUARE BY ¾" GALVANIZED
STEEL PLATE ON 1" GROUT BED

4"

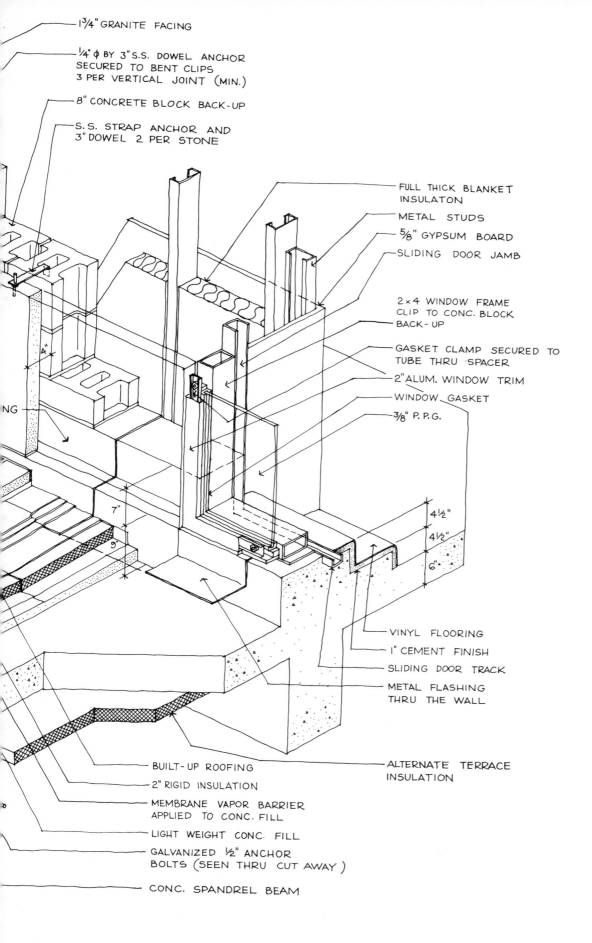

1¾" GRANITE FACING

¼" ⌀ BY 3" S.S. DOWEL ANCHOR
SECURED TO BENT CLIPS
3 PER VERTICAL JOINT (MIN.)

8" CONCRETE BLOCK BACK-UP

S.S. STRAP ANCHOR AND
3" DOWEL 2 PER STONE

FULL THICK BLANKET
INSULATON

METAL STUDS

⅝" GYPSUM BOARD

SLIDING DOOR JAMB

2 x 4 WINDOW FRAME
CLIP TO CONC. BLOCK
BACK-UP

GASKET CLAMP SECURED TO
TUBE THRU SPACER

2" ALUM. WINDOW TRIM

WINDOW GASKET

⅜" P.P.G.

4½"

4½"

6"

7"

9"

4"

NG

VINYL FLOORING

1" CEMENT FINISH

SLIDING DOOR TRACK

METAL FLASHING
THRU THE WALL

BUILT-UP ROOFING

2" RIGID INSULATION

MEMBRANE VAPOR BARRIER
APPLIED TO CONC. FILL

LIGHT WEIGHT CONC. FILL

GALVANIZED ½" ANCHOR
BOLTS (SEEN THRU CUT AWAY)

CONC. SPANDREL BEAM

ALTERNATE TERRACE
INSULATION

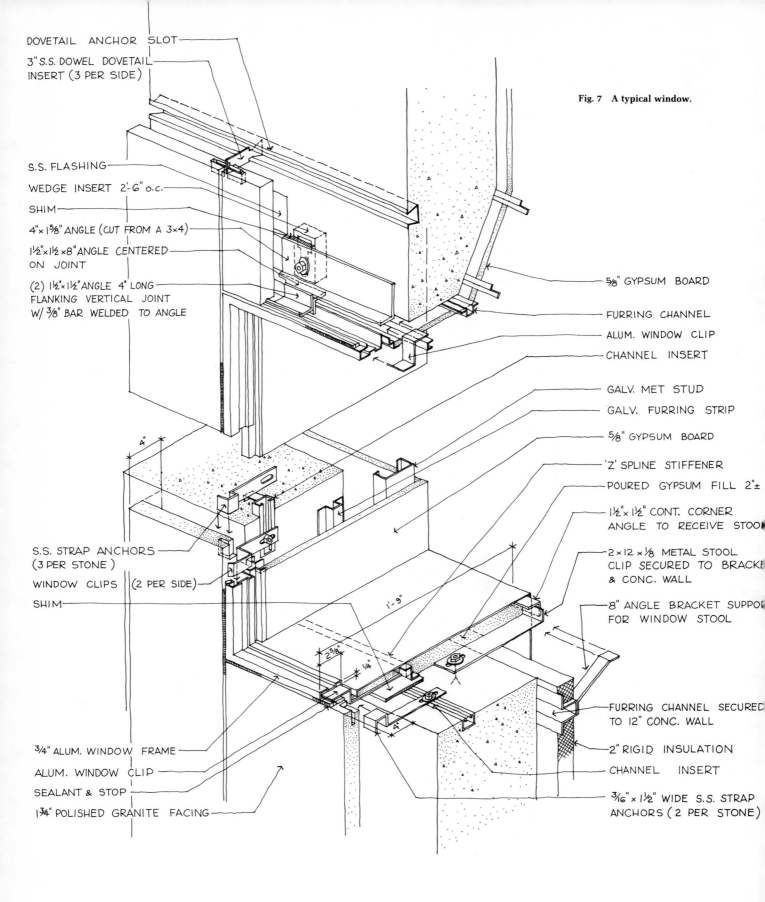

DOVETAIL ANCHOR SLOT

3" S.S. DOWEL DOVETAIL INSERT (3 PER SIDE)

Fig. 7 A typical window.

S.S. FLASHING

WEDGE INSERT 2'-6" o.c.

SHIM

4" x 1⅝" ANGLE (CUT FROM A 3×4)

1½" x 1½" x 8" ANGLE CENTERED ON JOINT

(2) 1½" x 1½" ANGLE 4" LONG FLANKING VERTICAL JOINT W/ ⅜" BAR WELDED TO ANGLE

⅝" GYPSUM BOARD

FURRING CHANNEL

ALUM. WINDOW CLIP

CHANNEL INSERT

GALV. MET STUD

GALV. FURRING STRIP

⅝" GYPSUM BOARD

'Z' SPLINE STIFFENER

POURED GYPSUM FILL 2"±

1½" x 1½" CONT. CORNER ANGLE TO RECEIVE STOOL

2 × 12 × ⅛ METAL STOOL CLIP SECURED TO BRACKET & CONC. WALL

8" ANGLE BRACKET SUPPORT FOR WINDOW STOOL

S.S. STRAP ANCHORS (3 PER STONE)

WINDOW CLIPS (2 PER SIDE)

SHIM

FURRING CHANNEL SECURED TO 12" CONC. WALL

2" RIGID INSULATION

CHANNEL INSERT

¾" ALUM. WINDOW FRAME

ALUM. WINDOW CLIP

SEALANT & STOP

1¾" POLISHED GRANITE FACING

³⁄₁₆" × 1½" WIDE S.S. STRAP ANCHORS (2 PER STONE)

4"

1'-9"

2⅝"

¼"

4"

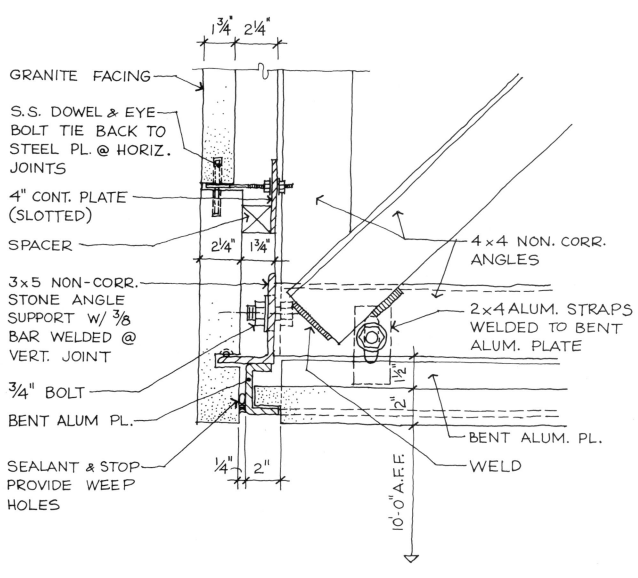

GRANITE FACING

S.S. DOWEL & EYE BOLT TIE BACK TO STEEL PL. @ HORIZ. JOINTS

4" CONT. PLATE (SLOTTED)

SPACER

3 x 5 NON-CORR. STONE ANGLE SUPPORT W/ ⅜ BAR WELDED @ VERT. JOINT

¾" BOLT

BENT ALUM PL.

SEALANT & STOP PROVIDE WEEP HOLES

1¾" 2¼"

2¼" 1¾"

¼" 2"

4 x 4 NON. CORR. ANGLES

2 x 4 ALUM. STRAPS WELDED TO BENT ALUM. PLATE

1½"

2"

BENT ALUM. PL.

WELD

10'-0" A.F.F.

Fig. 8 Vertical section through a typical intersection of a soffit and the wall.

The intersection between the soffit and the side wall is shown in Figure 9. Horizontal angles supporting the soffit are welded to steel plates that have been attached to wedge inserts cast into the structural concrete. Aluminum straps, noted in Figure 8, are bolted to the angles and welded to the miscellaneous elements that actually support the granite soffit. For example, the 3- by 3-inch extruded aluminum T receives the granite soffit in much the same way an inverted aluminum T receives an acoustic "lay-in" tile ceiling.

Fig. 9 Vertical section through the intersection of the soffit and side wall.

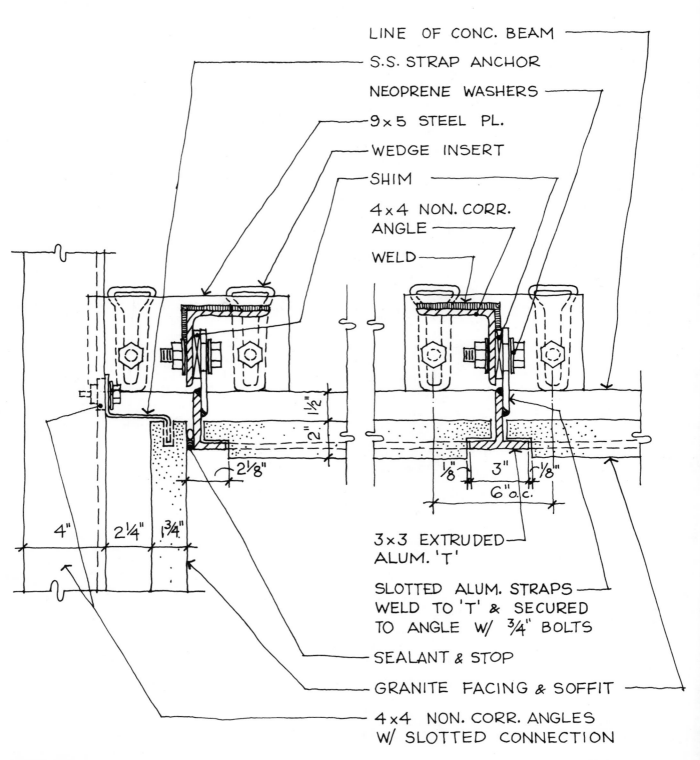

LINE OF CONC. BEAM

S.S. STRAP ANCHOR

NEOPRENE WASHERS

9 × 5 STEEL PL.

WEDGE INSERT

SHIM

4 × 4 NON. CORR. ANGLE

WELD

3 × 3 EXTRUDED ALUM. 'T'

SLOTTED ALUM. STRAPS WELD TO 'T' & SECURED TO ANGLE W/ ¾" BOLTS

SEALANT & STOP

GRANITE FACING & SOFFIT

4 × 4 NON. CORR. ANGLES W/ SLOTTED CONNECTION

Figure 10 is a vertical section through the glass curtain wall and the soffit and indicates the method used to develop a transition between these elements. The stone soffit is joined to the concrete structure by the wedge inserts, plates, and angles noted earlier. This assembly intersects the glass curtain wall, and a transition to the drapery pocket and the hung ceiling is made by a metal soffit.

Figure 5 is a continuation of this study and illustrates the relation of the eleventh-floor spandrel to the setback at the floor below. This drawing relates the head and sill details of the glazing to the interior of the building and to the heating system used to provide perimeter radiation. The aluminum sections supporting the projected soffit first observed in Figure 3 are illustrated, as are their struts and their connection to the structure. The interior concrete column is shown with various angles, metal studs, gypsum board, and insulation that define the interior portion of this assembly. The fin tube convector and enclosure are shown in relation to the glass.

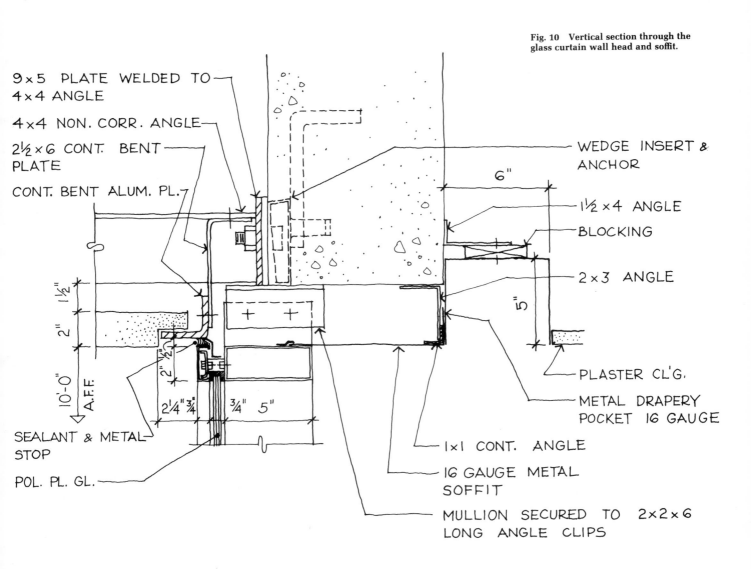

Fig. 10 Vertical section through the glass curtain wall head and soffit.

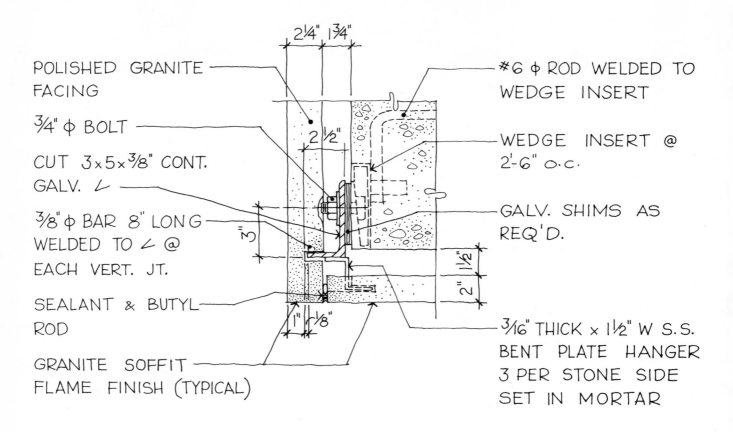

POLISHED GRANITE FACING

¾" φ BOLT

CUT 3 x 5 x ⅜" CONT. GALV. ∟

⅜" φ BAR 8" LONG WELDED TO ∟ @ EACH VERT. JT.

SEALANT & BUTYL ROD

GRANITE SOFFIT FLAME FINISH (TYPICAL)

2¼" 1¾"

2½"

3"

1" 1⅛"

2" 1½"

#6 φ ROD WELDED TO WEDGE INSERT

WEDGE INSERT @ 2'-6" O.C.

GALV. SHIMS AS REQ'D.

3/16" THICK x 1½" W S.S. BENT PLATE HANGER 3 PER STONE SIDE SET IN MORTAR

Fig. 11 Vertical section through stone soffit.

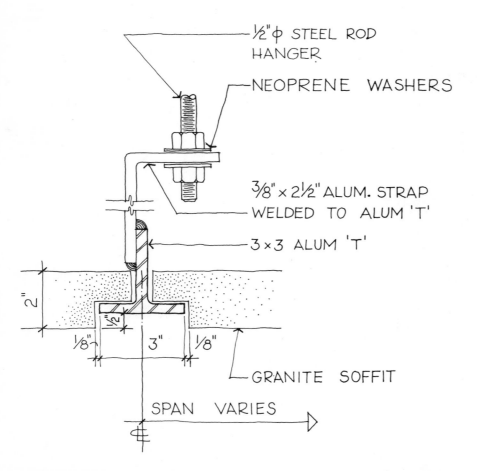

½" φ STEEL ROD HANGER

NEOPRENE WASHERS

⅜" x 2½" ALUM. STRAP WELDED TO ALUM 'T'

3 x 3 ALUM 'T'

2"

½"

⅛" 3" ⅛"

GRANITE SOFFIT

SPAN VARIES

Fig. 12 Vertical section through typical intermediate soffit support.

The detail shown in Figure 11 is a variation of the typical soffit detail in that this assembly calls for the vertical and horizontal transition to take place without a reveal. The installation of the soffit is made possible by the use of a concealed bent plate hanger secured to a continuous angle. The wedge insert required for this installation is shown in dotted lines and carries the angle that receives both the vertical and the horizontal granite. The soffit running perpendicularly back to the face of the building is shown in Figure 12. It is supported by an intermediate aluminum T suspended from the slab above by a bent strap and adjustable ½-inch steel hanger rod. Figure 13 shows the intersection of the glass curtain wall and the finished eleventh-floor slab and spandrel. The angle secured to the spandrel connects the glass sill mullion to the slab and secures the granite spandrel panel to the structure with a simple strap anchor. A clamp secures the glass and gaskets. The assembly is completed by the addition of a snap-on aluminum trim piece.

The relation of the tenth-floor terrace to the setback exterior wall is shown in Figure 6. A granite-sheathed precast concrete railing element, weighing approximately 1 ton, is shown here secured to the parapet. The railing is attached to a stainless steel post and heavy steel plate assembly bolted to the concrete spandrel beam. The contrast between terrace and roof construction is clearly shown in this diagram. Since the terrace is used for circulation, additional steps were taken to protect it from penetration and water leakage. A ¾-inch-thick asphalt setting bed, asphalt blocks, and grout were applied to the waterproofing membrane to create the wearing surface required for pedestrian traffic. Figure 6 includes a roof-insulation detail that was not used by Haines Lundberg Waehler in this project but is typical for the construction industry. This system can be installed from the floor below by impaling rigid insulation onto clips that are secured to the underside of the slab with epoxy cement. This method is accepted by most building codes and provides an effective reduction of heat loss and condensation. Also shown are the anchors that secure the granite facing stones to the concrete block backup wall at the horizontal and vertical joints.

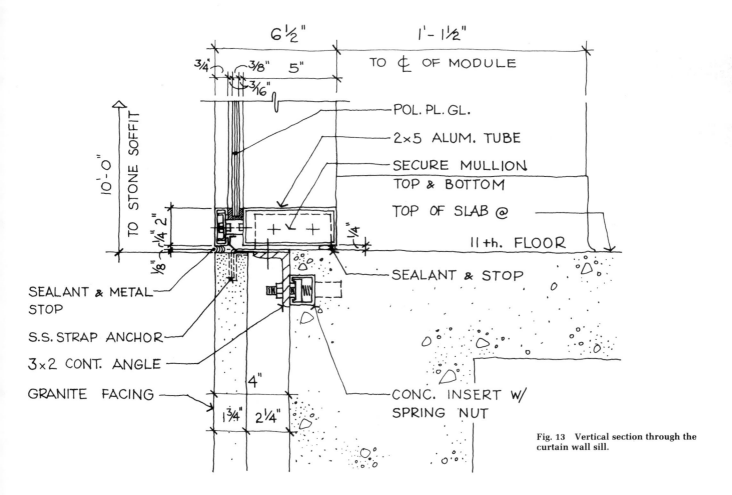

Fig. 13 Vertical section through the curtain wall sill.

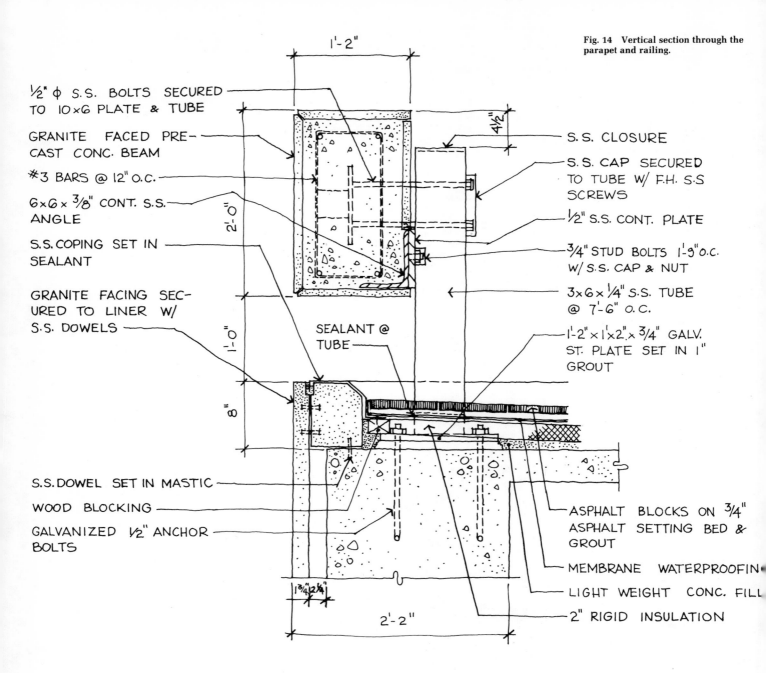

Fig. 14 Vertical section through the parapet and railing.

½" φ S.S. BOLTS SECURED TO 10×6 PLATE & TUBE

GRANITE FACED PRE-CAST CONC. BEAM

#3 BARS @ 12" O.C.

6×6 × ⅜" CONT. S.S. ANGLE

S.S. COPING SET IN SEALANT

GRANITE FACING SEC-URED TO LINER W/ S.S. DOWELS

1'-2"

4½"

2'-0"

1'-0"

8"

SEALANT @ TUBE

S.S. CLOSURE

S.S. CAP SECURED TO TUBE W/ F.H. S.S SCREWS

½" S.S. CONT. PLATE

¾" STUD BOLTS 1'-9" O.C. W/ S.S. CAP & NUT

3×6 × ¼" S.S. TUBE @ 7'-6" O.C.

1'-2" × 1'-2" × ¾" GALV. ST. PLATE SET IN 1" GROUT

S.S. DOWEL SET IN MASTIC

WOOD BLOCKING

GALVANIZED ½" ANCHOR BOLTS

ASPHALT BLOCKS ON ¾" ASPHALT SETTING BED & GROUT

MEMBRANE WATERPROOFING

LIGHT WEIGHT CONC. FILL

2" RIGID INSULATION

1¾" 2¼"

2'-2"

A vertical section through the parapet and railing of the tenth floor may be referred to in Figure 14. The construction of the railing and its relation to the structure is developed in this drawing. The granite facing at the terrace coping is a variation of the main roof detail and is treated accordingly. A horizontal section of the railing assembly showing the intersection of the prestressed units is illustrated in Figure 15. A 10- by 6-inch plate, cast into the left railing section, is wrapped with neoprene tape and receives the right-hand railing section, which is then inserted over it. The plate is welded to two stainless steel bolts that are secured to the 3- by 6-inch tubular post. This process is repeated successively until all the railing sections

are installed. The facing installation for the prestressed concrete railing sections is described in Figure 16, which shows the 8-gauge stainless steel anchor used to secure the ⅞-inch-thick granite veneer. The mitered corner and preformed sealant stop are used to waterproof this exterior section.

The relation of a typical window to the stone facade is illustrated in Figure 7. The window frame is composed of ¾-inch extruded aluminum sections and is designed to receive a pivotal sash. Windows and stone panels are secured to the concrete structure of the building with channel inserts. These inserts receive the anchorage devices for the stone panels, approximately three per stone on each side.

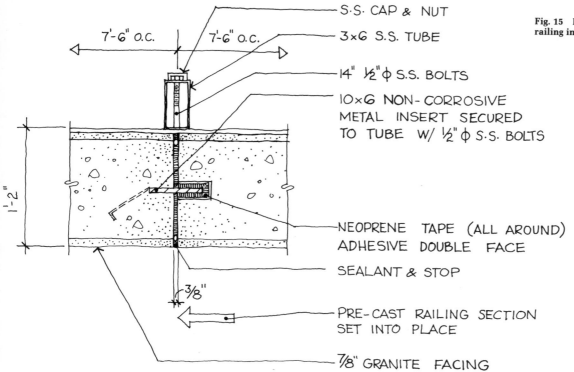

S.S. CAP & NUT

3×6 S.S. TUBE

7'-6" O.C.   7'-6" O.C.

14" ½"φ S.S. BOLTS

10×6 NON-CORROSIVE METAL INSERT SECURED TO TUBE W/ ½"φ S.S. BOLTS

1'-2"

NEOPRENE TAPE (ALL AROUND) ADHESIVE DOUBLE FACE

SEALANT & STOP

3/8"

PRE-CAST RAILING SECTION SET INTO PLACE

7/8" GRANITE FACING

Fig. 15 Horizontal section through the railing intersection.

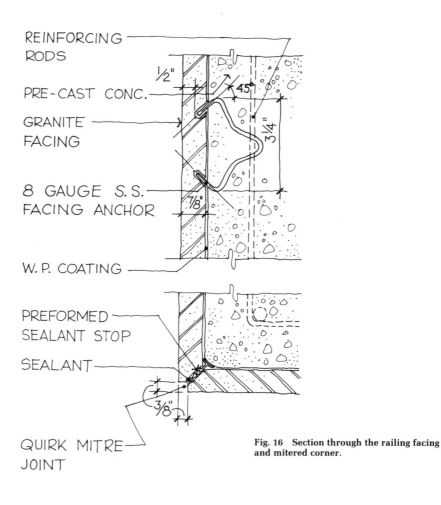

REINFORCING RODS

PRE-CAST CONC.

GRANITE FACING

½"

45°

3 1/4"

8 GAUGE S.S. FACING ANCHOR

7/8"

W. P. COATING

PREFORMED SEALANT STOP

SEALANT

3/8"

QUIRK MITRE JOINT

Fig. 16 Section through the railing facing and mitered corner.

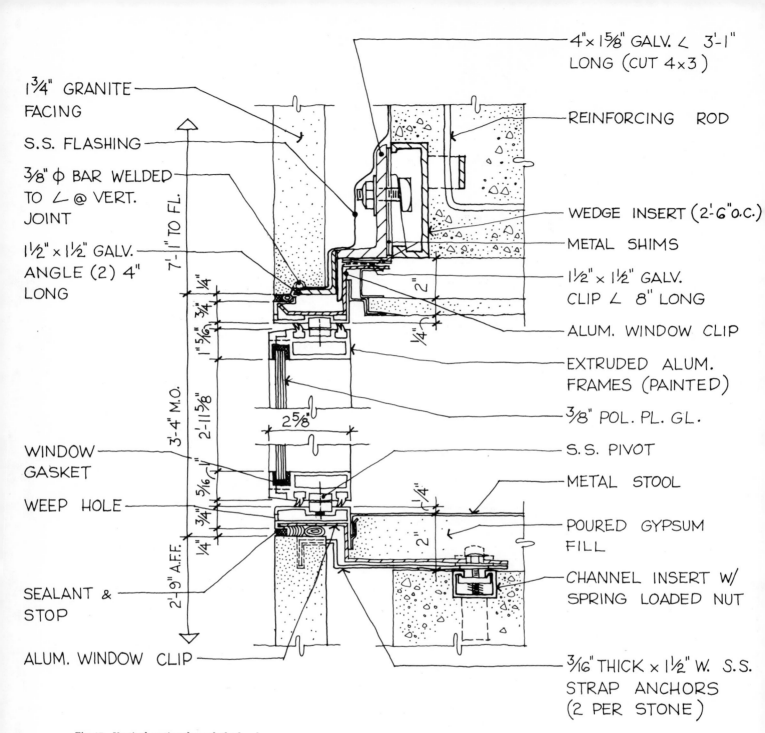

1¾" GRANITE FACING

S.S. FLASHING

⅜" ⌀ BAR WELDED TO ∠ @ VERT. JOINT

1½" × 1½" GALV. ANGLE (2) 4" LONG

WINDOW GASKET

WEEP HOLE

SEALANT & STOP

ALUM. WINDOW CLIP

4" × 1⅝" GALV. ∠ 3'-1" LONG (CUT 4×3)

REINFORCING ROD

WEDGE INSERT (2'-6" o.c.)

METAL SHIMS

1½" × 1½" GALV. CLIP ∠ 8" LONG

ALUM. WINDOW CLIP

EXTRUDED ALUM. FRAMES (PAINTED)

⅜" POL. PL. GL.

S.S. PIVOT

METAL STOOL

POURED GYPSUM FILL

CHANNEL INSERT W/ SPRING LOADED NUT

3/16" THICK × 1½" W. S.S. STRAP ANCHORS (2 PER STONE)

7'-1" TO FL.

¼"

¾"

1 5/16"

3'-4" M.O.

2'-11⅝"

5/16"

¾"

¼"

2'-9" A.F.F.

2 5/8"

2"

¼"

¼"

2"

Fig. 17 Vertical section through the head and sill of a typical window.

Window clips are also secured to the inserts, which are provided with spring-loaded connecting nuts. This diagram further delineates the relation of the interior wall finish to the window, head, and sill details. Figure 17 defines the method by which the granite facing and the head and sill of the window are secured to the building structure. In this detail the wedge insert is clearly shown in section, as is the wedge bolt that provides the vertical adjustment for this device. Note the ⅝-inch-diameter bar which is welded to the shelf angle only at the location of the vertical joints and which provides an important measure of support for adjacent stone panels in this assembly. The sill detail shows the connection between the stone panel and the window frame and their attachment to the structure by a strap anchor. A plan section through the window jamb is shown in Figure 18. The various

components of the window and stone facade are noted. The channel insert in this detail is shown receiving the window clip and the strap anchor for the stone panel. This insert is continuous along the height of the jamb and serves a dual purpose by securing both the window and the panel clips simultaneously.

The contemporary use of stone as a veneer rather than as a load-bearing material represents a radical departure from the past. Stone in this example was used as a curtain wall material with little or no functional relation to the load-bearing substance that is the basis of our architectural history. Coursing, arcuation, and mass are of little import to us in today's masonry vernacular. Clips, anchors, ties, and sealants are the controlling factors of stone veneer construction, and a study of this building allows us to become familiar with this new stone technology.

Fig. 18 Horizontal section through the window jamb.

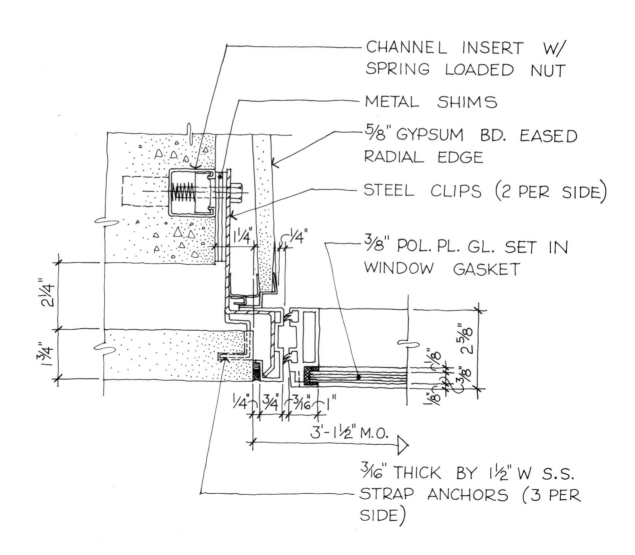

CHANNEL INSERT W/
SPRING LOADED NUT

METAL SHIMS

⅝" GYPSUM BD. EASED
RADIAL EDGE

STEEL CLIPS (2 PER SIDE)

⅜" POL. PL. GL. SET IN
WINDOW GASKET

3'-1½" M.O.

³⁄₁₆" THICK BY 1½" W S.S.
STRAP ANCHORS (3 PER
SIDE)

The W. C. Decker Engineering Building

Corning, New York   ARCHITECTS: Davis, Brody & Associates

Fig. 1 The Decker Building in its setting.

A competently designed building tends to endow its occupants with a sense of dignity that enhances the activities that take place within it. A pioneer in glass manufacturing would be expected to demand extremely high aesthetic and functional standards for its new research and engineering building. It was natural for Corning Glass Works to seek an ideal architectural expression of its technical mission by the innovative and forceful use of their key product. Davis, Brody & Associates were selected as architects for the W. C. Decker Engineering Building located in Corning, New York. It appears that the needs of the client and the capability of the architects meshed ideally for the development of this project.

In this structure the architects have introduced several innovative methods of construction that utilize state-of-the-art developments in glass technology. A major restraint placed upon the development of the project was that the Decker Building be compatible with its neighbors in the Houghton Park. Most of these structures were designed in the "international style" that emerged during the postwar period and are characterized by steel frame structures sheathed in metal and glass curtain walls and ribbon windows. Figure 1 shows a view of the Decker Building and its site location.

The building is three stories high with a lower level used primarily for parking and to a lesser degree for the mail room and some laboratories. The structure is raised on stilts because the Chemung River that flows to the south periodically floods the Corning valley. The Decker Building as seen in Figure 2 is subtly molded in glass and metal with curved convex lounge areas and an exterior stair that is reminiscent of Alvar Aalto's Massachusetts Institute of Technology dormitory. Semicircular tubes of aluminum form strong horizontal accents that define the spandrel panels and

Fig. 2 South and east elevations.

girdle the structure. The building's functions are joined by an atrium spine that runs down its center and forms two large triangular areas. One is located at the entry lobby, and the other contains the cafeteria at the far end of the building. This progression of interior space becomes the design focus of the building, and the skylights that cover the atriums can be seen from inside and outside the building. The spaces formed beckon people to enter the building and invite interaction of its occupants and visitors, which is consistent with the requirements of the client for a research facility that would promote the exchange and dissemination of information. Figures 3 and 4 show interior views of the atrium and skylight.

It becomes apparent upon inspection of the building that there are no vertical mullions whatsoever on the vision or spandrel glass. Glass panels appear to be continuous horizontal bands wrapping themselves around the outside of the structure. They are reintroduced on the interior elevations of the atrium as continuous horizontal mirrored accents at the floor spandrels. The only hint of discontinuity on the glass is the vertical lines that form the butt joints between the glass panels. The long elevations on the east and west are accented with full-height

Figs. 3 and 4   Interior views of atrium and skylight.

curved segments (see Figure 5) that identify lounge areas. Figure 6 is an interior view of the lounge area; its panels of vision glass form an unbroken curved wall that provides a panoramic view of the countryside.

The simple lines of the facade conceal an intricate cladding system that defies easy analysis. One does not immediately identify the construction methods used to secure the curtain wall elements to the perimeter of the structure. The design of the building is disciplined within a 32-foot structural grid, and this design is reflected on the exterior by a progression of six glass sections per bay, each section 5 feet 4 inches wide. The prefabricated spandrel assembly combines three of these panels into one 16-foot-long section which is the central element of the cladding system. Figure 7 illustrates a typical spandrel assembly and acquaints us with the highly refined glass technology that makes the elevations work. The butt-jointed vision glass panels shown below the spandrel are secured to the head and are also attached to the sill of the spandrel section. The segmented sill mullion shown here is designed to receive distinctive half-round molding trim that snaps into place. The bottom of each vertical extrusion is cut at an angle of 45 degrees to receive the mullion and the gutter extension that is used to drain condensate from the interior face of the spandrel assembly. This building's facade, expressed in a variation of the international style, becomes a brilliant juxtaposition of clear and opaque horizontal bands of glass. Absent are the structural vertical and horizontal mullions that have been the hallmark of an earlier metal and glass technology.

The spandrel assembly is composed of tempered glass, laminated rigid insulation, and four vertical aluminum extrusions. The sole function of the extrusions is to provide anchorage to the perimeter of the building structure. They vary in height from 4 to 7 feet depending upon the elevation condition. The innovative cladding system used in the Decker Building depends upon the composite action of high-strength structural glass and "space-age" adhesives. These materials together provide the necessary strength for the spandrel assembly to be fabricated on the ground and hoisted into position for attachment to the structure. Crucial to this assembly is the special heat-strengthened spandrel glass that is coated with a ceramic material that makes it opaque. The resulting 16-foot-long panel is a marvel of glass, plastic, and metal technologies. Not only must the glass be attached securely to the metal parts, but the glass must be allowed to expand and contract at different rates relative to the metal to which it is applied. The vertical aluminum extrusions which are used primarily to connect the spandrel to the structure also provide the assembly with the means to absorb vertical and horizontal building movements.

Fig. 5   Full-height curved segments identifying lounge areas.

Fig. 6   Interior view of lounge area.

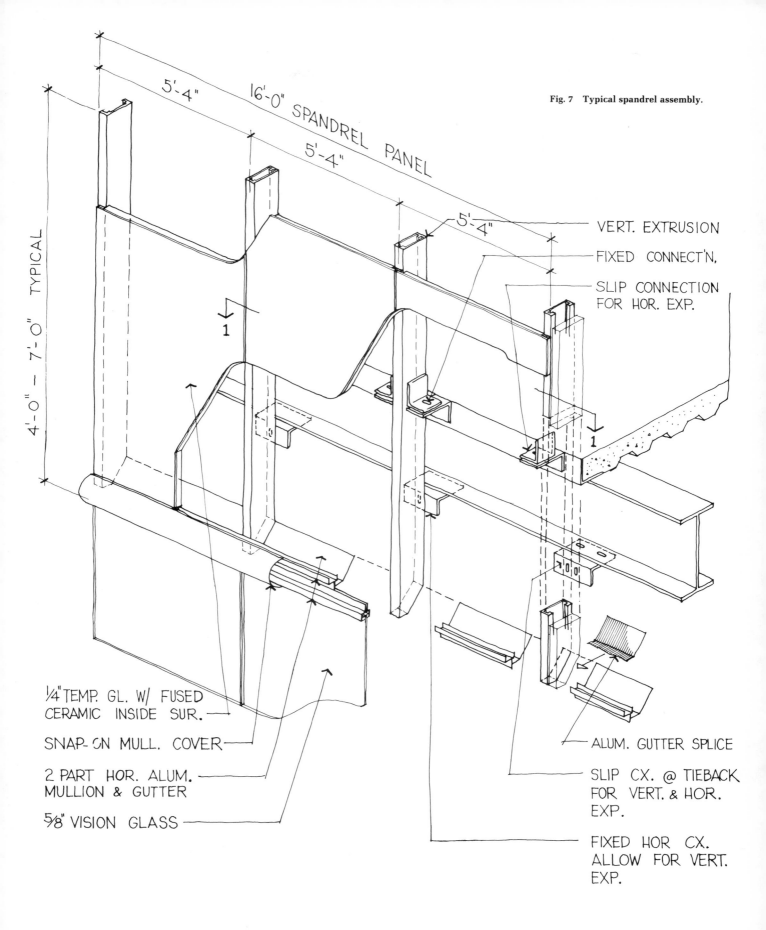

5'-4"

16'-0" SPANDREL PANEL

5'-4"

5'-4"

Fig. 7 Typical spandrel assembly.

4'-0" — 7'-0" TYPICAL

VERT. EXTRUSION

FIXED CONNECT'N,

SLIP CONNECTION
FOR HOR. EXP.

1

1

¼" TEMP. GL. W/ FUSED
CERAMIC INSIDE SUR.

SNAP-ON MULL. COVER

2 PART HOR. ALUM.
MULLION & GUTTER

⅝" VISION GLASS

ALUM. GUTTER SPLICE

SLIP CX. @ TIEBACK
FOR VERT. & HOR.
EXP.

FIXED HOR CX.
ALLOW FOR VERT.
EXP.

A section through the ¼-inch glass spandrel panels is shown in Figure 8, which indicates that they are secured to the intermediate mullion with structural silicone adhesive. This material is used to bond the glass to the vertical aluminum extrusions. A bond breaker which allows independent movement for the glass panels without introducing excessive internal stress is installed. The panels of glass are then sealed to each other with silicone caulking but not to the bond breaker, which resists this adhesion. Several days are required to allow the structural silicone to cure and acquire strength before the panels may be moved. Rigid insulation is applied to the inside face of the opaque glass before fabrication. Vertical aluminum extrusions at the end of each spandrel assembly are used to secure the system and provide the required horizontal expansion at this connection. This condition is shown in Figure 8, which illustrates how the 2½- by 5½-inch aluminum extrusions at the spandrel ends are designed to slip within

each other to provide the necessary flexibility between panels.

The length of the building requires vertical expansion joints to absorb movement caused by temperature changes. Horizontal sections A and B through the expansion joints are shown in Figure 9; these joints occur approximately 100 feet on center. Section A is a plan view taken through the spandrel section that indicates a weather-stripped slip joint that is secured to the typical vertical extrusions. The corresponding expansion joint at the vision glass is shown in Section B. Note the similarity of the extruded aluminum splice joints in these sections.

Fig. 8 Plan section of intermediate mullion and splice mullion.

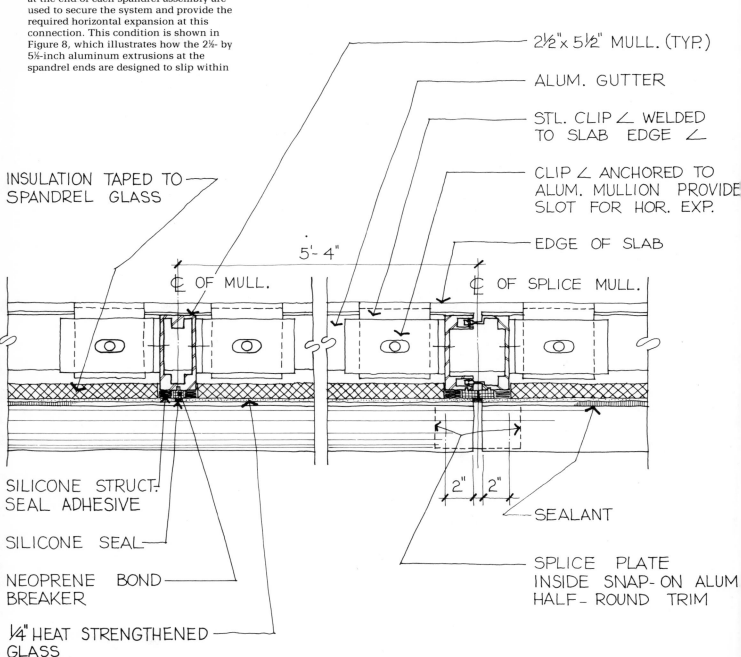

2½" x 5½" MULL. (TYP.)

ALUM. GUTTER

STL. CLIP ∠ WELDED TO SLAB EDGE ∠

CLIP ∠ ANCHORED TO ALUM. MULLION PROVIDE SLOT FOR HOR. EXP.

EDGE OF SLAB

INSULATION TAPED TO SPANDREL GLASS

5'- 4"

℄ OF MULL.   ℄ OF SPLICE MULL.

2" 2"

SEALANT

SILICONE STRUCT. SEAL ADHESIVE

SILICONE SEAL

NEOPRENE BOND BREAKER

¼" HEAT STRENGTHENED GLASS

SPLICE PLATE INSIDE SNAP- ON ALUM HALF- ROUND TRIM

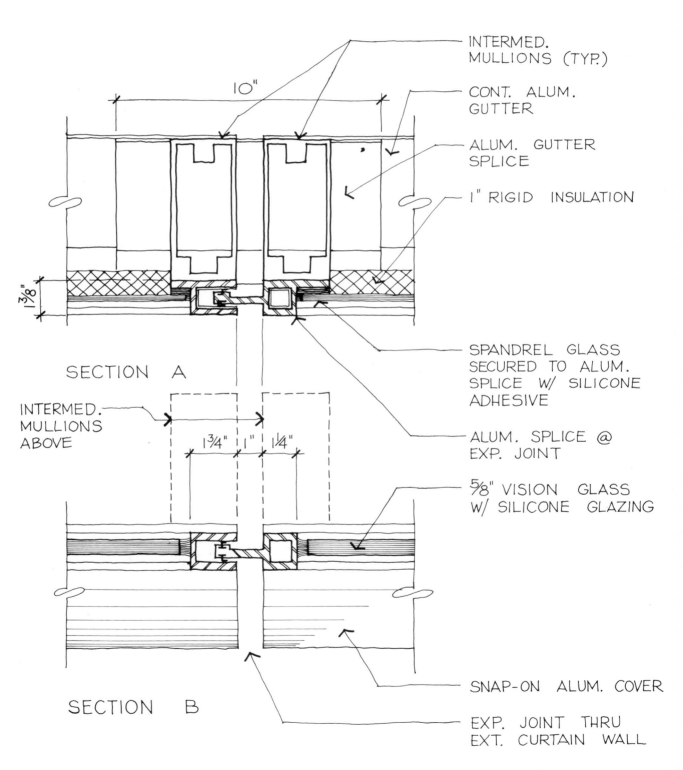

Fig. 9 Section A shows a horizontal section through the cladding expansion joint; section B shows a horizontal section through the expansion joint at the vision glass.

INTERMED.
MULLIONS (TYP.)

CONT. ALUM.
GUTTER

ALUM. GUTTER
SPLICE

1" RIGID INSULATION

10"

1 3/8"

SECTION A

SPANDREL GLASS
SECURED TO ALUM.
SPLICE W/ SILICONE
ADHESIVE

ALUM. SPLICE @
EXP. JOINT

INTERMED.
MULLIONS
ABOVE

1 3/4" 1" 1 1/4"

5/8" VISION GLASS
W/ SILICONE GLAZING

SECTION B

SNAP-ON ALUM. COVER

EXP. JOINT THRU
EXT. CURTAIN WALL

The next series of illustrations studies the roof and parapet. In Figure 10 is seen a typical vertical extrusion that is part of the spandrel assembly. It is clipped to the edge of the slab with sufficient height above the roof to form a low parapet. It is also secured to the spandrel beam with a clip angle and shims. The horizontal mullion that is at the top of the assembly and that normally receives the vision glass and snap-on molding here accepts the aluminum coping which makes the transition from exterior wall to roof. Figure 11 is a vertical section

Fig. 10 Parapet spandrel and roof

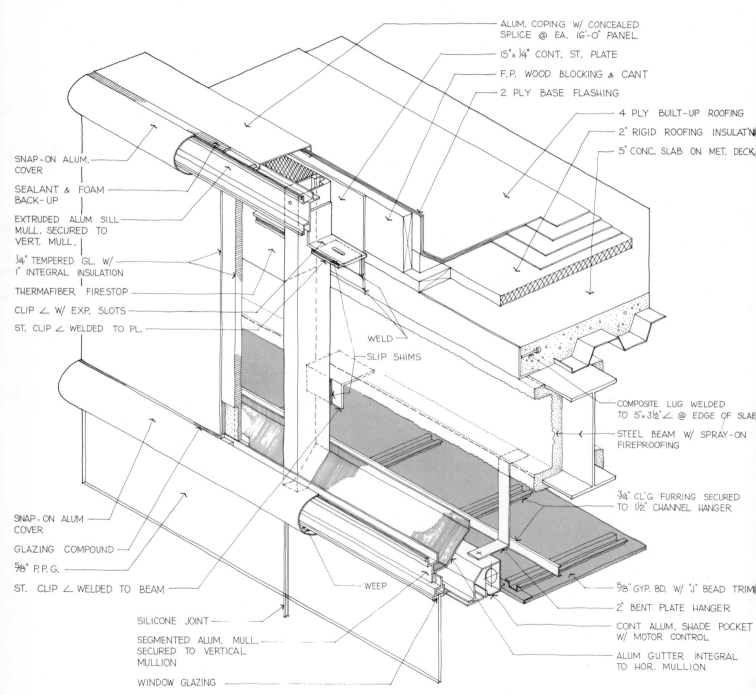

SNAP-ON ALUM. COVER

SEALANT & FOAM BACK-UP

EXTRUDED ALUM SILL MULL. SECURED TO VERT. MULL.

¼" TEMPERED GL. W/ 1" INTEGRAL INSULATION

THERMAFIBER FIRESTOP

CLIP ∠ W/ EXP. SLOTS

ST. CLIP ∠ WELDED TO PL.

SNAP-ON ALUM COVER

GLAZING COMPOUND

⅝" P. P. G.

ST. CLIP ∠ WELDED TO BEAM

SILICONE JOINT

SEGMENTED ALUM. MULL. SECURED TO VERTICAL MULLION

WINDOW GLAZING

ALUM. COPING W/ CONCEALED SPLICE @ EA. 16'-0" PANEL

15"x ¼" CONT. ST. PLATE

F.P. WOOD BLOCKING & CANT

2 PLY BASE FLASHING

4 PLY BUILT-UP ROOFING

2" RIGID ROOFING INSULAT'N

5" CONC. SLAB ON MET. DECK

WELD

SLIP SHIMS

WEEP

COMPOSITE LUG WELDED TO 5"x3½"∠ @ EDGE OF SLAB

STEEL BEAM W/ SPRAY-ON FIREPROOFING

¾" CL'G FURRING SECURED TO 1½" CHANNEL HANGER

⅝" GYP. BD. W/ "J" BEAD TRIM

2" BENT PLATE HANGER

CONT ALUM. SHADE POCKET W/ MOTOR CONTROL

ALUM GUTTER INTEGRAL TO HOR. MULLION

through this assembly that explains the relation of the spandrel to the roof parapet. The coping is tucked into the sill mullion and overlaps the inside face of the parapet. Note the sealant used to protect this installation from water penetration. Figures 10 and 11 both illustrate the use of the gutter extrusion at the head of the vision glass to conduct moisture out of the cladding system through weep holes. Also noted on these drawings are the composite lugs which are welded to the metal edge angle; this assembly reinforces the roof slab. Note the installation of the fire-stop secured by an impaling bracket in the parapet assembly. The segmented head mullion, in addition to securing the gutter, also receives the continuous aluminum shade pocket, which in turn makes the transition to the interior suspended gypsum board ceiling.

Fig. 11 Vertical section through the parapet, spandrel, and roof.

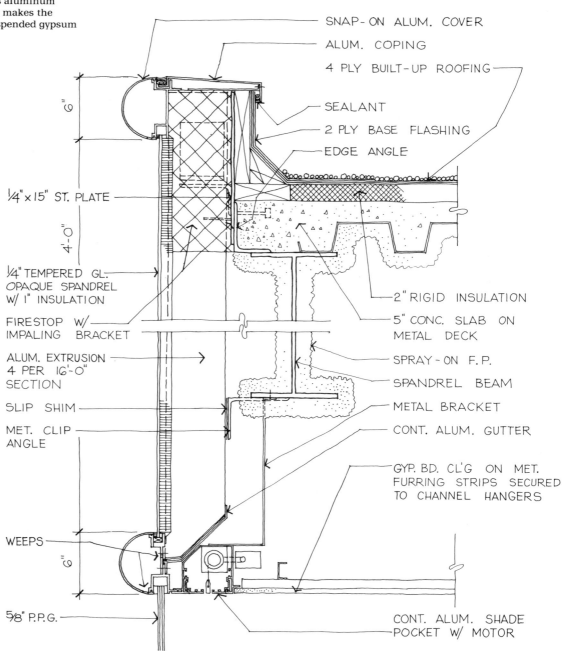

SNAP-ON ALUM. COVER

ALUM. COPING

4 PLY BUILT-UP ROOFING

SEALANT

2 PLY BASE FLASHING

EDGE ANGLE

1/4" × 15" ST. PLATE

1/4" TEMPERED GL. OPAQUE SPANDREL W/ 1" INSULATION

FIRESTOP W/ IMPALING BRACKET

ALUM. EXTRUSION 4 PER 16'-0" SECTION

SLIP SHIM

MET. CLIP ANGLE

WEEPS

5/8" P.P.G.

2" RIGID INSULATION

5" CONC. SLAB ON METAL DECK

SPRAY-ON F.P.

SPANDREL BEAM

METAL BRACKET

CONT. ALUM. GUTTER

GYP. BD. CL'G ON MET. FURRING STRIPS SECURED TO CHANNEL HANGERS

CONT. ALUM. SHADE POCKET W/ MOTOR

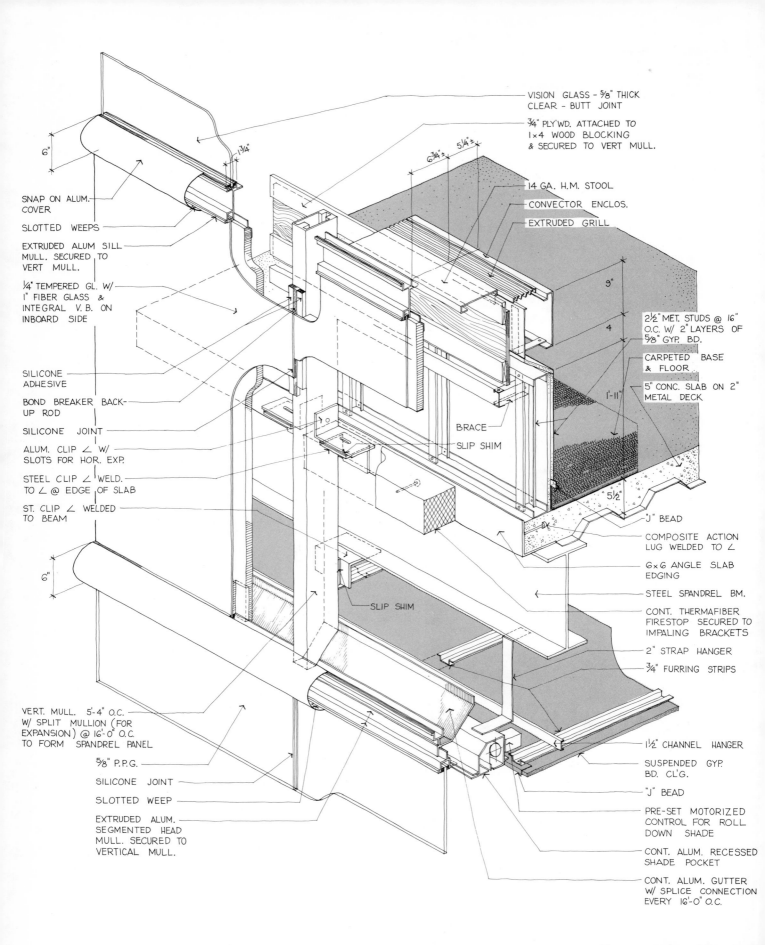

VISION GLASS - ⅝" THICK
CLEAR - BUTT JOINT

¾" PLY'WD. ATTACHED TO
1×4 WOOD BLOCKING
& SECURED TO VERT MULL.

6¾"±   5¼"±

14 GA. H.M. STOOL

CONVECTOR ENCLOS.

EXTRUDED GRILL

9"

4

2½" MET. STUDS @ 16"
O.C. W/ 2" LAYERS OF
⅝" GYP. BD.

CARPETED BASE
& FLOOR

5" CONC. SLAB ON 2"
METAL DECK

1'-11"

BRACE

SLIP SHIM

5½"

"J" BEAD

COMPOSITE ACTION
LUG WELDED TO ∠

6×6 ANGLE SLAB
EDGING

STEEL SPANDREL BM.

CONT. THERMAFIBER
FIRESTOP SECURED TO
IMPALING BRACKETS

2" STRAP HANGER

¾" FURRING STRIPS

1½" CHANNEL HANGER

SUSPENDED GYP.
BD. CL'G.

"J" BEAD

PRE-SET MOTORIZED
CONTROL FOR ROLL
DOWN SHADE

CONT. ALUM. RECESSED
SHADE POCKET

CONT. ALUM. GUTTER
W/ SPLICE CONNECTION
EVERY 16'-0" O.C.

6"

¾"

SNAP ON ALUM.
COVER

SLOTTED WEEPS

EXTRUDED ALUM SILL
MULL. SECURED TO
VERT. MULL.

¼" TEMPERED GL. W/
1" FIBER GLASS &
INTEGRAL V. B. ON
INBOARD SIDE

SILICONE
ADHESIVE

BOND BREAKER BACK-
UP ROD

SILICONE JOINT

ALUM. CLIP ∠ W/
SLOTS FOR HOR. EXP.

STEEL CLIP ∠ WELD.
TO ∠ @ EDGE OF SLAB

ST. CLIP ∠ WELDED
TO BEAM

6"

SLIP SHIM

VERT. MULL. 5'-4" O.C.
W/ SPLIT MULLION (FOR
EXPANSION) @ 16'-0" O.C.
TO FORM SPANDREL PANEL

⅝" P.P.G.

SILICONE JOINT

SLOTTED WEEP

EXTRUDED ALUM.
SEGMENTED HEAD
MULL. SECURED TO
VERTICAL MULL.

Fig. 12 Typical spandrel condition.

Figure 12 illustrates that portion of a spandrel assembly that is secured to a typical floor slab and forms the head and sill conditions for the vision glass. The sill and its relation to the vision glass and convector stool mark the transition to the interior spaces of the building. The spandrel beam, the fire-stop, and the edge angle are shown in relation to the cladding system. The segmented aluminum head, the gutter, and the shade pocket provide the transition to the lower vision glass panels and suspended ceiling. The gypsum board ceiling is applied to metal furring strips, which in turn are secured to a 1½-inch channel runner attached to the bottom of the slab by hanger rods spaced at 4 feet on center. The gypsum board is screwed to the furring strips, taped and spackled, and finished with a J bead at the ceiling intersection with the shade pocket. We see

here in greater detail how the vertical mullion is attached to the slab with slotted angle clips equipped with slip shims to provide for the inevitable panel movement caused by temperature changes. The continuous hollow metal stool sits on the horizontal sill mullion and is attached to it with a spring clip.

Figure 13 is a vertical section through the intermediate floor slab and illustrates the relation of the elements shown in Figure 12. Continuous wood grounds attached to the vertical extrusions receive the stool and allow the fin tube heating enclosure to be mounted on plywood. The remainder of the 3-foot-high sill is formed with metal studs and a double layer of gypsum board. The finished gypsum board layer is cut 4 inches shy of the slab and is finished with a J bead. This provides a neat detail for the development of a flush-carpeted base.

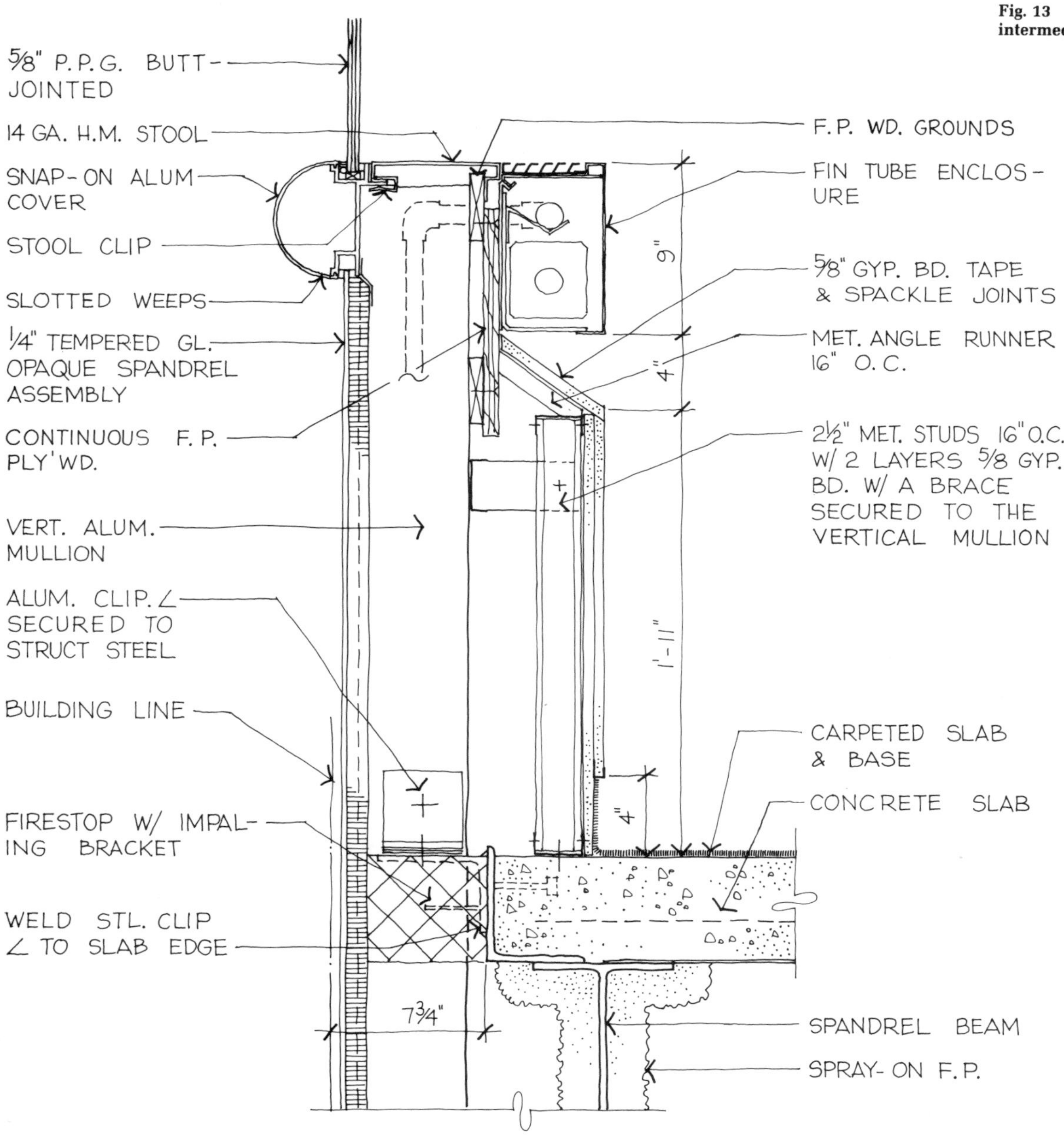

Fig. 13 Vertical section through the intermediate floor slab.

⅝" P.P.G. BUTT-JOINTED

14 GA. H.M. STOOL

SNAP-ON ALUM COVER

STOOL CLIP

SLOTTED WEEPS

¼" TEMPERED GL. OPAQUE SPANDREL ASSEMBLY

CONTINUOUS F.P. PLY'WD.

VERT. ALUM. MULLION

ALUM. CLIP. ∠ SECURED TO STRUCT STEEL

BUILDING LINE

FIRESTOP W/ IMPALING BRACKET

WELD STL. CLIP ∠ TO SLAB EDGE

F.P. WD. GROUNDS

FIN TUBE ENCLOSURE

⅝" GYP. BD. TAPE & SPACKLE JOINTS

MET. ANGLE RUNNER 16" O.C.

2½" MET. STUDS 16" O.C. W/ 2 LAYERS ⅝ GYP. BD. W/ A BRACE SECURED TO THE VERTICAL MULLION

CARPETED SLAB & BASE

CONCRETE SLAB

SPANDREL BEAM

SPRAY-ON F.P.

7¾"

Figure 14, a vertical section through an exterior soffit, demonstrates the versatility of the head mullion detail. This detail can be adapted for exterior soffits, as shown in this drawing, or used to receive a shade pocket or a suspended ceiling. The segmented head and sill elements must be capable of responding to a variety of requirements called for by the building design. The exterior gypsum board soffit is secured to furring strips and stud hangers, both of which receive insulation batts. An intermediate U-shaped aluminum extrusion receives the exterior gypsum board soffit and a variation of the shade pocket, which permits the installation of the vision glass and the continuation of the soffit as a suspended interior ceiling.

A relatively small portion of the building's lower level is enclosed, the majority of the area being turned over to parking. The danger of periodic flooding makes this a sensible response to a recurrent situation. Figure 15 illustrates the detailing used at the ground line of the building. A narrow horizontal strip window at the mail room and a corresponding open horizontal space at the perimeter of the parking area express a nearly continuous

band around the building at the ground level. An aluminum head channel is secured to a hung metal stud assembly and supports the narrow band of horizontal vision glass that is 1 foot 10 inches high. The segmented aluminum mullion is used to join the vertical spandrel assembly to a 12-inch-wide soffit of exterior gypsum board. The interior suspended ceiling consists of a 2- by 4-foot lay-in tile ceiling that is secured to the slab above.

The Decker Building has an exciting skylight that faithfully follows the plan development of the interior functions. In these interior spaces, the play of light and shade caused by changing weather conditions creates a variety of moods within the building. The skylight link between the triangular-shaped entry area and cafeteria is visible throughout the building and is punctuated by the peaked skylights overhead. The glass used on the skylight is a technical response to the building's energy program. It is a solar-reflective material which protects the interior atrium from glare and excessive solar gain while providing natural illumination.

Fig. 14 Vertical section through the exterior soffit.

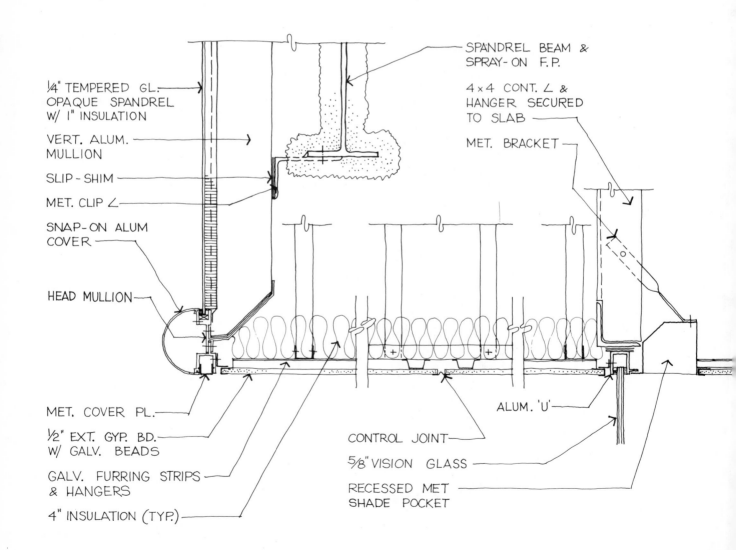

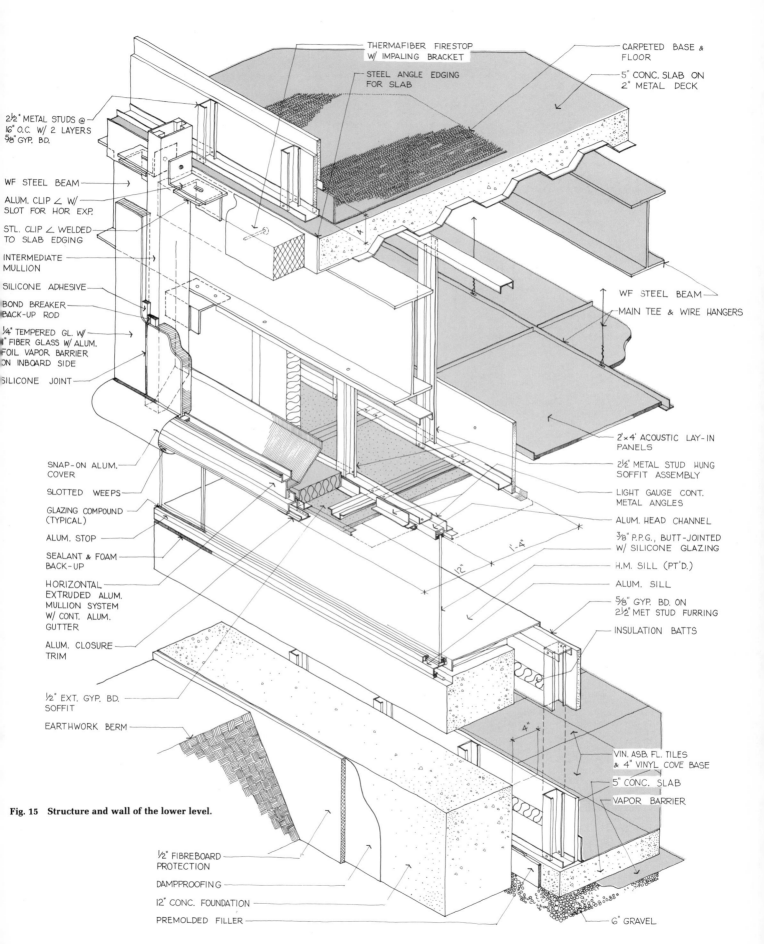

THERMAFIBER FIRESTOP
W/ IMPALING BRACKET

STEEL ANGLE EDGING
FOR SLAB

CARPETED BASE &
FLOOR

5" CONC. SLAB ON
2" METAL DECK

2½" METAL STUDS @
16" O.C. W/ 2 LAYERS
⅝" GYP. BD.

WF STEEL BEAM

ALUM. CLIP ∠ W/
SLOT FOR HOR EXP.

STL. CLIP ∠ WELDED
TO SLAB EDGING

INTERMEDIATE
MULLION

SILICONE ADHESIVE

BOND BREAKER
BACK-UP ROD

¼" TEMPERED GL. W/
" FIBER GLASS W/ ALUM.
FOIL VAPOR BARRIER
ON INBOARD SIDE

SILICONE JOINT

WF STEEL BEAM

MAIN TEE & WIRE HANGERS

2'×4' ACOUSTIC LAY-IN
PANELS

2½" METAL STUD HUNG
SOFFIT ASSEMBLY

LIGHT GAUGE CONT.
METAL ANGLES

ALUM. HEAD CHANNEL

⅜" P.P.G., BUTT-JOINTED
W/ SILICONE GLAZING

H.M. SILL (PT'D.)

ALUM. SILL

⅝" GYP. BD. ON
2½" MET STUD FURRING

INSULATION BATTS

SNAP-ON ALUM.
COVER

SLOTTED WEEPS

GLAZING COMPOUND
(TYPICAL)

ALUM. STOP

SEALANT & FOAM
BACK-UP

HORIZONTAL
EXTRUDED ALUM.
MULLION SYSTEM
W/ CONT. ALUM.
GUTTER

ALUM. CLOSURE
TRIM

½" EXT. GYP. BD.
SOFFIT

EARTHWORK BERM

VIN. ASB. FL. TILES
& 4" VINYL COVE BASE

5" CONC. SLAB

VAPOR BARRIER

Fig. 15 Structure and wall of the lower level.

½" FIBREBOARD
PROTECTION

DAMPPROOFING

12" CONC. FOUNDATION

PREMOLDED FILLER

6" GRAVEL

Figure 16 illustrates the shape of the skylight and its relation to the penthouses. The small skylights on the quadrants of the penthouse structures provide illumination for the spaces below. Figure 17, a vertical section through the skylight, indicates the various details studied here that are crucial to understanding this complex assembly. The exterior treatment of the elevations is echoed on the interior through the use of mirrors on the spandrel sections overlooking the atrium. The skylight, floors, walls, and people moving through the interior mall are reflected in these mirrored bands, providing an exciting visual experience not unlike a multiscreened light show.

Figure 18 analyzes the skylight details and traces their development from the horizontally banded exterior cladding system to the interior spandrels overlooking the atrium. As one approachs the building from the north, one notes that the cladding system is interrupted at the building's entrance. Walls of glass rise dramatically from the entry vestibule to an intersection with the hip roof portion of the

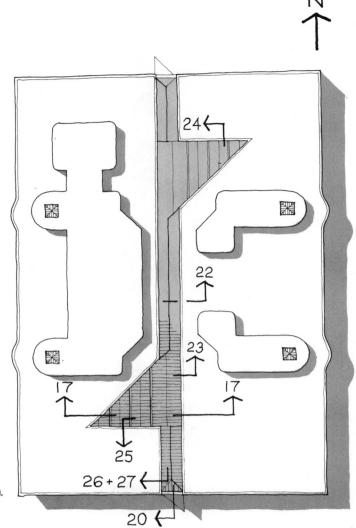

Fig. 16   Shape of skylight and its relation to the penthouses (see Figures 17, 20, and 22–27 for details).

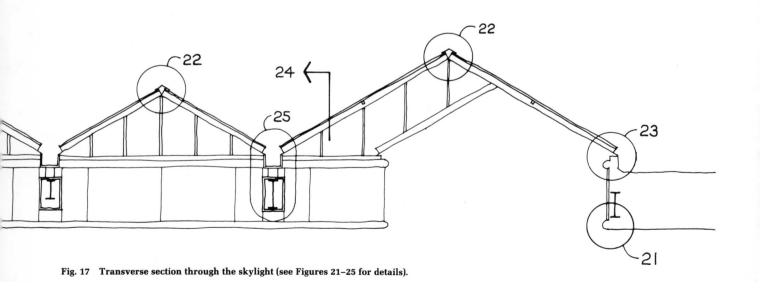

Fig. 17   Transverse section through the skylight (see Figures 21–25 for details).

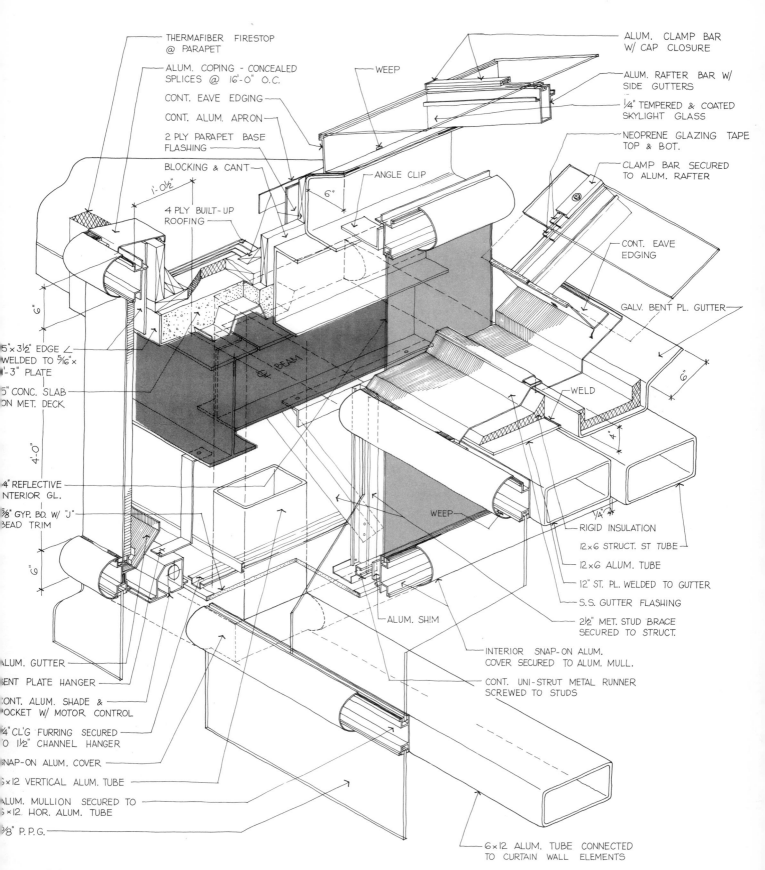

THERMAFIBER FIRESTOP @ PARAPET

ALUM. COPING - CONCEALED SPLICES @ 16'-0" O.C.

CONT. EAVE EDGING

CONT. ALUM. APRON

2 PLY PARAPET BASE FLASHING

BLOCKING & CANT

4 PLY BUILT-UP ROOFING

WEEP

ANGLE CLIP

ALUM. CLAMP BAR W/ CAP CLOSURE

ALUM. RAFTER BAR W/ SIDE GUTTERS

¼" TEMPERED & COATED SKYLIGHT GLASS

NEOPRENE GLAZING TAPE TOP & BOT.

CLAMP BAR SECURED TO ALUM. RAFTER

CONT. EAVE EDGING

GALV. BENT PL. GUTTER

5" × 3½" EDGE ∠ WELDED TO 5/16" × 1'-3" PLATE

5" CONC. SLAB ON MET. DECK

¼" REFLECTIVE INTERIOR GL.

⅝" GYP. BD. W/ "J" BEAD TRIM

WELD

WEEP

¼"

RIGID INSULATION

12×6 STRUCT. ST TUBE

12×6 ALUM. TUBE

12" ST. PL. WELDED TO GUTTER

S.S. GUTTER FLASHING

2½" MET. STUD BRACE SECURED TO STRUCT.

INTERIOR SNAP-ON ALUM. COVER SECURED TO ALUM. MULL.

CONT. UNI-STRUT METAL RUNNER SCREWED TO STUDS

ALUM. SHIM

ALUM. GUTTER

BENT PLATE HANGER

CONT. ALUM. SHADE & POCKET W/ MOTOR CONTROL

¼" CL'G FURRING SECURED TO 1½" CHANNEL HANGER

SNAP-ON ALUM. COVER

6×12 VERTICAL ALUM. TUBE

ALUM. MULLION SECURED TO 6×12 HOR. ALUM. TUBE

⅜" P.P.G.

6×12 ALUM. TUBE CONNECTED TO CURTAIN WALL ELEMENTS

Fig. 18   Skylight and exterior glass at the entry.

skylight. Figures 3, 18, and 19 illustrate the transition of the exterior cladding system to the interior spandrels and skylight. The opaque glass spandrel panels terminate at the fourth floor above the ground floor, and the vision glass is installed from that point to the other side of the entry. This development can be studied in Figure 4, which shows the south entry. This complex assembly is composed of 6- by 12-inch aluminum and steel tubes secured to a bent steel plate gutter. The strength of the steel elements in this assembly allows the structure to span the entry and support the considerable weight of the skylight hip. A vertical section through this assembly is shown in Figure 20, which illustrates the relation of the 6- by 12-inch metal tubes to the vision glass and hip end of the skylight. The gutter detail with its insulation and stainless steel flashing is shown as part of the roofing assembly. Note the 4-foot-high vertical aluminum tube that flanks the entry area and is aligned with the overhead structure.

Fig. 19 Transition of exterior cladding system to interior spandrels and skylight.

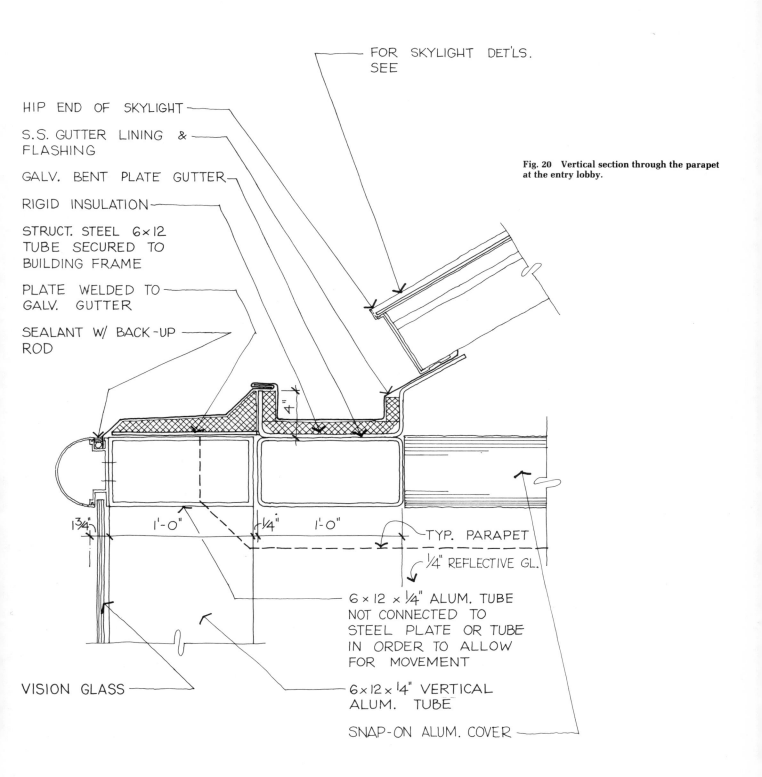

FOR SKYLIGHT DET'LS. SEE

HIP END OF SKYLIGHT

S.S. GUTTER LINING & FLASHING

GALV. BENT PLATE GUTTER

RIGID INSULATION

STRUCT. STEEL 6×12 TUBE SECURED TO BUILDING FRAME

PLATE WELDED TO GALV. GUTTER

SEALANT W/ BACK-UP ROD

Fig. 20 Vertical section through the parapet at the entry lobby.

4"

1¾"

1'-0"

¼"

1'-0"

TYP. PARAPET

¼" REFLECTIVE GL.

6×12×¼" ALUM. TUBE NOT CONNECTED TO STEEL PLATE OR TUBE IN ORDER TO ALLOW FOR MOVEMENT

6×12×¼" VERTICAL ALUM. TUBE

VISION GLASS

SNAP-ON ALUM. COVER

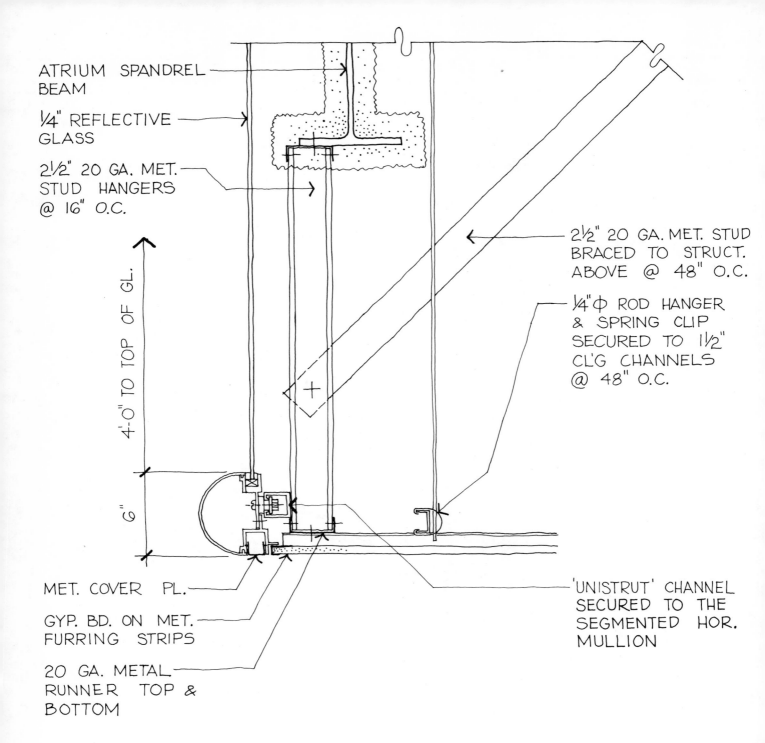

ATRIUM SPANDREL BEAM

1/4" REFLECTIVE GLASS

2 1/2" 20 GA. MET. STUD HANGERS @ 16" O.C.

4'-0" TO TOP OF GL.

6"

2 1/2" 20 GA. MET. STUD BRACED TO STRUCT. ABOVE @ 48" O.C.

1/4"φ ROD HANGER & SPRING CLIP SECURED TO 1 1/2" CL'G CHANNELS @ 48" O.C.

MET. COVER PL.

GYP. BD. ON MET. FURRING STRIPS

20 GA. METAL RUNNER TOP & BOTTOM

'UNISTRUT' CHANNEL SECURED TO THE SEGMENTED HOR. MULLION

Fig. 21 Vertical section through the interior spandrel.

Figure 21 illustrates the lower assembly of the interior spandrel and demonstrates the consistency with which the design theme of the building exterior is executed indoors. A Unistrut channel receives the segmented horizontal mullion at the point of transition between the mirrored spandrel and the suspended ceiling that intersects the mullion. Note the stud hanger braced to the slab, and the ¼-inch-diameter rod and channels that support the suspended gypsum board ceiling. The upper portion of this assembly may be found in Figure 23.

An examination, starting with Figure 22, of the skylight details shown in Figure 17 shows the typical ridge assembly of the skylight. The aluminum rafters are joined to the ridge by extruded aluminum bars secured by a bent plate. A brace clip welded to the ridge bars stabilizes this installation. An aluminum ridge cap is clipped into extruded neoprene fittings and is bolted through the aluminum rafters and bent plate. Intermediate tubular aluminum bars are installed at regular intervals to receive the segmented skylight glass. Figure 22 describes a typical method for the installation and waterproofing of this type of assembly. The cross bar that carries an integral condensate gutter is secured to the rafters and is designed to receive an

Fig. 22 Vertical section through the interior parapet spandrel and soffit.

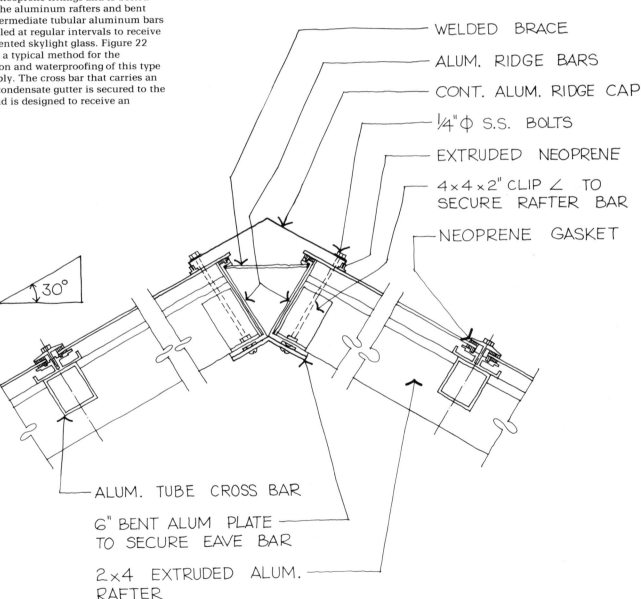

WELDED BRACE

ALUM. RIDGE BARS

CONT. ALUM. RIDGE CAP

¼" ⌀ S.S. BOLTS

EXTRUDED NEOPRENE

4 × 4 × 2" CLIP ∠ TO SECURE RAFTER BAR

NEOPRENE GASKET

30°

ALUM. TUBE CROSS BAR

6" BENT ALUM PLATE TO SECURE EAVE BAR

2 × 4 EXTRUDED ALUM. RAFTER

aluminum clamp that creates a waterproof sandwich of skylight glass and neoprene gaskets. Figure 23 traces the ridge down to the eave; this can be studied in Figure 18 as well. In this detail, running perpendicular to the exterior spandrel is a 12-inch channel on top of a beam. The channel secured to the interior spandrel beam forms the typical internal parapet and eaves. It receives wood blocking, a plate bent at the angle of the skylight, flashing, rafters, and eave edging. The edging is similar to the ridge bars shown in Figure 22. The glass is clamped to the aluminum rafters and is secured to a continuous neoprene glazing gasket that is designed to snap into the aluminum eave. Moisture formed within the skylight is conducted by condensate gutters to the aluminum eaves and drained through weep holes. The eave is seated on an aluminum apron that secures the skylight parapet base flashing. An angle bracket is attached to the ⅜-inch bent plate to receive the segmented aluminum mullion. This illustration and Figure 22 present a complete vertical section through the interior spandrel assembly. Lighting track is installed on selected rafters and is connected to electric conduit installed between the snap-on trim and the ⅜-inch bent plate. Note the spray-on fireproofing applied to the structural members.

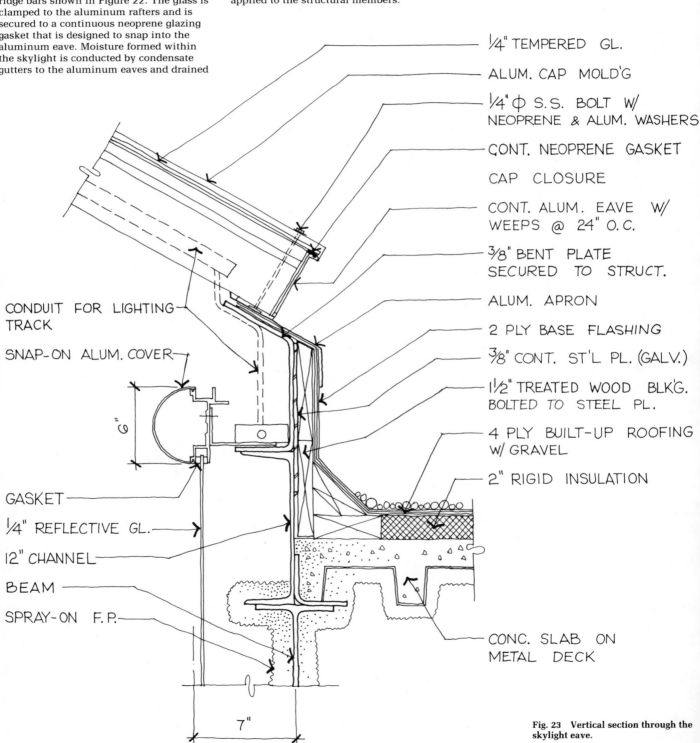

1/4" TEMPERED GL.

ALUM. CAP MOLD'G

1/4" ⌀ S.S. BOLT W/ NEOPRENE & ALUM. WASHERS

CONT. NEOPRENE GASKET

CAP CLOSURE

CONT. ALUM. EAVE W/ WEEPS @ 24" O.C.

3/8" BENT PLATE SECURED TO STRUCT.

ALUM. APRON

2 PLY BASE FLASHING

3/8" CONT. ST'L PL. (GALV.)

1 1/2" TREATED WOOD BLK'G. BOLTED TO STEEL PL.

4 PLY BUILT-UP ROOFING W/ GRAVEL

2" RIGID INSULATION

CONC. SLAB ON METAL DECK

CONDUIT FOR LIGHTING TRACK

SNAP-ON ALUM. COVER

GASKET

1/4" REFLECTIVE GL.

12" CHANNEL

BEAM

SPRAY-ON F.P.

6"

7"

Fig. 23 Vertical section through the skylight eave.

The vertical sides of the skylight and the way they are secured to the parapet are noted in Figure 24. A section of a rafter bar is shown with its integral extruded condensate gutters. The cap molding is clamped to the rafter bars and creates a complex sandwich composed of glass and neoprene gaskets that cushions and waterproofs this assembly. A firm connection here creates a virtually water-resistant joint. The vertical glass of the skylight sidewall is secured to gaskets that are attached to the edge rafter, which receives a finished aluminum apron. The vertical edge of the skylight is secured to the 12-inch channel. A series of vertical steel fins have been welded to the channel for its reinforcement so that it may receive a cantilevered 4- by 4-inch angle that is attached to the segmented interior head mullion.

Fig. 24   Vertical section through the sidewalls of the skylight.

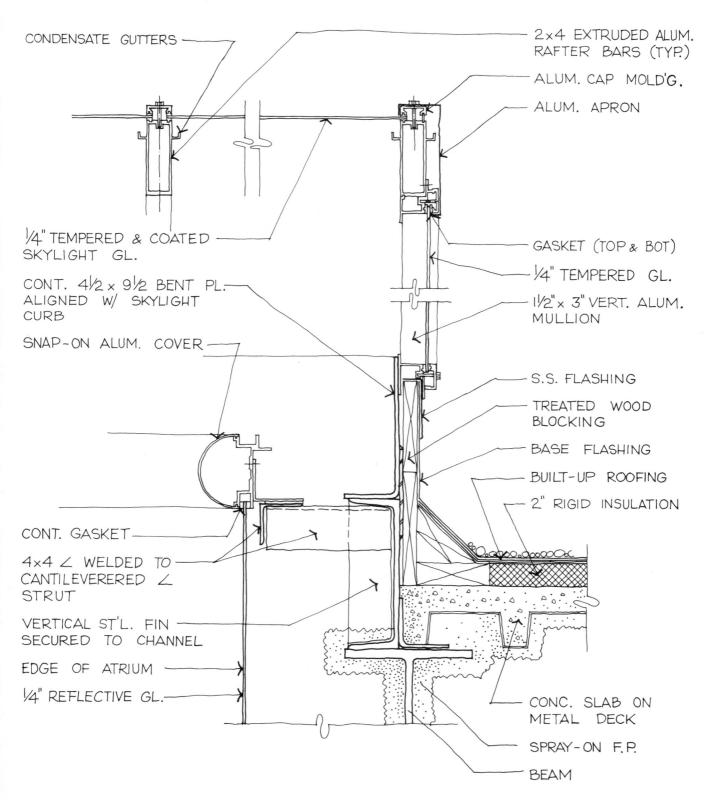

CONDENSATE GUTTERS

2×4 EXTRUDED ALUM. RAFTER BARS (TYP.)

ALUM. CAP MOLD'G.

ALUM. APRON

¼" TEMPERED & COATED SKYLIGHT GL.

CONT. 4½ × 9½ BENT PL. ALIGNED W/ SKYLIGHT CURB

SNAP-ON ALUM. COVER

GASKET (TOP & BOT)

¼" TEMPERED GL.

1½" × 3" VERT. ALUM. MULLION

S.S. FLASHING

TREATED WOOD BLOCKING

BASE FLASHING

BUILT-UP ROOFING

2" RIGID INSULATION

CONT. GASKET

4×4 ∠ WELDED TO CANTILEVERERED ∠ STRUT

VERTICAL ST'L. FIN SECURED TO CHANNEL

EDGE OF ATRIUM

¼" REFLECTIVE GL.

CONC. SLAB ON METAL DECK

SPRAY-ON F.P.

BEAM

The skylights over the large triangular atriums form valleys that must be drained. Figure 25 illustrates an example of how this assembly functions. Not only must water runoff be conducted away from the skylight, but the considerable weight of the glass and metal structure must be supported as well. The beams that carry the gutters form an impressive part of the atrium space (see Figure 3). A beam finished with gypsum board and designed to be coordinated with the interior spandrels supports a series of tubular steel elements that carry a ⅝-inch galvanized

steel bent plate that forms the gutter and receives the aluminum skylight eaves. A tie bar is welded at regular intervals to this plate in order to strengthen it. Aluminum aprons cover sheet neoprene, and rigid insulation is installed under the neoprene to prevent condensation from forming on the interior of the assembly.

Safety requirements call for the installation of venting devices in the skylight to remove smoke from the atrium in the event of fire. A space as large as this has a potential for smoke spread that is a major concern and is addressed by the

installation of smoke vents. Figures 26 and 27 indicate two complementary section views of these vents, which occur at both eaves of the skylight approximately 70 feet on center. It is interesting to note the flexibility of a system that allows a disruption of its original aesthetic design formula as neatly as this does. Figure 27 indicates the typical expansion joints for the rafters with their flexible expansion joint covers secured to the gaskets of the cap molding and rafters. Extruded sections bridge the rafters and receive a frame for the vent.

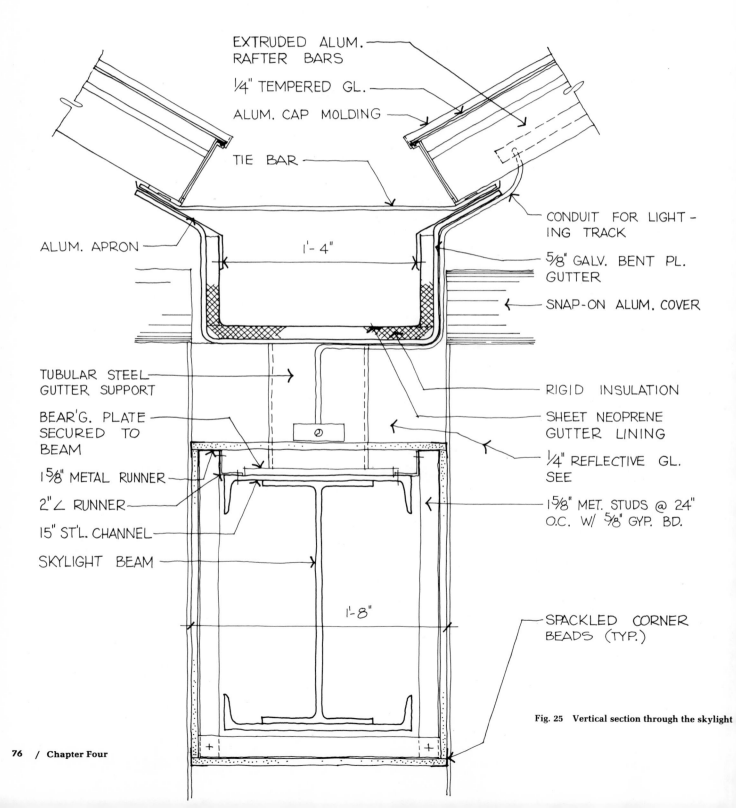

Fig. 25 Vertical section through the skylight

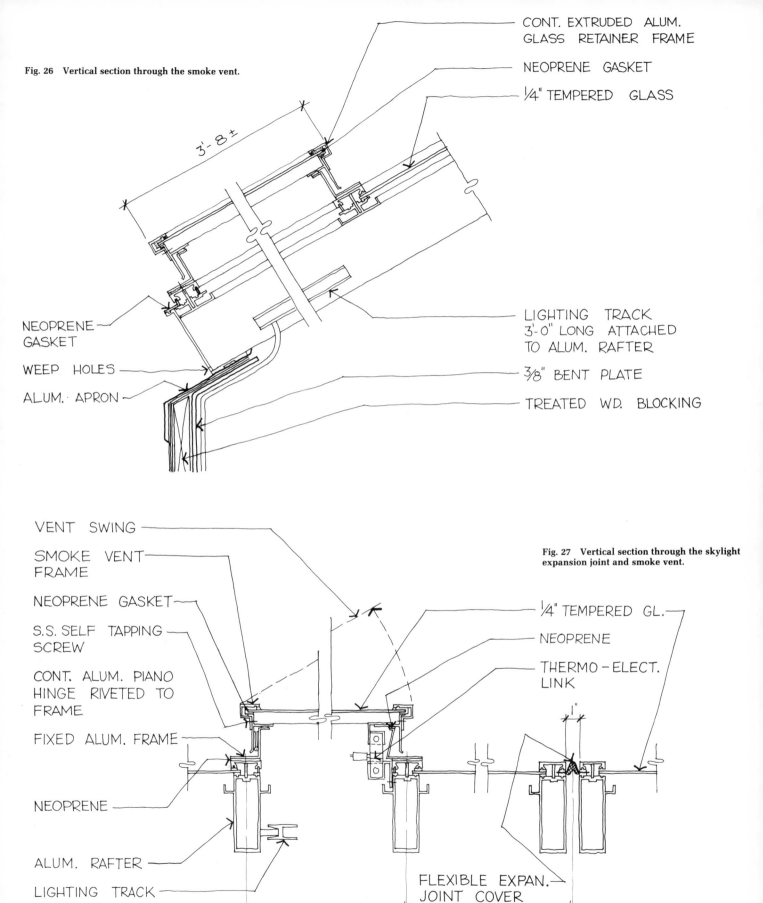

CONT. EXTRUDED ALUM.
GLASS RETAINER FRAME

NEOPRENE GASKET

1/4" TEMPERED GLASS

Fig. 26   Vertical section through the smoke vent.

3'-8 ±

LIGHTING TRACK
3'-0" LONG ATTACHED
TO ALUM. RAFTER

3/8" BENT PLATE

TREATED WD. BLOCKING

NEOPRENE
GASKET

WEEP HOLES

ALUM. APRON

VENT SWING

SMOKE VENT
FRAME

Fig. 27   Vertical section through the skylight
expansion joint and smoke vent.

NEOPRENE GASKET

S.S. SELF TAPPING
SCREW

1/4" TEMPERED GL.

NEOPRENE

CONT. ALUM. PIANO
HINGE RIVETED TO
FRAME

THERMO-ELECT.
LINK

FIXED ALUM. FRAME

1"

NEOPRENE

ALUM. RAFTER

LIGHTING TRACK

FLEXIBLE EXPAN.
JOINT COVER

2'-8"   2'-8"   2'-8"   2'-8"

RAFTER SPACING

2 Hammarskjold Plaza
New York, New York

ARCHITECTS: Raymond, Rado, Caddy & Bonnington Architects/Planners

Fig. 1 The building as seen from Second Avenue looking southeast.

Aluminum and glass are the basic curtain wall materials used on many office buildings throughout the United States. However, an almost universal sameness that is typical of this type of construction tends to dull the senses to real innovation. For most projects, manufacturers offer standardized curtain wall components that architects generally use as a starting point for design. It is hoped that the refinement of proportions and mullion patterning will be studied in an attempt to arrive at the expression of an original and noteworthy building.

Building code requirements for most projects—in addition to design and functional considerations—make heavy demands on the part of the architect's time and talent. These legal restraints very often determine the focus of a design effort. In the hands of a skilled designer, the needs of a program, budgetary constraints, zoning regulations, and code limitations sometimes encourage new lines of research that generate aesthetic dividends. Metal and glass curtain walls tend to be much lighter in weight than the more traditional forms of construction. Fire safety in this instance becomes a matter of paramount importance. Heavier, more fire resistant masonry and glass curtain walls have an obvious advantage with respect to limiting the spread of fire. A window surrounded by brick or concrete is an effective barrier against flames that might shatter adjacent non-fire-rated glass assemblies and attack parts of the same building or nearby structures.

Raymond, Rado, Caddy & Bonnington Architects/Planners are the designers of 2 Hammarskjold Plaza, an office building located on Second Avenue in New York City. This firm has developed a particularly simple and elegant curtain wall for the building. The cladding system is composed of slender vertical mullions, tinted gray glass, and a split sill horizontal mullion that occurs at every floor slab. There are no opaque spandrel assemblies, fire barriers, or other visible elements that detract from the simplicity of the floor-to-floor glass. Yet this building was designed in conformance with one of the most demanding fire and safety codes in the world.

There are several construction techniques used by architects in New York City in order to conform to code requirements and to minimize the spread of fire from one floor of a building to another. It is customary to install a vertical fire-rated barrier above and below the spandrel beam. The appearance of most office buildings, especially in New York City, reflects this fire safety requirement. One can observe clear or tinted glass from the top of the windowsill to the hung ceiling or window head. Concealed from sight are the spandrel beam, the perimeter radiation, the suspended ceiling plenum, and the vertical

Fig. 2 The plaza entry and a close-up view of part of the northwest corner.

fire-stops, which are usually fabricated of concrete block. These unseen assemblies require some kind of opaque covering panel such as metal or enameled tempered glass. In addition to vertical fire-stops, horizontal fire barriers or slab projections past the column line may be used as well. This tends to give a building a strong horizontal accent and generates very deep shadows on the perimeter glass. A third possibility with respect to fire-prevention requirements depends on the proximity of the building to adjacent structures. A building placed on a plaza can be constructed with a minimal fire-protected spandrel section if it is more than 30 feet from other buildings and utilizes a projected horizontal fire-stop at the floor slabs.

2 Hammarskjold Plaza as seen from Second Avenue looking southeast can be studied in Figure 1. This is a view of the building showing the very simple curtain wall system, the plaza, and the masonry-sheathed service core located on the eastern face of the tower. This building sits on a plaza that is used for entry, recreation, and the display of sculpture. Figure 2 provides a view of the plaza entry and a close-up view of part of the northwest corner indicating the glass and mullions. Note that the vertical mullions shown in this photograph are extruded with an integral recessed track that receives the window-washing scaffold. The exterior columns break free of the building at the plaza level and form a partial arcade around the lobby area.

The curtain wall for this building relies on continuous vertical mullions 3 feet 4 inches on center and a split sill horizontal mullion that is approximately 10 inches high. This mullion is the only expression of a horizontal line that appears on the elevations of the tower. As can be seen in subsequent details, the mullion conceals the projected floor slab from view. The net design effect as seen from the interior of the office floor looking out is of a clear glass vista from floor to ceiling that is broken only by an interior horizontal line composed of the perimeter radiation enclosure. The exterior service core of the office tower is located on the east side of the building and is sheathed in face brick that serves as a contrast to the very light feeling of the metal and glass curtain wall. Figure 3 indicates the juxtaposition of the curtain wall and masonry reveal of the service core. Seen dimly behind the glass is a horizontal element that is the perimeter radiation. A floating convector cover is secured to the vertical mullions at approximately 2 feet 4 inches above the finished floor and provides comfort and a degree of security for the occupants of the building at the height of a normal windowsill.

Fig. 3 Juxtaposition of the curtain wall and masonry reveal of the service core.

The southwest corner of the building is shown in Figure 4, in which the transition of the first floor and plaza is studied. The exterior corner column is shown engaging a metal and suspended tile soffit over the lobby area. The distinction between the interior and exterior construction can be easily observed in this drawing. The treatment of the column in this diagram is a case in point. At the plaza level the column is fireproofed with poured concrete and sheathed in interlocking aluminum panel strips. The fireproofing of the same column is changed to spray-on material at the interior first-floor level, and the column is finished with gypsum board secured to metal furring. The fin tube cabinet enclosure is shown secured to the corner mullions and wrapping around the column. Note the insulated supply and return lines that provide heated water to the perimeter convection and radiation system of this building.

The exterior aluminum facing is composed of 4½-inch-wide interlocking aluminum strips and is used on the first-floor spandrel, the exterior columns, the roof parapet, and miscellaneous metal trim throughout the building. The floor slab is shown cantilevered approximately 1 foot past the centerline of the spandrel beam. It is this slab extension that develops a fire barrier for the structure, and it is this detail that is repeated for every floor of the building. In addition, the curtain wall can be installed as an unbroken plane without any interference with the structure. Note the cast insert set into the edge of the slab. This insert receives the vertical mullion. The soffit trim that surrounds the perimeter of the building is secured to studs and furring hangers that also form the subassembly that receives the spandrel facing panels. Note the spray-on fireproofing for the spandrel beam and the insulation batts installed in the spandrel assembly. The lower left portion of Figure 4 indicates the suspended ceiling soffit for the arcade and lobby area below. A ¼-inch hanger rod suspends channel runners and wire lath that receive mortar and a mosaic tile soffit finish. The vision glass used to complete the curtain wall assembly is installed in neoprene window gaskets secured to the mullions.

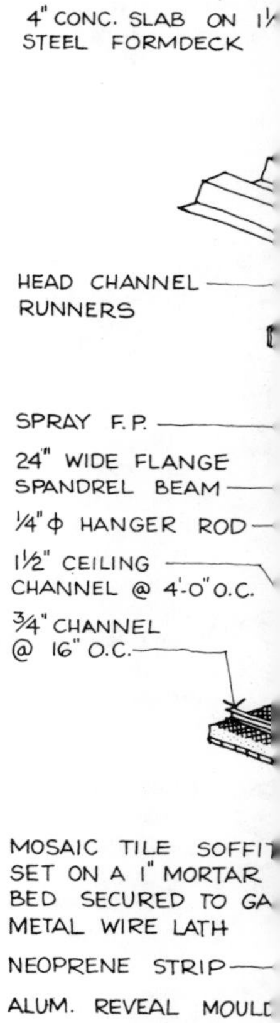

4" CONC. SLAB ON 1½ STEEL FORMDECK

HEAD CHANNEL
RUNNERS

SPRAY F.P.
24" WIDE FLANGE
SPANDREL BEAM
¼" φ HANGER ROD
1½" CEILING
CHANNEL @ 4'-0" O.C.
¾" CHANNEL
@ 16" O.C.

MOSAIC TILE SOFFIT
SET ON A 1" MORTAR
BED SECURED TO GA
METAL WIRE LATH

NEOPRENE STRIP

ALUM. REVEAL MOULD

Fig. 4 A view of the corner column the lobby and first floor.

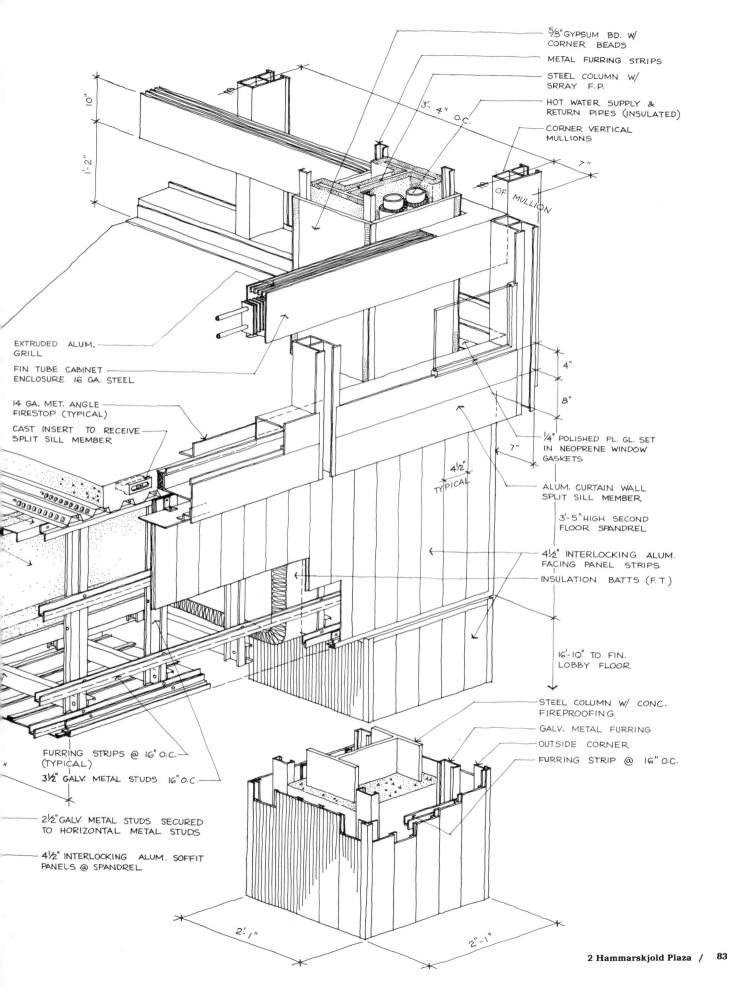

⅝" GYPSUM BD. W/
CORNER BEADS

METAL FURRING STRIPS

STEEL COLUMN W/
SRRAY F.P.

HOT WATER SUPPLY &
RETURN PIPES (INSULATED)

CORNER VERTICAL
MULLIONS

10"

1'-2"

3'-4" O.C.

7"

OF MULLION

EXTRUDED ALUM.
GRILL

FIN TUBE CABINET
ENCLOSURE 16 GA. STEEL

14 GA. MET. ANGLE
FIRESTOP (TYPICAL)

CAST INSERT TO RECEIVE
SPLIT SILL MEMBER

4"

8"

7"

4½"
TYPICAL

¼" POLISHED PL. GL. SET
IN NEOPRENE WINDOW
GASKETS

ALUM. CURTAIN WALL
SPLIT SILL MEMBER

3'-5" HIGH SECOND
FLOOR SPANDREL

4½" INTERLOCKING ALUM.
FACING PANEL STRIPS

INSULATION BATTS (F.T.)

16'-10" TO FIN.
LOBBY FLOOR

STEEL COLUMN W/ CONC.
FIREPROOFING

GALV. METAL FURRING

OUTSIDE CORNER

FURRING STRIP @ 16" O.C.

FURRING STRIPS @ 16" O.C.
(TYPICAL)

3½" GALV. METAL STUDS 16" O.C.

2½" GALV. METAL STUDS SECURED
TO HORIZONTAL METAL STUDS

4½" INTERLOCKING ALUM. SOFFIT
PANELS @ SPANDREL

2'-1"

2'-1"

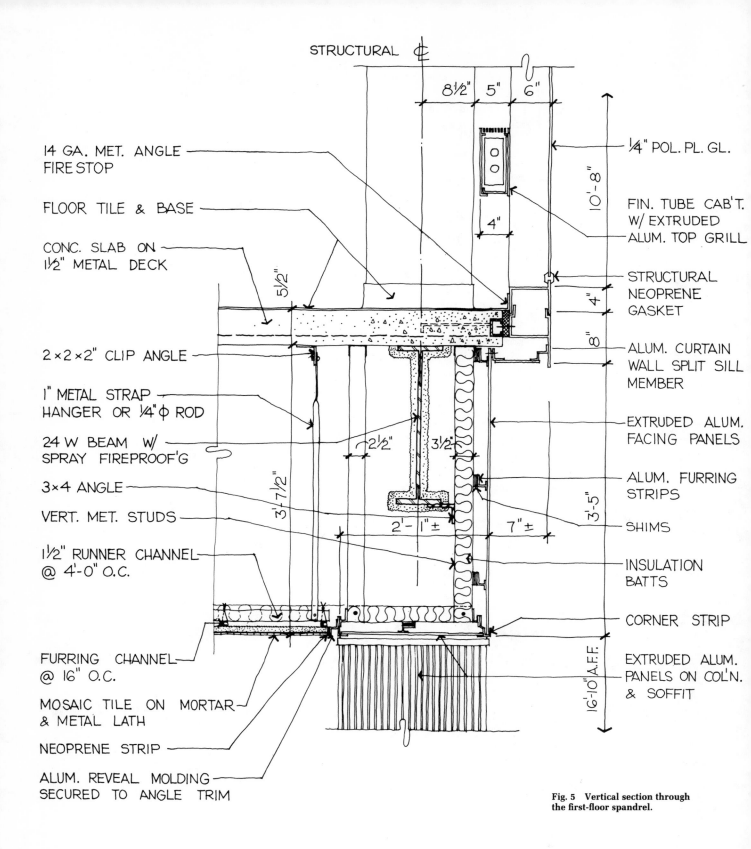

STRUCTURAL ℄

8½" 5" 6"

4"

10'-8"

14 GA. MET. ANGLE FIRE STOP

FLOOR TILE & BASE

CONC. SLAB ON 1½" METAL DECK

2×2×2" CLIP ANGLE

1" METAL STRAP HANGER OR ¼" φ ROD

24 W BEAM W/ SPRAY FIREPROOF'G

3×4 ANGLE

VERT. MET. STUDS

1½" RUNNER CHANNEL @ 4'-0" O.C.

FURRING CHANNEL @ 16" O.C.

MOSAIC TILE ON MORTAR & METAL LATH

NEOPRENE STRIP

ALUM. REVEAL MOLDING SECURED TO ANGLE TRIM

5½"

2½" 3½"

3'-7½"

2'-1"± 7"±

¼" POL. PL. GL.

FIN. TUBE CAB'T. W/ EXTRUDED ALUM. TOP GRILL

STRUCTURAL NEOPRENE GASKET

4" 8"

ALUM. CURTAIN WALL SPLIT SILL MEMBER

EXTRUDED ALUM. FACING PANELS

ALUM. FURRING STRIPS

SHIMS

3'-5"

INSULATION BATTS

CORNER STRIP

EXTRUDED ALUM. PANELS ON COL'N. & SOFFIT

16'-10" A.F.F.

Fig. 5 Vertical section through the first-floor spandrel.

Figure 5 is a vertical section through the first-floor spandrel and indicates the various components used in this assembly. This view shows an alternative approach to the suspended lobby ceiling. A 1-inch metal strap hanger is shown supporting the channel runner instead of the ¼-inch rod shown in Figure 4. The facing panels are secured to aluminum furring strips that are attached to vertical metal studs used as furring. Shims are installed wherever necessary to maintain the proper interval between the facing panels and the metal studs forming the fascia and soffit of the first floor. The convector enclosure is shown installed between the face of the column and the inside face of the vertical mullion. The full-height glass is indicated at the sill.

Figure 6 is an isometric view of the interlocking aluminum panel facing system. Note the special furring strips that are attached to the metal studs every 16 inches on center. They are designed to receive a friction clip that is used to secure the interlocking panels. Each panel is individually cut and is installed by engaging the adjacent panel through a tongue-and-groove connection and securing the loose side of the panel to the furring strip with friction clips. The vertical striations on the aluminum panel tend to conceal the actual joint line, and the result is a consistently handsome texture for this assembly.

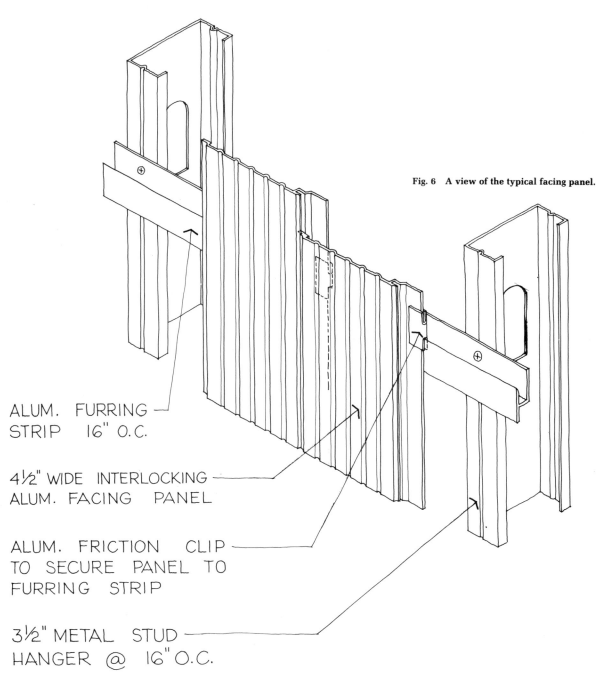

Fig. 6   A view of the typical facing panel.

ALUM. FURRING STRIP 16" O.C.

4½" WIDE INTERLOCKING ALUM. FACING PANEL

ALUM. FRICTION CLIP TO SECURE PANEL TO FURRING STRIP

3½" METAL STUD HANGER @ 16" O.C.

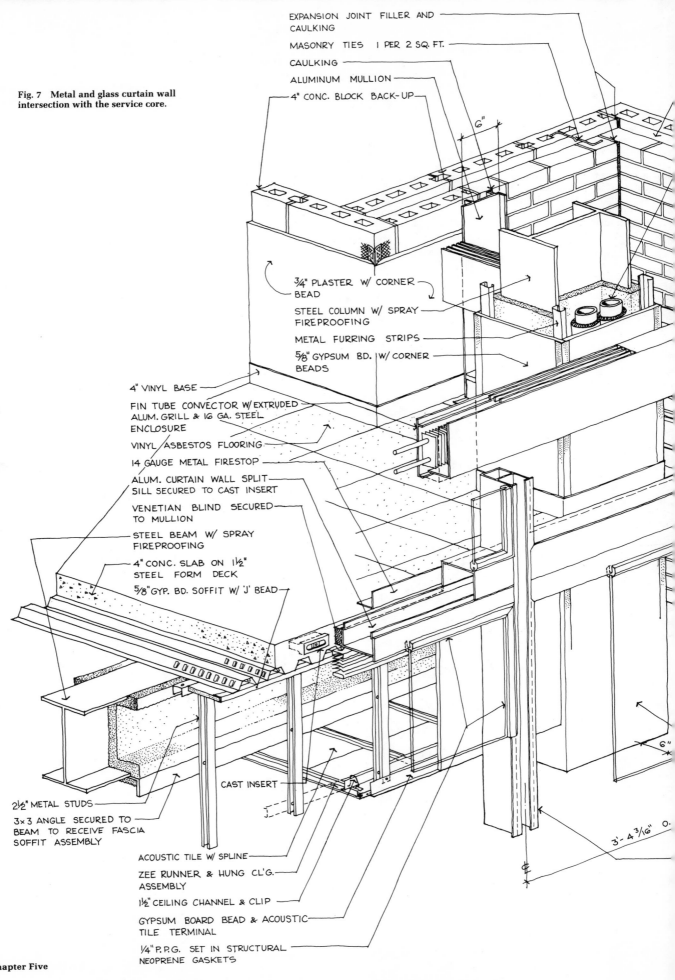

EXPANSION JOINT FILLER AND CAULKING

MASONRY TIES 1 PER 2 SQ. FT.

CAULKING

ALUMINUM MULLION

4" CONC. BLOCK BACK-UP

6"

Fig. 7   Metal and glass curtain wall intersection with the service core.

¾" PLASTER W/ CORNER BEAD

STEEL COLUMN W/ SPRAY FIREPROOFING

METAL FURRING STRIPS

⅝" GYPSUM BD. W/ CORNER BEADS

4" VINYL BASE

FIN TUBE CONVECTOR W/ EXTRUDED ALUM. GRILL & 16 GA. STEEL ENCLOSURE

VINYL ASBESTOS FLOORING

14 GAUGE METAL FIRESTOP

ALUM. CURTAIN WALL SPLIT SILL SECURED TO CAST INSERT

VENETIAN BLIND SECURED TO MULLION

STEEL BEAM W/ SPRAY FIREPROOFING

4" CONC. SLAB ON 1½" STEEL FORM DECK

⅝" GYP. BD. SOFFIT W/ 'J' BEAD

2½" METAL STUDS

3 x 3 ANGLE SECURED TO BEAM TO RECEIVE FASCIA SOFFIT ASSEMBLY

CAST INSERT

ACOUSTIC TILE W/ SPLINE

ZEE RUNNER & HUNG CL'G. ASSEMBLY

1½" CEILING CHANNEL & CLIP

GYPSUM BOARD BEAD & ACOUSTIC TILE TERMINAL

¼" P. P. G. SET IN STRUCTURAL NEOPRENE GASKETS

6"

3'-4 3/16" O.

- 2" MASONRY CAVITY
- HOT WATER SUPPLY & RETURN PIPES
- STEEL COLUMN W/ MASONRY UNIT FIREPROOFING
- FACE BRICK

CORNER VERTICAL MULLIONS

10"

ALIGNED PLANES

2'-5½"

- INTERIOR COLUMN SHEATHED WITH ⅝" GYPSUM BOARD

- TYPICAL VERTICAL MULLION

Figure 7, in addition to indicating a typical wall section at the spandrel beam, also delineates the relation of the curtain wall to the service core. Figure 3 is a view of a similar condition as viewed from the plaza level. The column rising through the service core is fireproofed by the masonry enclosure composed of the exterior face brick and interior concrete backup block. This indicates yet another method of fireproofing the structure. The typical column spray-on fireproofing is shown at the corner of the curtain wall assembly. Figure 8 is a plan section of the northeast corner reveal that indicates the relation of the service core to the metal and glass cladding system. A variation of the vertical mullion receives the glazing gaskets and vision glass at the intersection of the curtain wall and masonry.

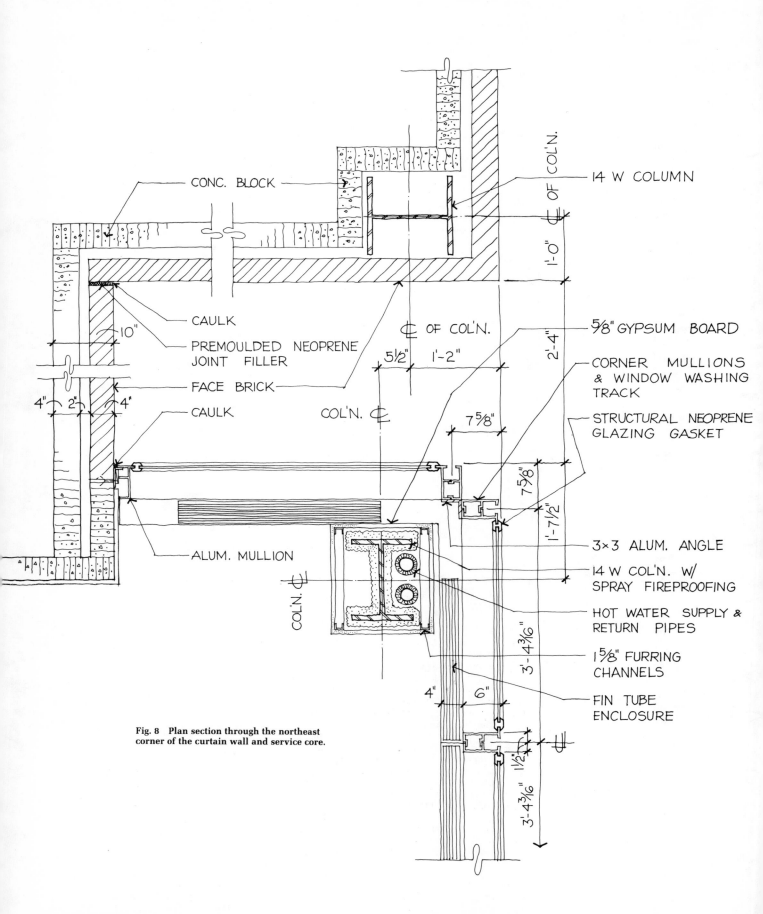

CONC. BLOCK

14 W COLUMN

1'-0" ℄ OF COL'N.

CAULK

PREMOULDED NEOPRENE JOINT FILLER

5/8" GYPSUM BOARD

CORNER MULLIONS & WINDOW WASHING TRACK

STRUCTURAL NEOPRENE GLAZING GASKET

10"

FACE BRICK

4" 2" 4"

CAULK

℄ OF COL'N.

5½" 1'-2"

2'-4"

COL'N. ℄

7 5/8"

7 5/8"

1'-7½"

ALUM. MULLION

3×3 ALUM. ANGLE

14 W COL'N. W/ SPRAY FIREPROOFING

HOT WATER SUPPLY & RETURN PIPES

COL'N. ℄

3'-4 3/16"

1 5/8" FURRING CHANNELS

FIN TUBE ENCLOSURE

Fig. 8 Plan section through the northeast corner of the curtain wall and service core.

4" 6"

1½"

3'-4 3/16"

The metal studs suspended from the slab as shown in Figure 7 support the gypsum board fascia assembly and the return for the suspended acoustic tile ceiling. The 1½-inch channel runner supports a concealed spline that receives the acoustic tile ceiling. The space between the gypsum board fascia and the curtain wall receives the drapery pocket, which in this case is used to house venetian blinds. Figure 9 is a vertical section through a curtain wall assembly at a typical floor spandrel and should be viewed in conjunction with Figure 7. The convector enclosure is shown mounted 2 feet 4 inches above the finished floor. The glass assembly with its glazing gaskets and split sill mullion is indicated in this

Fig. 9 Vertical section through a typical spandrel beam assembly.

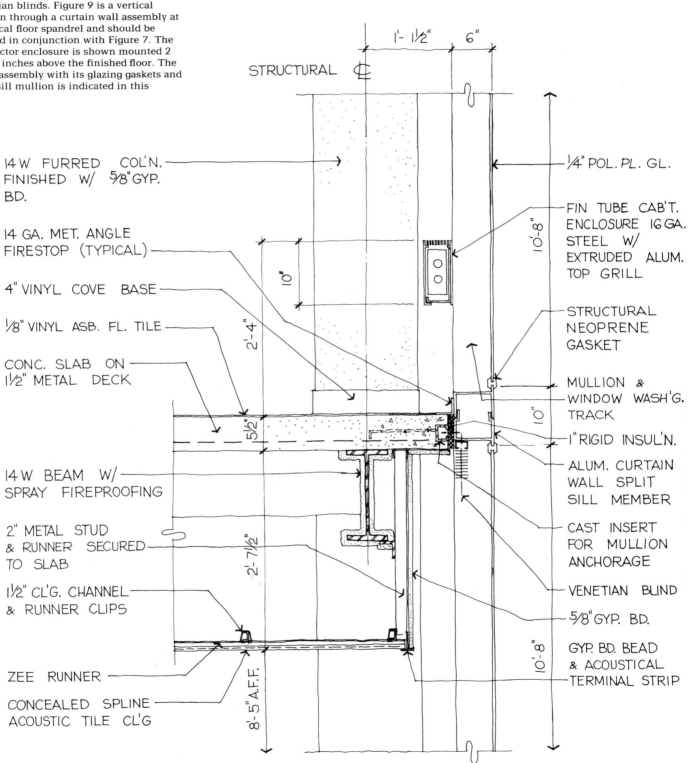

STRUCTURAL ℄

1'-1½"   6"

14 W FURRED COL'N. FINISHED W/ ⅝"GYP. BD.

14 GA. MET. ANGLE FIRESTOP (TYPICAL)

4" VINYL COVE BASE

⅛" VINYL ASB. FL. TILE

CONC. SLAB ON 1½" METAL DECK

14 W BEAM W/ SPRAY FIREPROOFING

2" METAL STUD & RUNNER SECURED TO SLAB

1½" CL'G. CHANNEL & RUNNER CLIPS

ZEE RUNNER

CONCEALED SPLINE ACOUSTIC TILE CL'G

10"

2'-4"

5½"

2'-7½"

8'-5" A.F.F.

¼" POL. PL. GL.

FIN TUBE CAB'T. ENCLOSURE 16 GA. STEEL W/ EXTRUDED ALUM. TOP GRILL

STRUCTURAL NEOPRENE GASKET

MULLION & WINDOW WASH'G. TRACK

1" RIGID INSUL'N.

ALUM. CURTAIN WALL SPLIT SILL MEMBER

CAST INSERT FOR MULLION ANCHORAGE

VENETIAN BLIND

⅝" GYP. BD.

GYP. BD. BEAD & ACOUSTICAL TERMINAL STRIP

10'-8"

10"

10'-8"

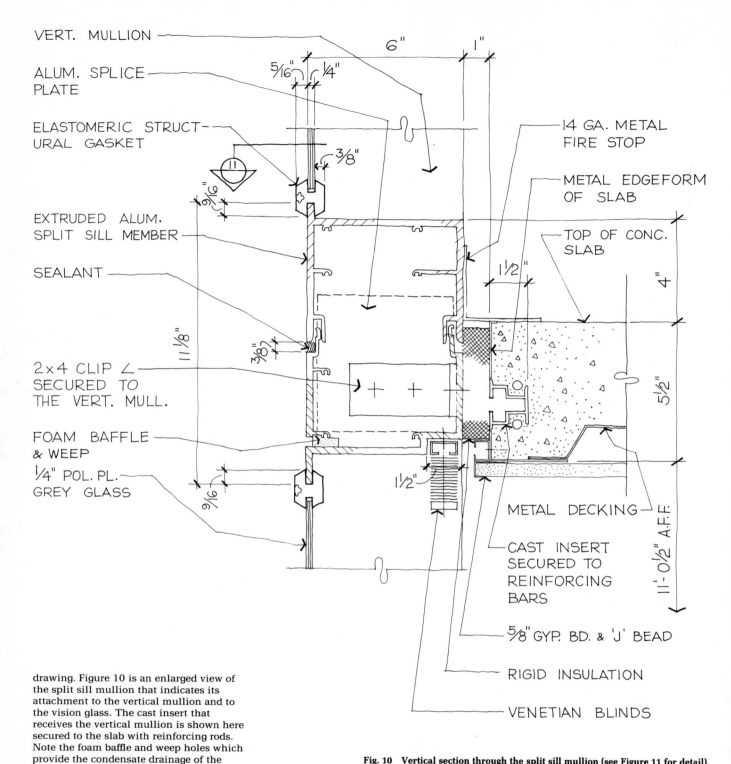

VERT. MULLION

ALUM. SPLICE PLATE

ELASTOMERIC STRUCTURAL GASKET

EXTRUDED ALUM. SPLIT SILL MEMBER

SEALANT

2×4 CLIP ∠ SECURED TO THE VERT. MULL.

FOAM BAFFLE & WEEP

¼" POL. PL. GREY GLASS

6"

1"

5/16"

¼"

3/8"

9/16"

1½"

11 1/8"

3/8"

4"

5½"

9/16"

1½"

11'-0½" A.F.F.

14 GA. METAL FIRE STOP

METAL EDGEFORM OF SLAB

TOP OF CONC. SLAB

METAL DECKING

CAST INSERT SECURED TO REINFORCING BARS

5/8" GYP. BD. & 'J' BEAD

RIGID INSULATION

VENETIAN BLINDS

drawing. Figure 10 is an enlarged view of the split sill mullion that indicates its attachment to the vertical mullion and to the vision glass. The cast insert that receives the vertical mullion is shown here secured to the slab with reinforcing rods. Note the foam baffle and weep holes which provide the condensate drainage of the mullion assembly. Figure 11 is a horizontal section through a typical vertical mullion that also serves as a window-washing track. The mullion is secured to the slab with a Z clip that is bolted to the cast insert shown in dotted lines.

Fig. 10   Vertical section through the split sill mullion (see Figure 11 for detail).

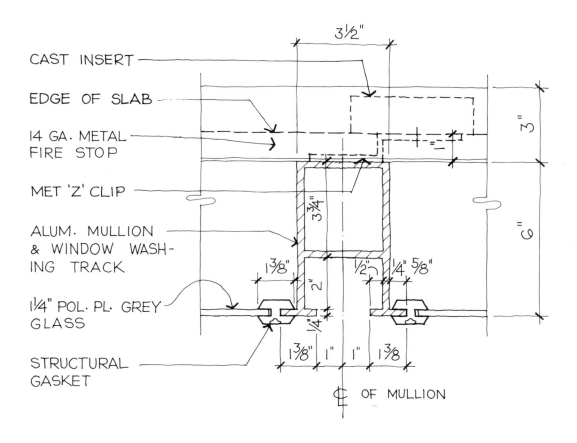

Fig. 11 Horizontal section through
a vertical mullion.

CAST INSERT

EDGE OF SLAB

14 GA. METAL
FIRE STOP

MET 'Z' CLIP

ALUM. MULLION
& WINDOW WASH-
ING TRACK

1¼" POL· PL· GREY
GLASS

STRUCTURAL
GASKET

3½"

3"

3¾"

6"

1⅜"

2"

½"

¼" ⅝"

¼"

1⅜"   1"   1"   1⅜

℄ OF MULLION

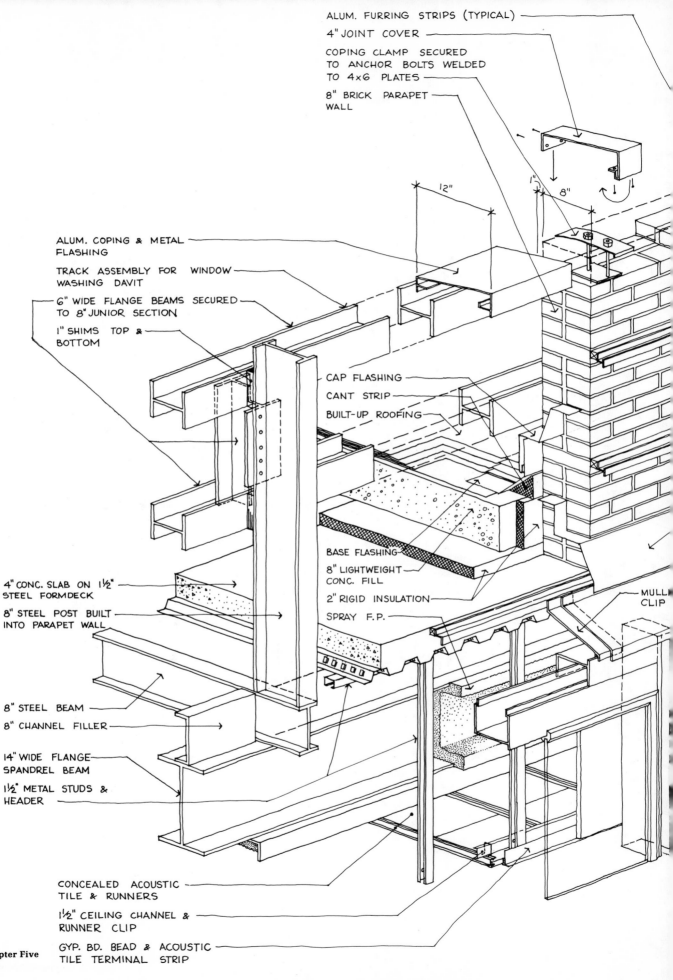

ALUM. FURRING STRIPS (TYPICAL)

4" JOINT COVER

COPING CLAMP SECURED
TO ANCHOR BOLTS WELDED
TO 4x6 PLATES

8" BRICK PARAPET
WALL

12"

1" 8"

ALUM. COPING & METAL
FLASHING

TRACK ASSEMBLY FOR WINDOW
WASHING DAVIT

6" WIDE FLANGE BEAMS SECURED
TO 8" JUNIOR SECTION

1" SHIMS TOP &
BOTTOM

CAP FLASHING

CANT STRIP

BUILT-UP ROOFING

BASE FLASHING

8" LIGHTWEIGHT
CONC. FILL

2" RIGID INSULATION

SPRAY F.P.

4" CONC. SLAB ON 1½"
STEEL FORMDECK

8" STEEL POST BUILT
INTO PARAPET WALL

MULL
CLIP

8" STEEL BEAM

8" CHANNEL FILLER

14" WIDE FLANGE
SPANDREL BEAM

1½" METAL STUDS &
HEADER

CONCEALED ACOUSTIC
TILE & RUNNERS

1½" CEILING CHANNEL &
RUNNER CLIP

GYP. BD. BEAD & ACOUSTIC
TILE TERMINAL STRIP

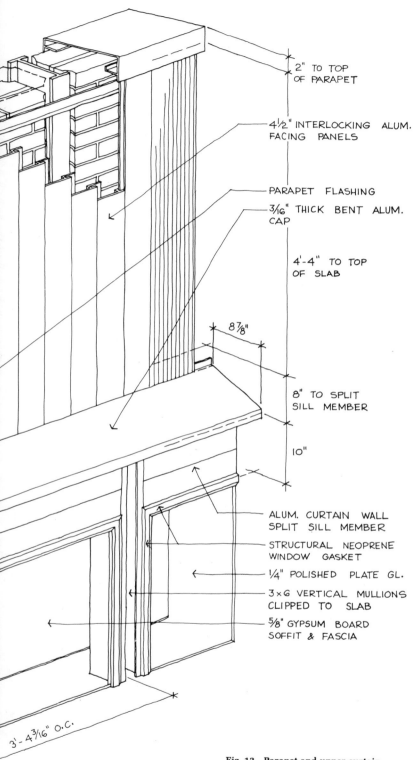

2" TO TOP
OF PARAPET

4½" INTERLOCKING ALUM.
FACING PANELS

PARAPET FLASHING

3/16" THICK BENT ALUM.
CAP

4'-4" TO TOP
OF SLAB

8 7/8"

8" TO SPLIT
SILL MEMBER

10"

ALUM. CURTAIN WALL
SPLIT SILL MEMBER

STRUCTURAL NEOPRENE
WINDOW GASKET

¼" POLISHED PLATE GL.

3×6 VERTICAL MULLIONS
CLIPPED TO SLAB

5/8" GYPSUM BOARD
SOFFIT & FASCIA

3'- 4 3/16" O.C.

Fig. 12   Parapet and upper curtain wall section.

The parapet, the upper curtain wall, and the track assembly for the window-washing davits are shown in Figure 12. There are several modifications to the typical spandrel beam assembly noted earlier that should be pointed out when dealing with the roof and parapet of this building. An 8-inch channel is installed directly on the spandrel beam, and 8-inch beams serve as purlins that support the slab. These structural elements are used to secure and reinforce vertical 8-inch posts that carry the track assembly for the window-washing davits. Figure 13 is a vertical section through the parapet structure. This drawing allows us to view the structural assembly unhampered by other components that make up the parapet. The track assembly is composed of 6-inch beams that are secured to the 8-inch posts. This entire structural system is designed to be received by the 8-inch masonry parapet wall so that the cladding system may be installed without structural interference.

Figure 12 further indicates the roof slab, the insulation, the 8 inches of lightweight concrete fill, and the built-up roofing. Base and cap flashing are shown sealing the inner face of the parapet assembly from moisture. Shims are installed as noted in

Figure 13 so that the track assembly is kept at a small distance from the inner face of the wall and does not interfere with its waterproofing. The steel posts that support the track assembly are built into the masonry wall, and sealant is used to prevent moisture penetration at these vertical joints. A coping clamp anchored to the masonry wall receives the combined metal coping and flashing. A 4-inch joint cover is set in mastic over each intersection of the metal coping and screwed into position as shown. The parapet flashing shown on the face of the building is locked into the masonry construction and engages the bent aluminum cap that terminates the curtain wall. The vertical distance between the cap and coping is finished with the same 4½-inch interlocking aluminum strips found on the plaza level and column covers. Aluminum furring secures these vertical strips to the parapet wall. The cap molding is secured to the top of the split sill mullion by 3-inch-wide bent metal clips that snap over the upper flange of the mullion. The gypsum board fascia and the suspended acoustic tile ceiling are similar to the typical ones shown earlier. Figure 14 is a vertical section through the parapet assembly and indicates the material noted in Figures 12 and 13. Shown here in two dimensions are most of the components that were indicated earlier. This drawing is a basic architectural detail for the assembly.

The architects for this building have developed an office tower that is both simple and elegant and have set it so skillfully on an urban plaza that it demands attention from the casual passerby. An imaginative and technologically innovative solution to the problems of a commercial structure is in evidence throughout this project. A firm grasp of the building code and an appreciation of economical construction are noteworthy.

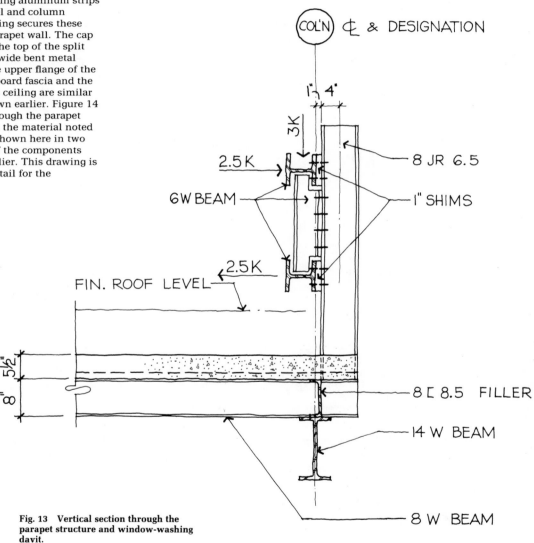

Fig. 13   Vertical section through the parapet structure and window-washing davit.

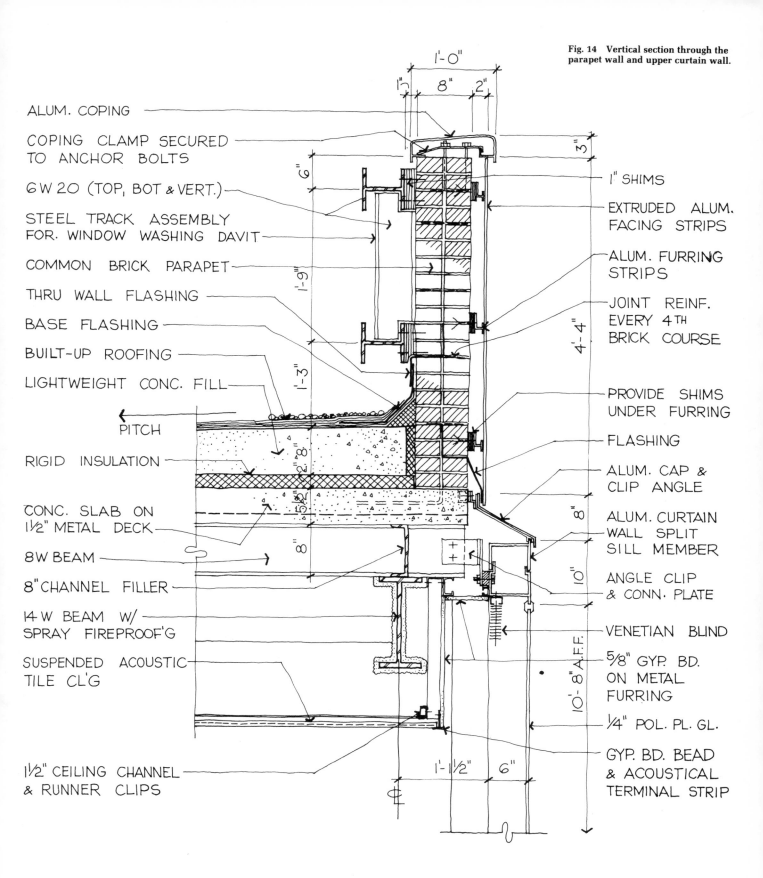

Fig. 14 Vertical section through the parapet wall and upper curtain wall.

ALUM. COPING

COPING CLAMP SECURED TO ANCHOR BOLTS

6 W 20 (TOP, BOT & VERT.)

STEEL TRACK ASSEMBLY FOR WINDOW WASHING DAVIT

COMMON BRICK PARAPET

THRU WALL FLASHING

BASE FLASHING

BUILT-UP ROOFING

LIGHTWEIGHT CONC. FILL

PITCH

RIGID INSULATION

CONC. SLAB ON 1½" METAL DECK

8W BEAM

8"CHANNEL FILLER

14 W BEAM W/ SPRAY FIREPROOF'G

SUSPENDED ACOUSTIC TILE CL'G

1½" CEILING CHANNEL & RUNNER CLIPS

1" SHIMS

EXTRUDED ALUM. FACING STRIPS

ALUM. FURRING STRIPS

JOINT REINF. EVERY 4TH BRICK COURSE

PROVIDE SHIMS UNDER FURRING

FLASHING

ALUM. CAP & CLIP ANGLE

ALUM. CURTAIN WALL SPLIT SILL MEMBER

ANGLE CLIP & CONN. PLATE

VENETIAN BLIND

5/8" GYP. BD. ON METAL FURRING

¼" POL. PL. GL.

GYP. BD. BEAD & ACOUSTICAL TERMINAL STRIP

The Gilbane Building
New Haven, Connecticut

ARCHITECTS: Shreve Lamb & Harmon Associates, PC Architects/Planners

Fig. 1 A view from Church Street.

Many building materials and construction systems used today were considered to be experimental or to have a limited application capability a scant generation ago. A substance as common as aluminum was looked down upon by many conservative architectural detailers since, under exterior conditions, the material did have a tendency to fade, pit, discolor, and generally behave badly. Concrete, another material that had acquired a dubious reputation, either was relegated to heavy structural use or was found in assemblies that were subsequently covered with more acceptable facing materials.

High-strength precast reinforced concrete was considered experimental in the United States until recently. Most building codes developed requirements for concrete strength that tended to limit the structural range of the material. Many municipalities were not willing to entertain the use of high-strength concrete at all, in spite of the fact that the material had become an almost universal expression of structure throughout the world. By the 1960s it appeared to the casual observer that we were a backward country with respect to concrete technology. Pier Luigi Nervi in Italy, Felix Candela in Mexico, Oscar Niemeyer in Brazil, and many other architects outside the United States were making significant contributions to the use of concrete well in advance of its acceptance by American design professionals. There were of course exceptions, unique designers who appreciated the potential of concrete and followed their intuition with respect to its use. Frank Lloyd Wright maintained a continuing relationship with the material beginning in 1906 when he designed the Unity Church in Oak Park, Illinois. Buildings such as the S. C. Johnson and Son—Administrative Building, built 1936 to 1939, and the Guggenheim Museum, New York City, 1946 to 1959, demonstrated Wright's ability to work successfully with this material. Louis Kahn was another architect who used concrete innovatively, and the Richards Medical Research Building, Medical & Biology Laboratories, Philadelphia, Pennsylvania, 1957 to 1960, established precast concrete as a material that, like steel, could be produced off-site under factory conditions and shipped anywhere. This trail blazing by a relatively small number of American practitioners helped establish the almost universal use of the material today with all its technological refinements.

This chapter explores concrete as a cladding system using precast wall panels. The office building at 55 Church Street in New Haven, Connecticut, designed by Shreve Lamb & Harmon Associates, PC Architects/Planners, takes advantage of the casting potential of plastic concrete. The resultant material is applied to the structure in the form of prismatic column covers and spandrel covers to form a building facade that is both sculptural and economical.

Figure 1 shows the building viewed from

Fig. 2 Relation of first-floor column covers to the third-floor spandrel.

Church Street and indicates its relation to a traditional bank building to the south and another vintage structure six stories tall to the north. This photograph indicates the south and west elevations of the tower. The building is eight stories high and is sheathed in heat-absorbent glass and precast concrete panels. The lobby area is enclosed in a simple glass and metal curtain wall two stories high, forming an aesthetic link to the adjacent bank. The third-floor spandrel is approximately on line with the bottom of the neoclassical pediment of the bank and is 26 feet above the sidewalk level. Figure 2 indicates the relation of the first-floor column covers to the third-floor spandrel. An illusion of height appears to combine the first- and second-floor curtain wall system in an unbroken vertical plane to the third-floor soffit. The building, although contemporary in nature, has by virtue of its proportions and elegant simplicity something of a classical quality that fits the site well.

A review of the working drawings indicates that the architects have been careful to plan and design the configuration of the various panel assemblies used in the cladding system. However, connecting details, inserts, and other pertinent precast concrete information required for fabrication are striking by their omission. The contract documents for this building called for the curtain wall contractor to submit a ''performance'' package embodying a complete statement of fabrication, including technique, accessories, and finished shop drawings that would satisfy the architect's design and technical requirements for the project.

Allied Building Systems Incorporated, located in Manchester, Connecticut, was selected by the architect and the general

contractor to provide the precast concrete curtain wall system for this structure. I used primarily their shop drawings for reference in the preparation of the diagrams and details in this chapter. It appears that this project benefited by a specialization of skills and a division of expertise between the architect and the curtain wall contractor. There was little or no overlap of the efforts made by these two principals in the construction process. The architect's engineering consultants, Ames and Selnick Structural Engineers of New York City, reviewed the contractor's submission with respect to the engineering requirements of the building's frame structure.

The third-floor spandrel and its intersection with the building's corner column is analyzed in Figure 3. This view allows us to study the relation between the spandrel beam and its cover. The bottom of the spandrel beam is secured to a hung lintel that receives the precast concrete spandrel cover. The end of the spandrel cover engages the concrete column cover and building slab. The tubular metal curtain wall sections of the storefront are shown secured to the bottom of the spandrel cover and to the vertical return of the column cover. Shown here are adjustable inserts that make the connection of the curtain wall elements possible. These inserts must be installed during the casting of the concrete and become the responsibility of the curtain wall contractor, who must coordinate and supervise the various trades involved in these assemblies. The weight of the concrete sections is considerable, and it should be observed that a 3- by 3-inch diagonal angle brace secured at regular intervals to the purlin is required to prevent the lintel from deflecting inward.

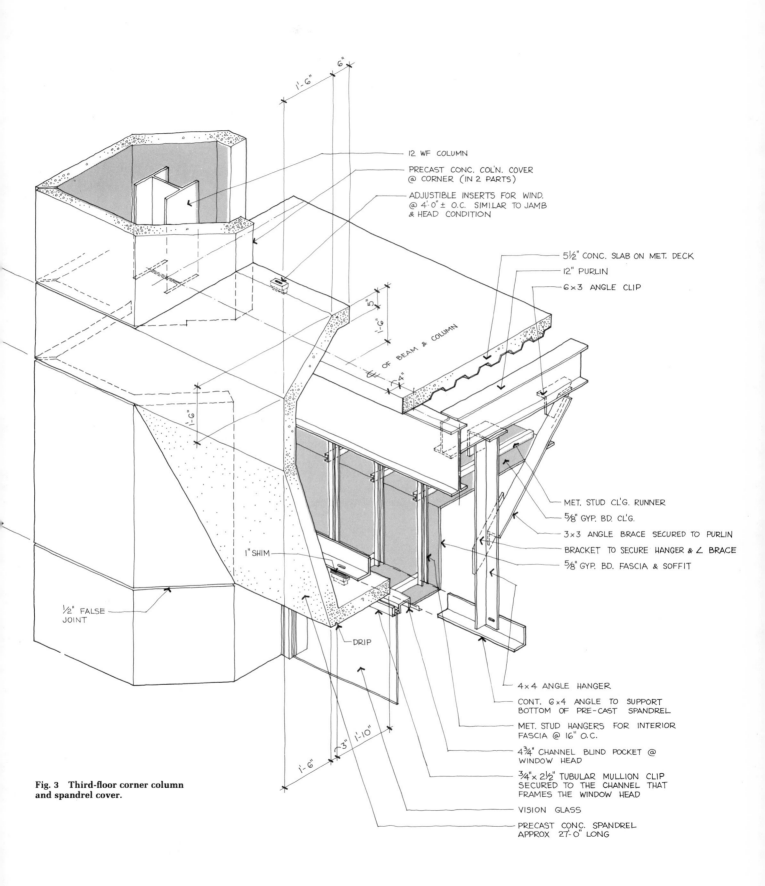

12 WF COLUMN

PRECAST CONC. COL'N. COVER
@ CORNER (IN 2 PARTS)

ADJUSTIBLE INSERTS FOR WIND.
@ 4'-0" ± O.C. SIMILAR TO JAMB
& HEAD CONDITION

5½" CONC. SLAB ON MET. DECK

12" PURLIN

6×3 ANGLE CLIP

OF BEAM & COLUMN

MET. STUD CL'G. RUNNER

⅝" GYP. BD. CL'G.

3×3 ANGLE BRACE SECURED TO PURLIN

BRACKET TO SECURE HANGER & ∠ BRACE

⅝" GYP. BD. FASCIA & SOFFIT

1" SHIM

½" FALSE
JOINT

DRIP

4×4 ANGLE HANGER

CONT. 6×4 ANGLE TO SUPPORT
BOTTOM OF PRE-CAST SPANDREL

MET. STUD HANGERS FOR INTERIOR
FASCIA @ 16" O.C.

4¾" CHANNEL BLIND POCKET @
WINDOW HEAD

¾"× 2½" TUBULAR MULLION CLIP
SECURED TO THE CHANNEL THAT
FRAMES THE WINDOW HEAD

VISION GLASS

PRECAST CONC. SPANDREL
APPROX 27'-0" LONG

1'-6"   6"

5"

1'-6"

4"

1'-6"

1'-6"   3"   1'-10"

**Fig. 3 Third-floor corner column
and spandrel cover.**

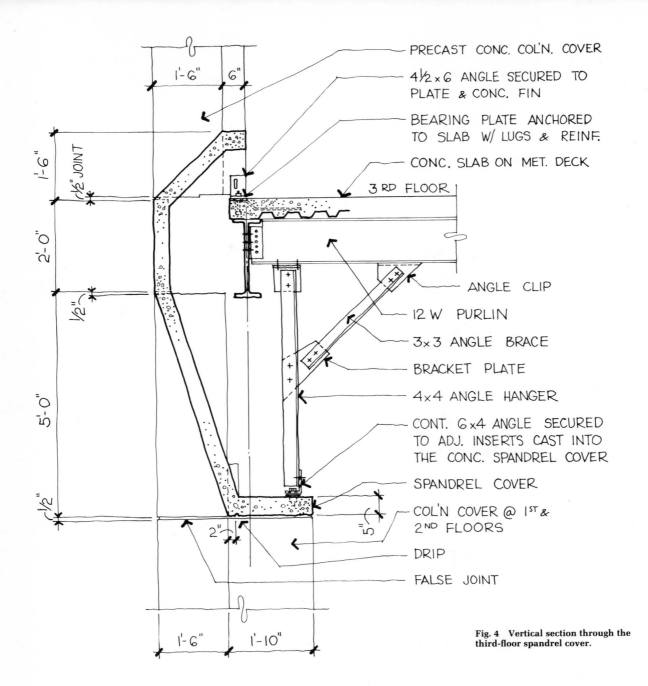

PRECAST CONC. COL'N. COVER

4½ × 6 ANGLE SECURED TO PLATE & CONC. FIN

BEARING PLATE ANCHORED TO SLAB W/ LUGS & REINF.

CONC. SLAB ON MET. DECK

3 RD FLOOR

ANGLE CLIP

12 W PURLIN

3 × 3 ANGLE BRACE

BRACKET PLATE

4 × 4 ANGLE HANGER

CONT. 6 × 4 ANGLE SECURED TO ADJ. INSERTS CAST INTO THE CONC. SPANDREL COVER

SPANDREL COVER

COL'N COVER @ 1ST & 2ND FLOORS

DRIP

FALSE JOINT

1'-6"   6"

1'-6"

1½" JOINT

2'-0"

½"

5'-0"

½"

2"

5"

1'-6"   1'-10"

Fig. 4   Vertical section through the third-floor spandrel cover.

The gypsum board soffit and interior fascia are shown framed into the drapery pocket and are supported by stud hangers and ceiling runners. Figure 4 is a vertical section through the third-floor spandrel that explores the relation of the spandrel covers, the building structure, and the supporting lintel. The glazing and window mullions are not indicated in this section but are covered elsewhere in this chapter. Primary emphasis is placed on the attachment of the spandrel cover to the slab and to the miscellaneous sections that make up the hung lintel.

The continuation and lower section of this isometric drawing may be found in Figure 5, which indicates the corner

column and cover brought down to the sidewalk level. Shown here as well is a part view of the second-floor slab, the spandrel beam, and the curtain wall system. Here we can evaluate the architect's effort to create a seemingly unbroken curtain wall plane from the sidewalk to the third floor. Note that the second-floor structural intersection is concealed by opaque spandrel glass contained within the curtain wall mullions. The second-floor spandrel beam shown in Figure 5 is secured to the corner column and is protected with spray-on fireproofing. Shown here is the conventional method for hanging a suspended plaster ceiling on metal lath secured to channel runners and the slab above. The intersection of the first

floor, the sidewalk, and the foundation wall is indicated in this view. The 18-inch beam, which supports the first-floor slab and the precast sidewalk curb, is framed into the corner column at the cellar level. The sill for the curtain wall and its relation to the first-floor convector cover is accompanied by a jog upward of the concrete slab in order to maintain an advantage with respect to water penetration. Note the application of fabric flashing that protects the first-floor slab and the cellar area from street water. The balance of the foundation walls are dampproofed to the line of the footings below the cellar.

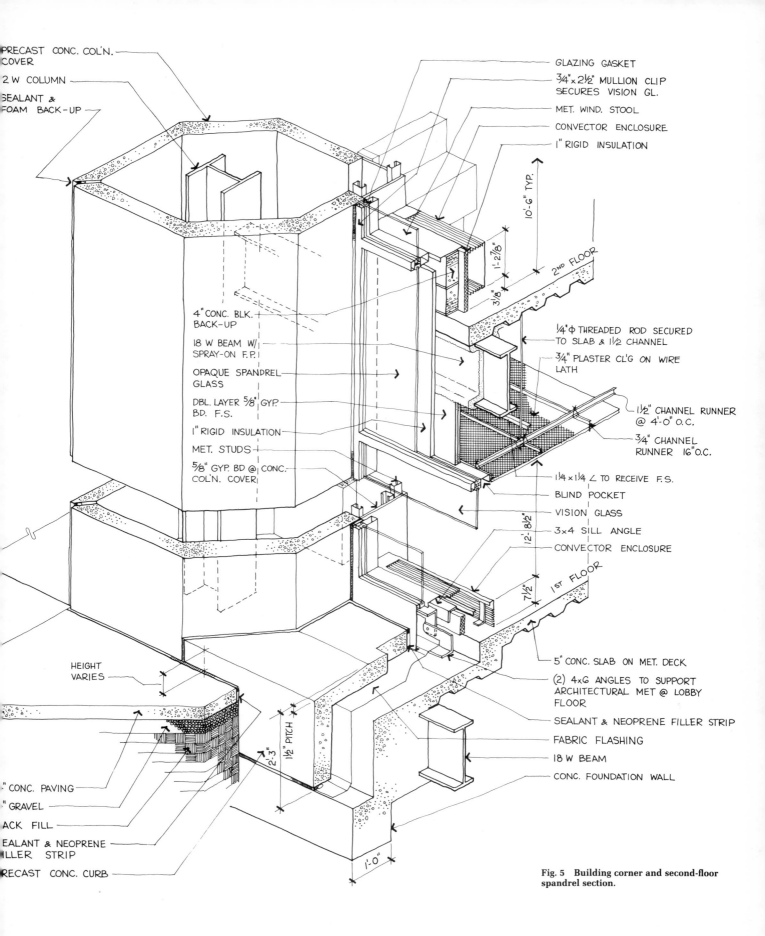

PRECAST CONC. COL'N. COVER

2 W COLUMN

SEALANT & FOAM BACK-UP

GLAZING GASKET

¾" x 2½" MULLION CLIP SECURES VISION GL.

MET. WIND. STOOL

CONVECTOR ENCLOSURE

1" RIGID INSULATION

10'-6" TYP.

2ND FLOOR

1'-2⅞"

3/8"

4" CONC. BLK. BACK-UP

18 W BEAM W/ SPRAY-ON F.P.

OPAQUE SPANDREL GLASS

DBL. LAYER ⅝" GYP. BD. F.S.

1" RIGID INSULATION

MET. STUDS

⅝" GYP. BD @ CONC. COL'N. COVER

¼"⌀ THREADED ROD SECURED TO SLAB & 1½ CHANNEL

¾" PLASTER CL'G ON WIRE LATH

1½" CHANNEL RUNNER @ 4'-0" O.C.

¾" CHANNEL RUNNER 16" O.C.

1¼ x 1¼ ∠ TO RECEIVE F.S.

BLIND POCKET

VISION GLASS

3 x 4 SILL ANGLE

CONVECTOR ENCLOSURE

12'-8½"

7½"

1ST FLOOR

HEIGHT VARIES

2'-3"

1½" PITCH

" CONC. PAVING

" GRAVEL

ACK FILL

EALANT & NEOPRENE ILLER STRIP

RECAST CONC. CURB

1'-0"

5" CONC. SLAB ON MET. DECK

(2) 4x6 ANGLES TO SUPPORT ARCHITECTURAL MET @ LOBBY FLOOR

SEALANT & NEOPRENE FILLER STRIP

FABRIC FLASHING

18 W BEAM

CONC. FOUNDATION WALL

Fig. 5   Building corner and second-floor spandrel section.

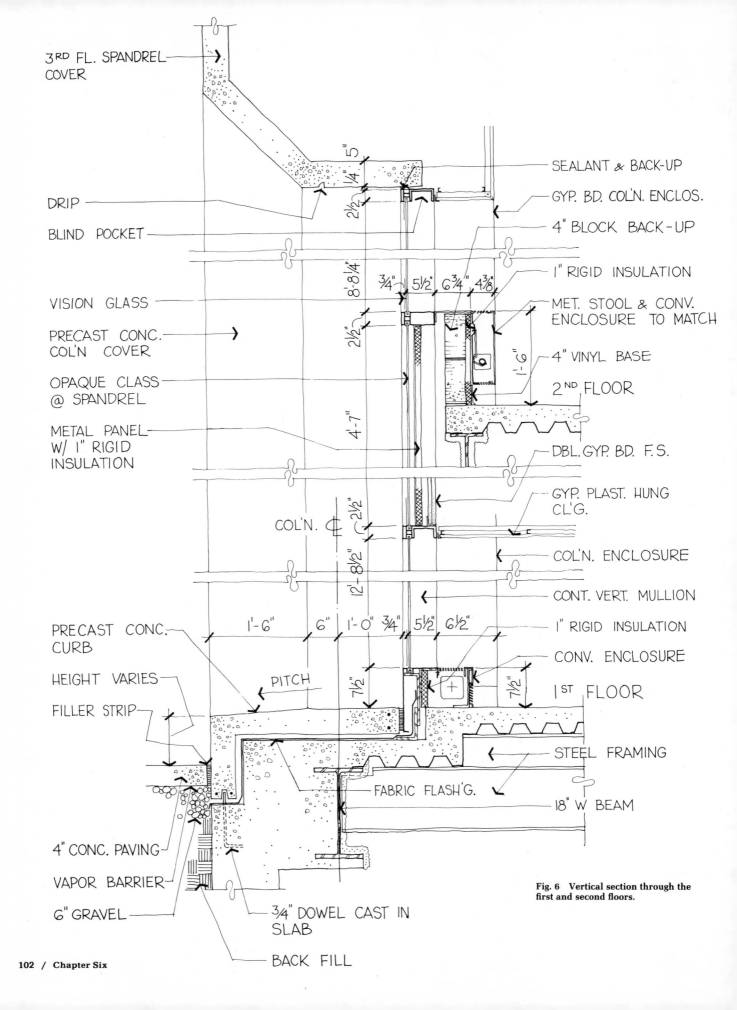

3RD FL. SPANDREL COVER

DRIP

BLIND POCKET

VISION GLASS

PRECAST CONC. COL'N COVER

OPAQUE CLASS @ SPANDREL

METAL PANEL W/ 1" RIGID INSULATION

PRECAST CONC. CURB

HEIGHT VARIES

FILLER STRIP

4" CONC. PAVING

VAPOR BARRIER

6" GRAVEL

3/4" DOWEL CAST IN SLAB

BACK FILL

PITCH

COL'N. C

5"

1/4"

2 1/2"

8'-8 1/4"

2 1/2"

3/4"   5 1/2"   6 3/4"   4 3/8"

4'-7"

1'-6"

2 1/2"

12'-8 1/2"

1'-6"   6"   1'-0"   3/4"   5 1/2"   6 1/2"

7 1/2"

7 1/2"

SEALANT & BACK-UP

GYP. BD. COL'N. ENCLOS.

4" BLOCK BACK-UP

1" RIGID INSULATION

MET. STOOL & CONV. ENCLOSURE TO MATCH

4" VINYL BASE

2ND FLOOR

DBL. GYP. BD. F. S.

GYP. PLAST. HUNG CL'G.

COL'N. ENCLOSURE

CONT. VERT. MULLION

1" RIGID INSULATION

CONV. ENCLOSURE

1ST FLOOR

STEEL FRAMING

FABRIC FLASH'G.

18" W BEAM

Fig. 6   Vertical section through the first and second floors.

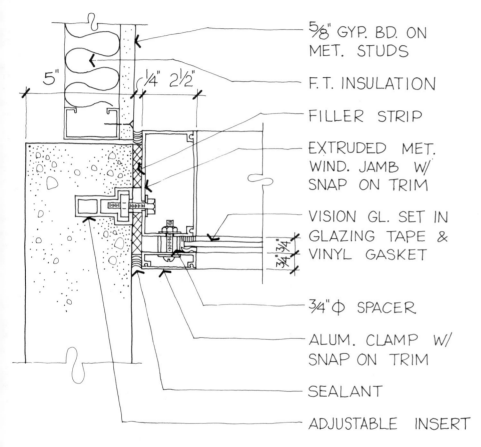

5/8" GYP. BD. ON MET. STUDS

F.T. INSULATION

FILLER STRIP

EXTRUDED MET. WIND. JAMB W/ SNAP ON TRIM

VISION GL. SET IN GLAZING TAPE & VINYL GASKET

3/4" ⌀ SPACER

ALUM. CLAMP W/ SNAP ON TRIM

SEALANT

ADJUSTABLE INSERT

Fig. 7 Horizontal section through the storefront curtain wall at the first and second floors.

Figure 6 is a vertical section through the exterior wall at the first and second floors and, in a two-dimensional format that serves as a review of Figure 5, describes the elements required for this installation. It may be helpful for the reader to compare the isometric diagrams with this material in order to better understand the relation of the construction elements in two and three dimensions. A horizontal section cut through the column cover and curtain wall may be studied in Figure 7. The adjustable insert that receives the storefront curtain wall must be set into the column cover at the factory during the time of casting in order to secure this assembly. Note the filler strip and sealant installation. The glass is set with glazing tape and compression gaskets and is held in place by an aluminum clamp that receives snap-on trim.

Figure 8 takes us into the building and points us outward facing the corner column. Here we can see the contribution made by the cladding contractor with respect to the attachment of the concrete curtain walls. The entire cladding system and its interaction of form and function come into sharp focus. The two panels forming the column cover are shown attached to each other and to the steel column by a system of concrete haunches cast into the panel assemblies. Cantilevered from the 12-inch column are two brackets formed of steel plates that are designed to receive the concrete haunches. Angle clips complete this part of the assembly, while the remainder of the column cover is

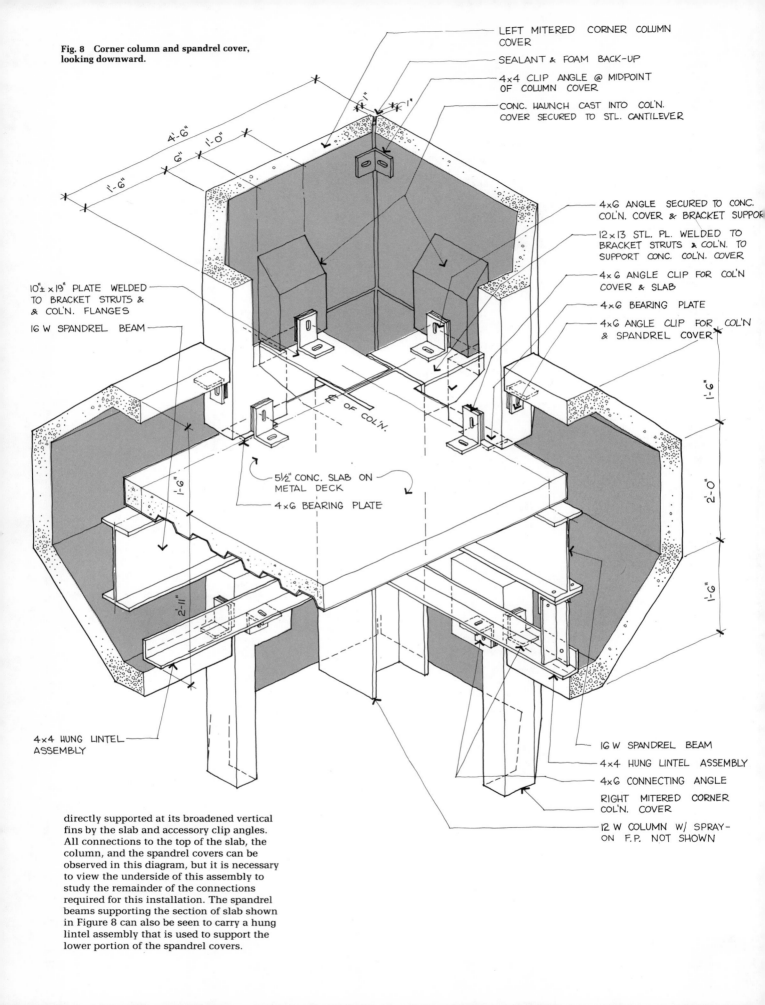

Fig. 8 Corner column and spandrel cover, looking downward.

LEFT MITERED CORNER COLUMN COVER

SEALANT & FOAM BACK-UP

4x4 CLIP ANGLE @ MIDPOINT OF COLUMN COVER

CONC. HAUNCH CAST INTO COL'N. COVER SECURED TO STL. CANTILEVER

4x6 ANGLE SECURED TO CONC. COL'N. COVER & BRACKET SUPPOR

12x13 STL. PL. WELDED TO BRACKET STRUTS & COL'N. TO SUPPORT CONC. COL'N. COVER

4x6 ANGLE CLIP FOR COL'N COVER & SLAB

4x6 BEARING PLATE

4x6 ANGLE CLIP FOR COL'N & SPANDREL COVER

10"± x 19" PLATE WELDED TO BRACKET STRUTS & & COL'N. FLANGES

16 W SPANDREL BEAM

4'-6"
6"
1'-0"
1'-6"
1"
1"

℄ OF COL'N.

5½" CONC. SLAB ON METAL DECK

4x6 BEARING PLATE

1'-6"

1'-6"

2'-0"

1'-6"

2'-11"

4x4 HUNG LINTEL ASSEMBLY

16 W SPANDREL BEAM

4x4 HUNG LINTEL ASSEMBLY

4x6 CONNECTING ANGLE

RIGHT MITERED CORNER COL'N. COVER

12 W COLUMN W/ SPRAY-ON F.P. NOT SHOWN

directly supported at its broadened vertical fins by the slab and accessory clip angles. All connections to the top of the slab, the column, and the spandrel covers can be observed in this diagram, but it is necessary to view the underside of this assembly to study the remainder of the connections required for this installation. The spandrel beams supporting the section of slab shown in Figure 8 can also be seen to carry a hung lintel assembly that is used to support the lower portion of the spandrel covers.

Figure 9 presents another view of the corner column and spandrel intersection viewed from below and looking upward and out. The steel frame and slab are defined in this drawing. The spandrel beam is supported by the steel column in a conventional manner, and the secondary structural elements shown support the spandrel and column covers. It is possible in this view to study the hung lintel assembly and the column cover clip angles. Steel lintel hangers positioned at regular intervals support a 4- by 4-inch lintel that performs two vital functions. It secures the lower edges of the precast spandrel covers and also engages the outer edges of the

corner column covers. These attachments are made with clip angles that are connected by bolts to adjustable inserts that have been cast into the concrete panels. Metal shims are used to solidly fill the spaces between the clip angles and the panels so that tight construction joints may be made. The concrete column covers are attached directly to the steel column

through two long 4- by 4-inch angles that run perpendicularly to each other and are clipped to the anchor inserts of the precast concrete. These angles are welded to the column to provide the necessary strength for the connection. The mitered corners of

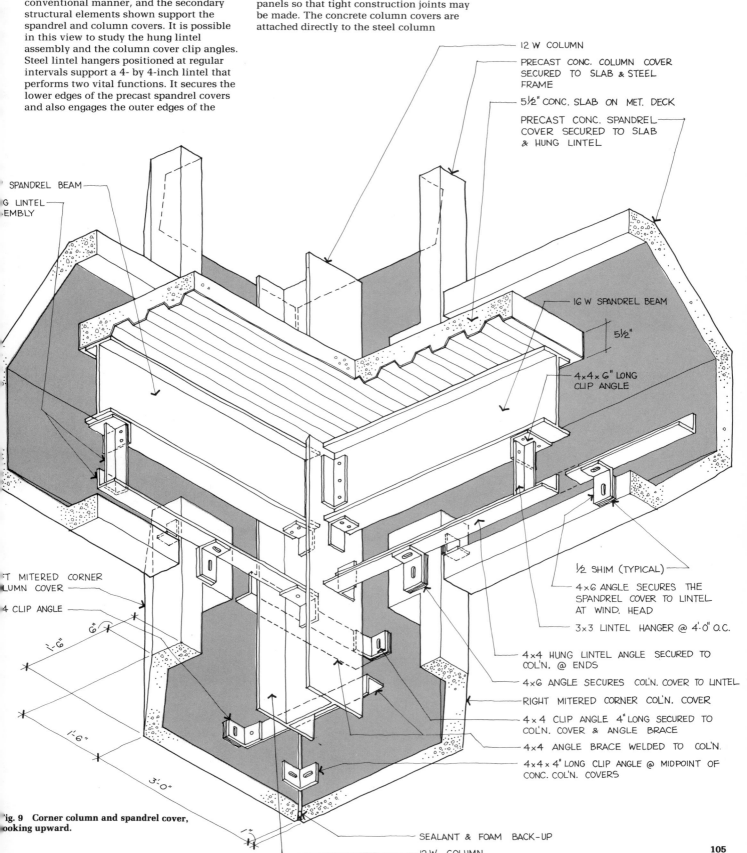

SPANDREL BEAM

G LINTEL
EMBLY

12 W COLUMN

PRECAST CONC. COLUMN COVER SECURED TO SLAB & STEEL FRAME

5½" CONC. SLAB ON MET. DECK

PRECAST CONC. SPANDREL COVER SECURED TO SLAB & HUNG LINTEL

16 W SPANDREL BEAM

5½"

4 x 4 x 6" LONG CLIP ANGLE

T MITERED CORNER
LUMN COVER

4 CLIP ANGLE

6"

1'-6"

1'-6"

3'-0"

1"

½ SHIM (TYPICAL)

4 x 6 ANGLE SECURES THE SPANDREL COVER TO LINTEL AT WIND. HEAD

3 x 3 LINTEL HANGER @ 4'-0" O.C.

4 x 4 HUNG LINTEL ANGLE SECURED TO COL'N. @ ENDS

4 x 6 ANGLE SECURES COL'N. COVER TO LINTEL

RIGHT MITERED CORNER COL'N. COVER

4 x 4 CLIP ANGLE 4" LONG SECURED TO COL'N. COVER & ANGLE BRACE

4 x 4 ANGLE BRACE WELDED TO COL'N.

4 x 4 x 4" LONG CLIP ANGLE @ MIDPOINT OF CONC. COL'N. COVERS

SEALANT & FOAM BACK-UP

12 W COLUMN

Fig. 9 Corner column and spandrel cover, looking upward.

105

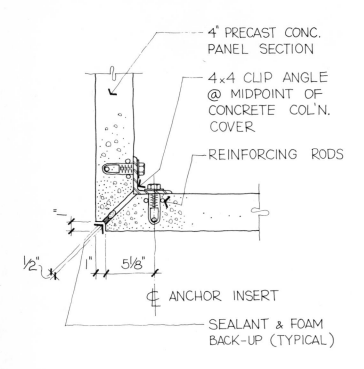

4" PRECAST CONC. PANEL SECTION

4x4 CLIP ANGLE @ MIDPOINT OF CONCRETE COL'N. COVER

REINFORCING RODS

½" 1" 5⅛"

℄ ANCHOR INSERT

SEALANT & FOAM BACK-UP (TYPICAL)

Fig. 10   Plan section through the column cover connection.

the concrete column covers are shown attached to each other with an angle at the midpoint of the cover panels. Figure 10 is a plan section through this intersection. The anchor inserts that receive the clip angle are shown approximately 5 inches from the edge of the reentrant corner. These devices must be set into the concrete panels and anchored before casting. The ½-inch space between the panels at the mitered corner receives a foam backup rod and sealant that waterproofs this joint. This detail is representative of the general sealant system for all the panel assemblies in this project.

Figure 11, a typical floor and corner bay, indicates the vision glass, the concrete spandrel, and the column covers and their relation to the corner of the building. Shown in dotted lines is the location of the vertical fins used for panel reinforcement and attachment. Figure 12 is a vertical section through the midpoint of the typical spandrel cover and indicates the main connections for this element. At this location the center concrete fin is secured to a 4- by 12-inch bearing plate set into the slab with composite lugs and additional reinforcing. As previously described, the bottom of the spandrel cover is secured to a continuous hung lintel. The end connections for the spandrel cover are shown in Figure 13. This drawing indicates the termination of the hung lintel at the column and the attachment of the spandrel cover to the slab and to the concrete

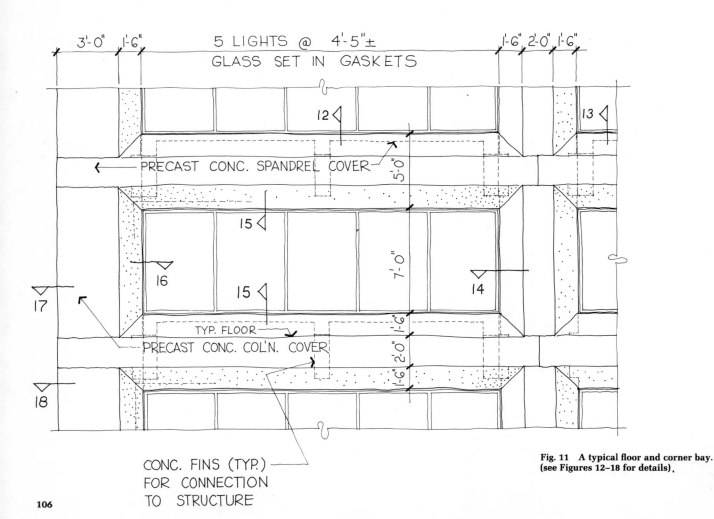

3'-0" 1'-6"   5 LIGHTS @ 4'-5"±   1'-6" 2'-0" 1'-6"
GLASS SET IN GASKETS

12

13

PRECAST CONC. SPANDREL COVER   5'-0"

15

7'-0"

16

15

14

TYP. FLOOR

17

PRECAST CONC. COL'N. COVER   1'-6" 2'-0" 1'-6"

18

CONC. FINS (TYP.) FOR CONNECTION TO STRUCTURE

Fig. 11   A typical floor and corner bay. (see Figures 12–18 for details).

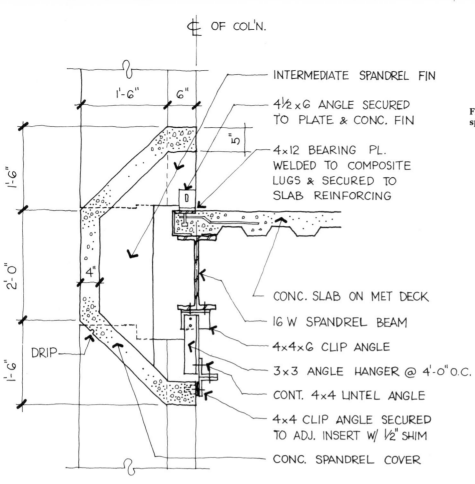

C OF COL'N.

1'-6" 6"
5"
1'-6"
2'-0"
4"
1'-6"
DRIP

INTERMEDIATE SPANDREL FIN

4½ × 6 ANGLE SECURED TO PLATE & CONC. FIN

4 × 12 BEARING PL. WELDED TO COMPOSITE LUGS & SECURED TO SLAB REINFORCING

CONC. SLAB ON MET DECK

16 W SPANDREL BEAM

4 × 4 × 6 CLIP ANGLE

3 × 3 ANGLE HANGER @ 4'-0" O.C.

CONT. 4 × 4 LINTEL ANGLE

4 × 4 CLIP ANGLE SECURED TO ADJ. INSERT W/ ½" SHIM

CONC. SPANDREL COVER

Fig. 12 Vertical section through spandrel at the midpoint of the bay.

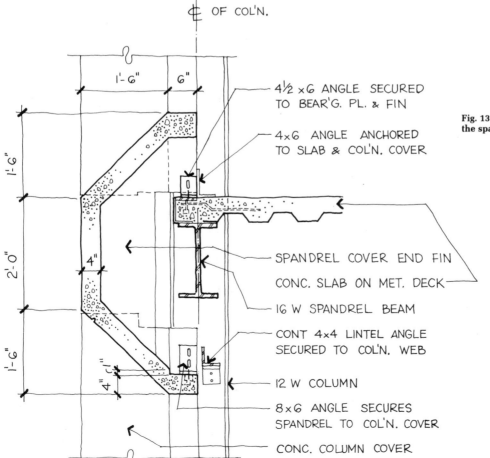

C OF COL'N.

1'-6" 6"
5"
1'-6"
2'-0"
4"
1'-6"
4"

4½ × 6 ANGLE SECURED TO BEAR'G. PL. & FIN

4 × 6 ANGLE ANCHORED TO SLAB & COL'N. COVER

SPANDREL COVER END FIN

CONC. SLAB ON MET. DECK

16 W SPANDREL BEAM

CONT 4 × 4 LINTEL ANGLE SECURED TO COL'N. WEB

12 W COLUMN

8 × 6 ANGLE SECURES SPANDREL TO COL'N. COVER

CONC. COLUMN COVER

Fig. 13 Vertical section through the spandrel at the column support.

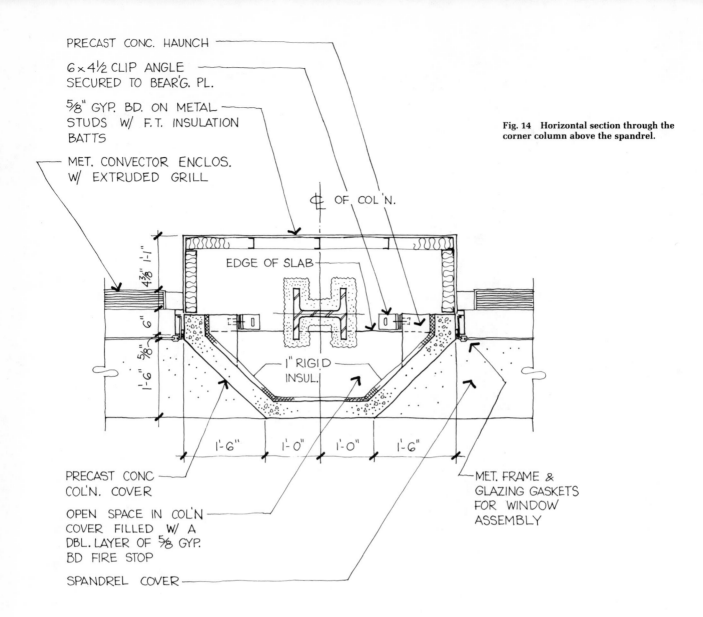

PRECAST CONC. HAUNCH

6 × 4½ CLIP ANGLE SECURED TO BEAR'G. PL.

⅝" GYP. BD. ON METAL STUDS W/ F.T. INSULATION BATTS

MET. CONVECTOR ENCLOS. W/ EXTRUDED GRILL

℄ OF COL'N.

EDGE OF SLAB

1" RIGID INSUL.

4⅜" 1'-1"

6" ⅝" 6"

1'-6"

1'-6"   1'-0"   1'-0"   1'-6"

PRECAST CONC COL'N. COVER

OPEN SPACE IN COL'N COVER FILLED W/ A DBL. LAYER OF ⅝ GYP. BD FIRE STOP

SPANDREL COVER

MET. FRAME & GLAZING GASKETS FOR WINDOW ASSEMBLY

Fig. 14   Horizontal section through the corner column above the spandrel.

column cover. Figure 14 is a horizontal section through a typical column cover; it indicates the structural attachment of the concrete haunches to the slab. Note the horizontal gypsum board fire-stop between the face of the slab and the inside of the column cover. This is installed in order to prevent the column enclosure assemblies from becoming fire flues.

A view of the head and sill section of the glazing is shown in Figure 15. One may observe typical dimensions, materials, and various structural and mechanical systems in this view. The anchor inserts for the structural attachment of the spandrel covers and the glazing mullions are shown in dotted lines. Figure 16 is a large-scale view of the glazing installation at the jamb section of the column cover. Extreme

caution must be exercised in the planning stages of construction detailing when the application of the glazing assembly is so heavily dependent upon the successful fabrication of other related items, namely the precast cladding system. The bent plate composing the mullion assembly is designed to receive the neoprene glazing gaskets that make the installation of the vision glass possible. A Z clip attached to the bent plate receives the metal window jamb. The ⅜-inch space between the concrete cover and the mullion is sealed inside and out as noted. The interior gypsum board partition is shown intersecting the column cover at this point. All the concrete covers are insulated with a 1-inch rigid insulation panel secured to the inside face of the concrete cladding

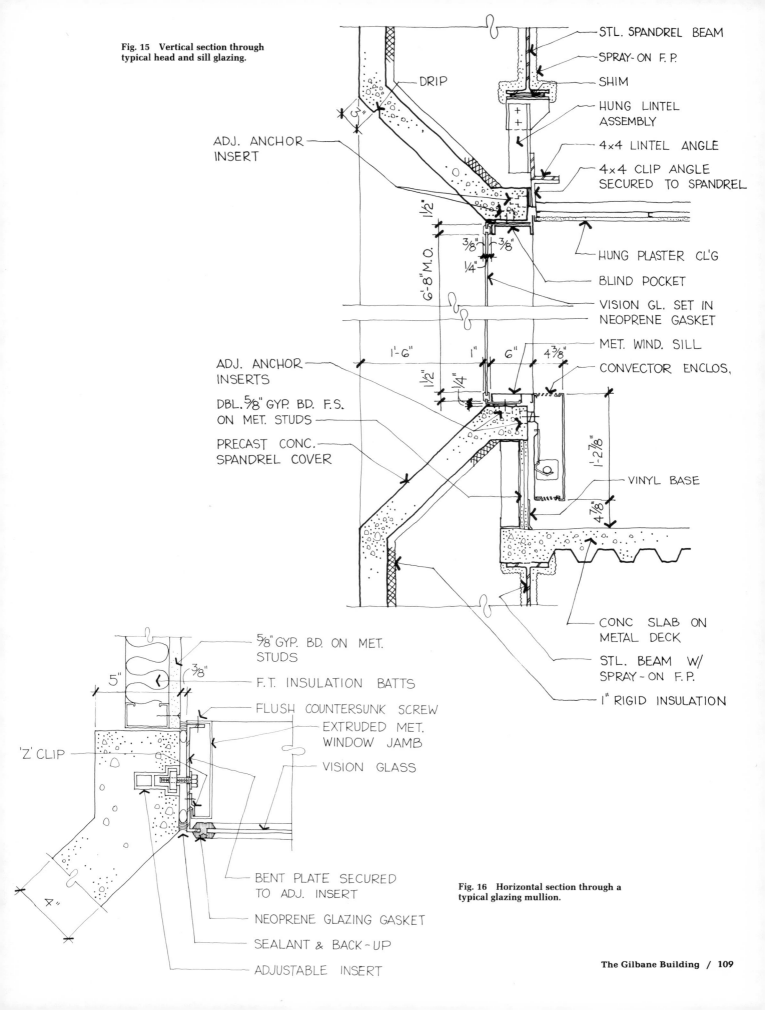

Fig. 15 Vertical section through typical head and sill glazing.

STL. SPANDREL BEAM

SPRAY-ON F. P.

SHIM

HUNG LINTEL ASSEMBLY

4×4 LINTEL ANGLE

4×4 CLIP ANGLE SECURED TO SPANDREL

DRIP

ADJ. ANCHOR INSERT

HUNG PLASTER CL'G

BLIND POCKET

VISION GL. SET IN NEOPRENE GASKET

MET. WIND. SILL

CONVECTOR ENCLOS.

ADJ. ANCHOR INSERTS

DBL. ⅝" GYP. BD. F.S. ON MET. STUDS

PRECAST CONC. SPANDREL COVER

VINYL BASE

CONC SLAB ON METAL DECK

STL. BEAM W/ SPRAY-ON F. P.

1" RIGID INSULATION

1½
3⁄8" 3⁄8"
¼"
6'-8" M.O.
1'-6"   1"   6"   4 3⁄8"
1½" ¼"
1'-2 7⁄8"
4 7⁄8"
3"

⅝" GYP. BD. ON MET. STUDS

F.T. INSULATION BATTS

FLUSH COUNTERSUNK SCREW

EXTRUDED MET. WINDOW JAMB

VISION GLASS

'Z' CLIP

5"
3⁄8"
4"

BENT PLATE SECURED TO ADJ. INSERT

NEOPRENE GLAZING GASKET

SEALANT & BACK-UP

ADJUSTABLE INSERT

Fig. 16 Horizontal section through a typical glazing mullion.

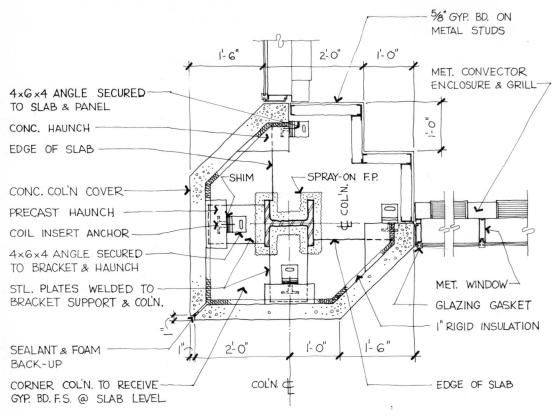

4×6×4 ANGLE SECURED
TO SLAB & PANEL

CONC. HAUNCH

EDGE OF SLAB

CONC. COL'N COVER

PRECAST HAUNCH

COIL INSERT ANCHOR

4×6×4 ANGLE SECURED
TO BRACKET & HAUNCH

STL. PLATES WELDED TO
BRACKET SUPPORT & COL'N.

SEALANT & FOAM
BACK-UP

CORNER COL'N. TO RECEIVE
GYP. BD. F.S. @ SLAB LEVEL

5/8" GYP. BD. ON
METAL STUDS

MET. CONVECTOR
ENCLOSURE & GRILL

SHIM

SPRAY-ON F.P.

℄ COL'N.

MET. WINDOW

GLAZING GASKET

1" RIGID INSULATION

COL'N. ℄

EDGE OF SLAB

1'-6"   2'-0"   1'-0"

1'-0"

1"   2'-0"   1'-0"   1'-6"

**Fig. 17   Horizontal section through a
typical column and cover
above the floor slab.**

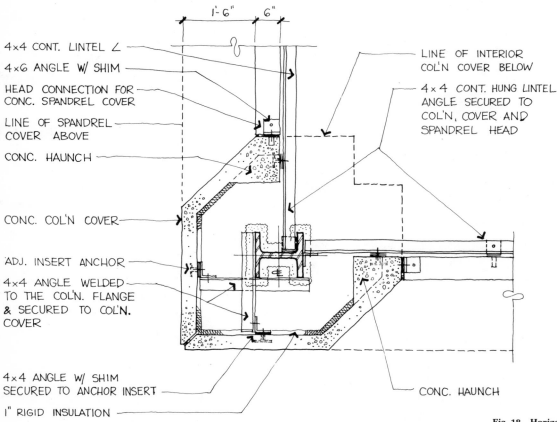

4×4 CONT. LINTEL ∠

4×6 ANGLE W/ SHIM

HEAD CONNECTION FOR
CONC. SPANDREL COVER

LINE OF SPANDREL
COVER ABOVE

CONC. HAUNCH

CONC. COL'N COVER

ADJ. INSERT ANCHOR

4×4 ANGLE WELDED
TO THE COL'N. FLANGE
& SECURED TO COL'N.
COVER

4×4 ANGLE W/ SHIM
SECURED TO ANCHOR INSERT

1" RIGID INSULATION

1'-6"   6"

LINE OF INTERIOR
COL'N COVER BELOW

4×4 CONT. HUNG LINTEL
ANGLE SECURED TO
COL'N, COVER AND
SPANDREL HEAD

CONC. HAUNCH

**Fig. 18   Horizontal section through a
typical column and cover below the floor slab.**

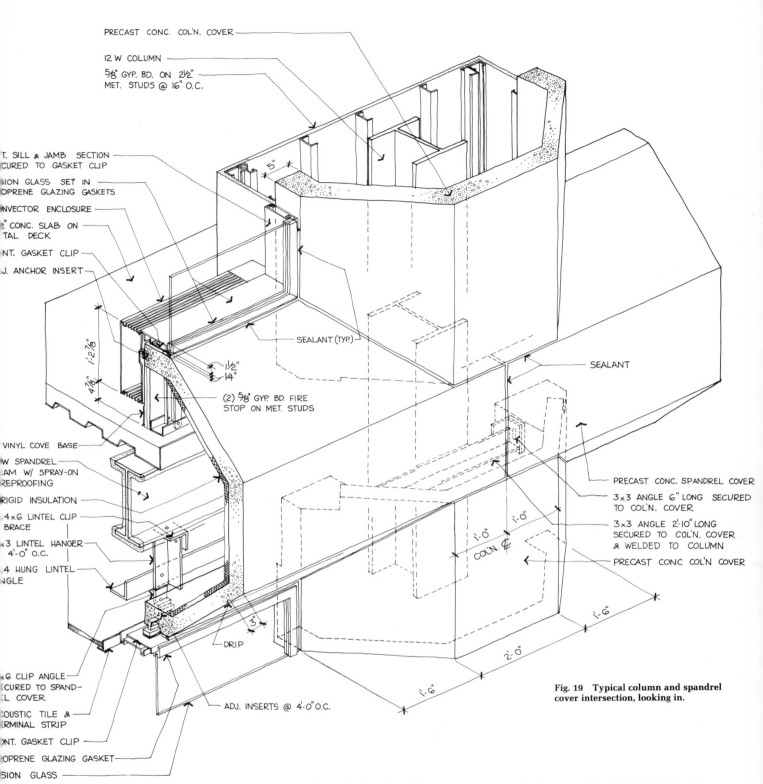

PRECAST CONC. COL'N. COVER

12 W COLUMN

5/8" GYP. BD. ON 2½"
MET. STUDS @ 16" O.C.

T. SILL & JAMB SECTION
CURED TO GASKET CLIP

SION GLASS SET IN
OPRENE GLAZING GASKETS

NVECTOR ENCLOSURE

2" CONC. SLAB ON
TAL DECK

NT. GASKET CLIP

J. ANCHOR INSERT

5"

1'-2 7/8"

4 7/8"

1½"
1/4"

(2) 5/8" GYP. BD. FIRE
STOP ON MET. STUDS

SEALANT (TYP.)

SEALANT

VINYL COVE BASE

W SPANDREL
AM W/ SPRAY-ON
REPROOFING

RIGID INSULATION

4 x G LINTEL CLIP
BRACE

3 LINTEL HANGER
4'-0" O.C.

4 HUNG LINTEL
NGLE

PRECAST CONC. SPANDREL COVER

3 x 3 ANGLE 6" LONG SECURED
TO COL'N. COVER

3 x 3 ANGLE 2'-10" LONG
SECURED TO COL'N. COVER
& WELDED TO COLUMN

PRECAST CONC. COL'N COVER

1'-0"

1'-0"

COL'N. ℄

1'-6"

2'-0"

1'-6"

3"

DRIP

ADJ. INSERTS @ 4'-0" O.C.

G CLIP ANGLE
CURED TO SPAND-
L COVER

COUSTIC TILE &
RMINAL STRIP

NT. GASKET CLIP

OPRENE GLAZING GASKET

SION GLASS

**Fig. 19 Typical column and spandrel
cover intersection, looking in.**

sections. Figure 17 is a horizontal section
through the column as seen above the slab
and is a plan equivalent of Figure 8. The
relation of the interior walls, the convector
covers, and the slab is noted here with
dimensions. Figure 18 is a view of this
same corner column cover as seen from a
point below the slab and is a plan detail
variation of the material covered in Figure
9.

An exterior view of a typical intersection
of a column and spandrel cover can be

found in Figure 19. The dotted lines
representing the unseen portions of the
column covers indicate the extent of these
assemblies. Also shown in dotted lines is
the bracing angle that ties the column
covers back to the steel angle. This is the
only view of this connection that can be
indicated practically. The fireproofed
spandrel beam is shown supporting the
slab and receiving the hung lintel
assembly. The sill section in this isometric
view indicates the vision glass, the glazing

gaskets, the extruded aluminum stool, and
the convector enclosure. The enclosure is
secured to an adjustable anchor insert, and
the opening between the slab and the
bottom of the spandrel cover is closed with
a fire-stop fabricated of a double layer of ⅝-
inch gypsum board on metal furring. The
spandrel beam supports the lintel hangers
shown here, and a cutaway view of the
anchor inserts indicates the method used to
fasten the head assembly of the window to
the spandrel cover.

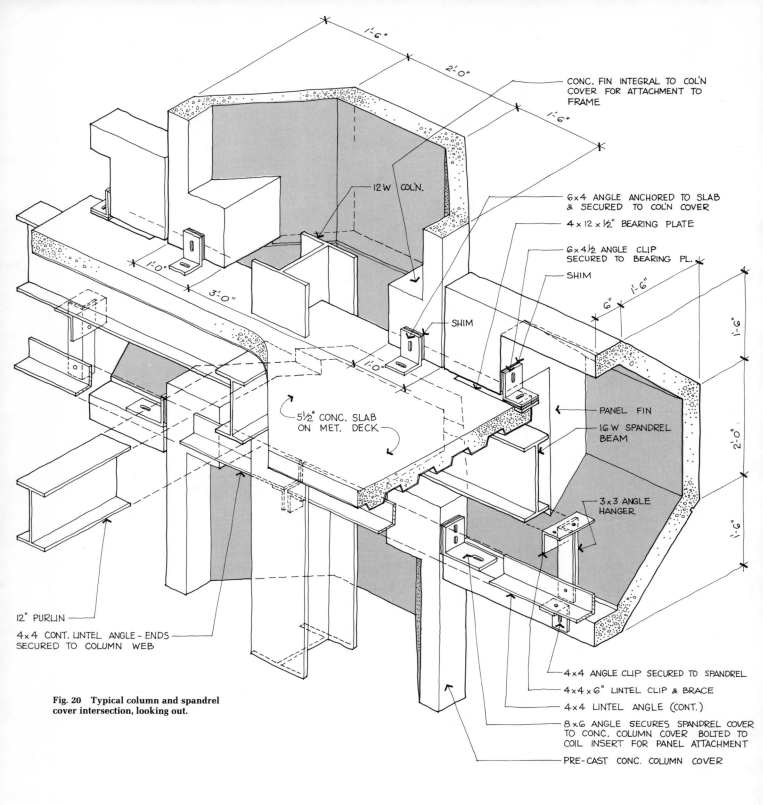

1'-6"
2'-0"
1'-6"

CONC. FIN INTEGRAL TO COL'N COVER FOR ATTACHMENT TO FRAME

12 W COL'N.

6x4 ANGLE ANCHORED TO SLAB & SECURED TO COL'N COVER

4 x 12 x ½" BEARING PLATE

6x4½ ANGLE CLIP SECURED TO BEARING PL.

SHIM

1'-6"

6"

1'-0"

3'-0"

SHIM

PANEL FIN

16 W SPANDREL BEAM

1'-6"

2'-0"

5½" CONC. SLAB ON MET. DECK

3x3 ANGLE HANGER

1'-6"

12" PURLIN

4x4 CONT. LINTEL ANGLE – ENDS SECURED TO COLUMN WEB

4x4 ANGLE CLIP SECURED TO SPANDREL

4x4 x 6" LINTEL CLIP & BRACE

4x4 LINTEL ANGLE (CONT.)

8 x6 ANGLE SECURES SPANDREL COVER TO CONC. COLUMN COVER BOLTED TO COIL INSERT FOR PANEL ATTACHMENT

PRE-CAST CONC. COLUMN COVER

Fig. 20 Typical column and spandrel cover intersection, looking out.

Figure 20 describes the intersection of a typical intermediate column and spandrel intersection as seen from the interior of the tower looking outward. The 12-inch purlin intersecting the column and 16-inch spandrel beam establishes the relationship of the main structural elements. A part view of the slab is shown, and it is here that the critical attachments to the precast concrete panels are made. The column cover side fins rest on the slab and are secured to it with clip angles. Metal shims

are used to bring the column cover to the proper elevation. The spandrel cover is secured to the top of the slab by an angle clip bolted to the anchor inserts and by a 4- by 12-inch bearing plate cast into the slab. The lower portion of the concrete spandrel cover is attached to a hung lintel assembly that is supported by the spandrel beam. The upper portion of the column cover is secured to the spandrel and to the structural column itself, as shown in this diagram.

The flat precast panels that form the penthouse and the south elevation of this building can be studied in Figure 21. Two concrete haunches per 10-foot panel rest on the concrete slab and are secured to it with angle clips. A coil insert is cast into the panel, and this receives the bolted connection through the required shims. A 6- by 5-inch bearing plate cast into the slab with composite bolts and additional reinforcing receives the horizontal leg of the clip angle. The upper portion of the flat

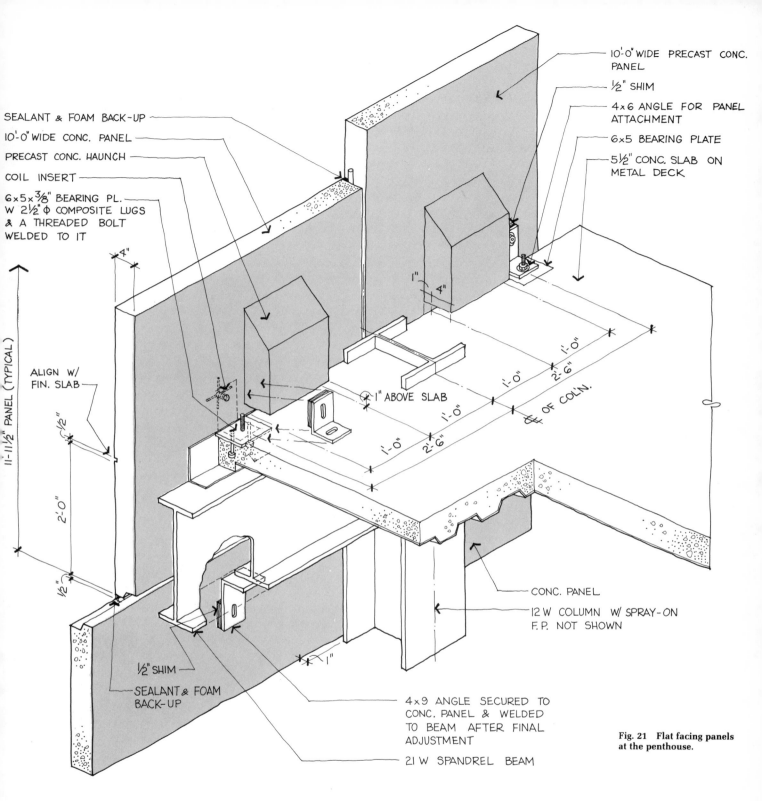

SEALANT & FOAM BACK-UP
10'-0" WIDE CONC. PANEL
PRECAST CONC. HAUNCH
COIL INSERT
6x5x3/8" BEARING PL.
W 2 1/2" Φ COMPOSITE LUGS
& A THREADED BOLT
WELDED TO IT

4"

ALIGN W/
FIN. SLAB

11-11 1/2" PANEL (TYPICAL)

1/2"

2'-0"

1/2"

10'-0" WIDE PRECAST CONC.
PANEL
1/2" SHIM
4x6 ANGLE FOR PANEL
ATTACHMENT
6x5 BEARING PLATE
5 1/2" CONC. SLAB ON
METAL DECK

1"

4"

1" ABOVE SLAB

1'-0"   1'-0"   2'-6"
2'-6"   1'-0"   ₵ OF COL'N.

CONC. PANEL
12 W COLUMN W/ SPRAY-ON
F. P. NOT SHOWN

1/2" SHIM
SEALANT & FOAM
BACK-UP

1"

4x9 ANGLE SECURED TO
CONC. PANEL & WELDED
TO BEAM AFTER FINAL
ADJUSTMENT

21 W SPANDREL BEAM

**Fig. 21 Flat facing panels
at the penthouse.**

panel is secured to the 21-inch spandrel beam with clip angles. Note the method by which both panels interlock horizontally and develop a seal against the weather. The vertical seam between the panels is sealed, and splice plates (not shown here) connect the panels at their midpoint height.

Concrete has not always delivered the exterior performance hoped for. Excess water content, segregation of aggregates, improper placement, and sloppy formwork have all contributed to the general problem

in a great many buildings throughout the world. It therefore becomes a singular event when all these difficulties can be resolved consistently for all installations calling for precast concrete panels. Precasting makes it possible to apply quality control during manufacture. Water content, which ultimately determines the strength of this material, can be carefully monitored during a factory process. High-quality metal or plastic formwork used repeatedly with vibration or other consolidation methods

produces a high-strength, high-quality finish that is virtually unavailable in on-site concrete casting operations.

From a camouflaged and, in terms of quality, a deficient material, concrete has become a visible, highly finished structural component suitable for use as a cladding material. Improvements in the quality and increases in the kinds of applications of the material will no doubt continue in the future.

7 Sibley's Department Store

Fayetteville, New York

ARCHITECTS: Raymond, Rado, Caddy & Bonnington Architects/Planners

Fig. 1 Main entrance of store.

The application of rigid materials such as steel and precast concrete to a sculptural building requires that the designer pay special attention with respect to construction detailing and fabrication. The design of Sibley's Department Store at the East Gate Mall in Fayetteville, New York, illustrates some important points with respect to the successful development of a complex facade for a commercial project. The architects for this building are Raymond, Rado, Caddy & Bonnington Architects/Planners. They have translated a sweeping design concept into a practical construction statement.

The store must conform to both building codes and contractual standards of construction established by the mall management. In fact, shopping centers impose construction regulations that are at times more stringent than local ordinances. These management requirements often govern design development, graphics, security, and mechanical performance. The architects were able to conform to all these demands and managed also to express the exterior of the building in a bold, sculptured way that significantly complements the simplicity of the shopping mall itself.

The department store is freestanding on three sides and is attached at its north elevation to the mall. A soaring play of prismatic concrete panels contrasted with a dark-brown masonry base and an inclined decorative soffit form the main entrance of the store, as seen in Figure 1. The net effect of this design is the creation of a three-dimensional funnel-like vestibule that directs pedestrians into the store lobby. An observer of this building requires a moment to realize that the cladding system is not actually made of poured concrete but is composed of rigid 4-foot-wide precast concrete panels.

The structure of the building is a simple steel frame composed of 32-foot-square bays two stories high forming a building approximately 340 feet long by 220 feet wide. A secondary steel structure that articulates the sculptured facade is composed of miscellaneous steel angles and channels. The precast concrete used in this project is 6 inches thick throughout and is prestressed for maximum strength. Since these panels were cast in a factory remote from the construction site, elements such as reinforcement, structural connections, hoisting inserts, and anchors had to be engineered into the system well in advance of the actual fabrication of the facade. The many problems related to the intersection of the cladding system and the structure had to be understood and dealt with in the construction detailing process many months before the project was fabricated.

Figure 2 illustrates the symmetry of the precast concrete panels forming the wings on either side of the main entry. Referring to Figure 1 again, we see an eye-level view of the protected entry area. This exterior vestibule is formed by inclined planes of concrete and an angled soffit finished with illuminated plastic pans leading to the entry lobby. A strong feeling of enclosure is centered on the entry of the building; this is exciting and functionally effective for shoppers using the parking lot access to the store.

Fig. 2   South elevation—entry.

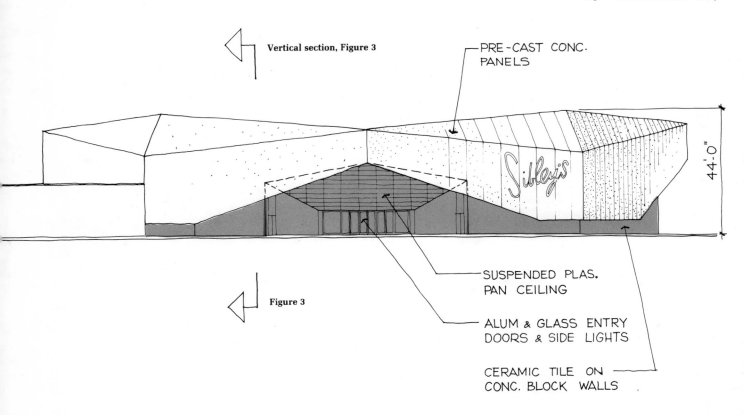

Vertical section, Figure 3

PRE-CAST CONC. PANELS

Sibley's

44'-0"

Figure 3

SUSPENDED PLAS. PAN CEILING

ALUM & GLASS ENTRY DOORS & SIDE LIGHTS

CERAMIC TILE ON CONC. BLOCK WALLS

Fig. 3 Vertical section through south entry wall.

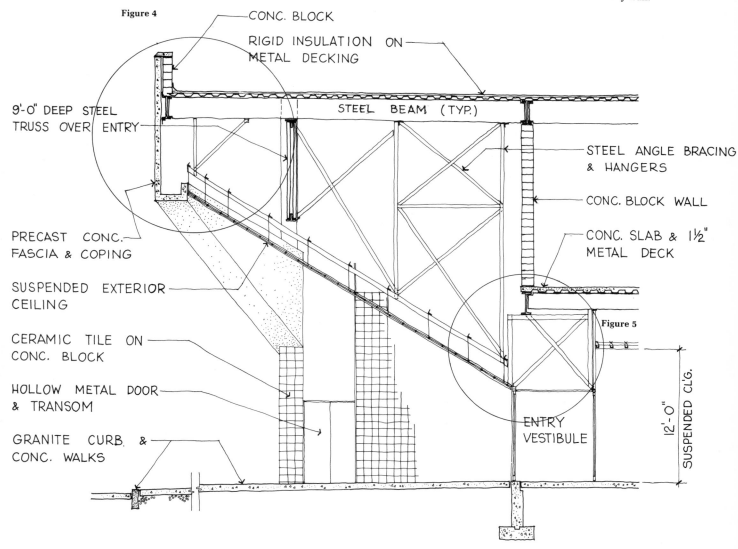

Figure 4

CONC. BLOCK

RIGID INSULATION ON METAL DECKING

STEEL BEAM (TYP.)

9'-0" DEEP STEEL TRUSS OVER ENTRY

STEEL ANGLE BRACING & HANGERS

CONC. BLOCK WALL

CONC. SLAB & 1½" METAL DECK

PRECAST CONC. FASCIA & COPING

SUSPENDED EXTERIOR CEILING

CERAMIC TILE ON CONC. BLOCK

HOLLOW METAL DOOR & TRANSOM

GRANITE CURB. & CONC. WALKS

Figure 5

ENTRY VESTIBULE

12'-0" SUSPENDED CL'G.

A vertical cross section through the entry area is shown in Figure 3. The concrete panels, the masonry walls, and the lobby are indicated. The primary steel structure and the miscellaneous secondary elements can be studied here. Special attention should be given the 9-foot-deep truss over the entryway since it supports heavy steel beams that are cantilevered from it to carry the precast concrete panels at the face of the building. The facade of the building forms an irregular cavity, running alongside the walls, that defines the store interior. Outlined for further analysis in this drawing are two areas of construction that are explained in isometric diagrams as follows.

Figure 4 is a view of the structure of the upper entry area showing the relation of the parapet, the roof, the precast concrete panels, and the beginning of the inclined soffit. The main truss spanning the width of the entry area is shown supporting cantilevered steel beams, which in turn carry the suspended soffit assembly. The entire steel structure, including the metal decking, receives spray-on fireproofing. Although the drawing does not indicate this fire protection, such protection must nevertheless be considered part of the overall requirements of the project. The cantilevered 24-inch beam supports an 18-inch spandrel beam that carries the parapet and satisfies several other structural requirements. A cut 18-inch beam with one flange removed is installed below the spandrel to secure the upper part of the precast parapet panel. A 9-inch beam acting as a structural hanger is clipped to the spandrel assembly and secures two 10-inch channels that directly support the bottom of the precast assembly. The concrete block backup for the parapet bears directly on the spandrel beam. Steel angles clipped to the cantilevered beams are suspended to form the 30-degree angle required for the plane of the inclined soffit. These hangers support 6-inch channels that are parallel to the inclined soffit and support the hanger assembly for the plastic pan ceiling. Note the 4- by 4-inch angles spaced 4 feet on center. These actually carry the 1-inch strap hangers that receive the channel runners and furring strips for the sheathed plywood soffit. As indicated in Figure 3, the drawing for this assembly is continued in Figure 5.

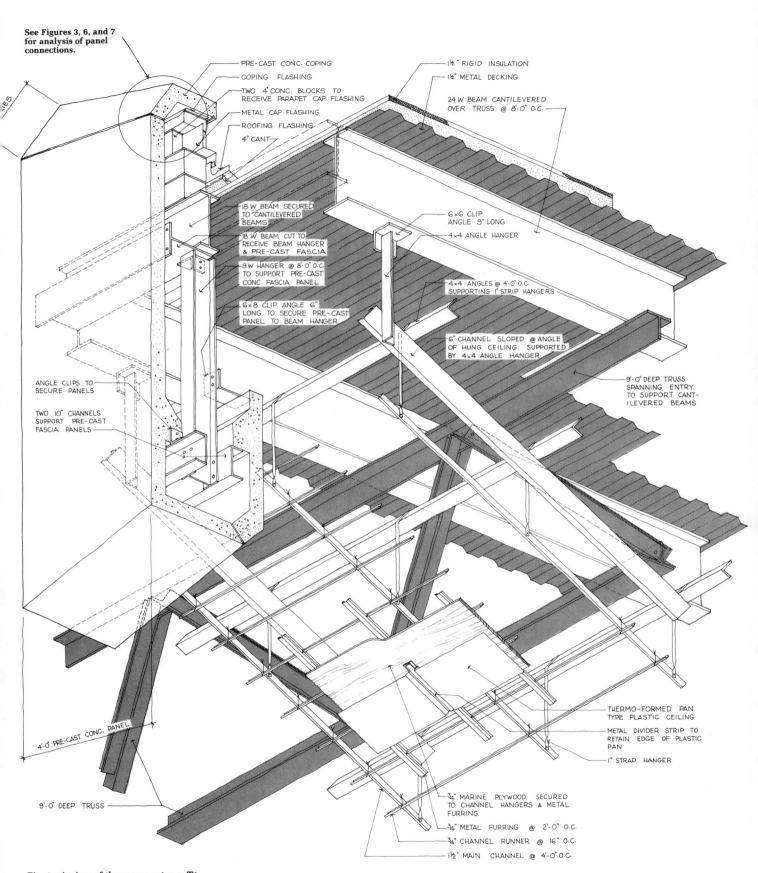

See Figures 3, 6, and 7 for analysis of panel connections.

PRE-CAST CONC. COPING
COPING FLASHING
TWO 4" CONC. BLOCKS TO RECEIVE PARAPET CAP FLASHING
METAL CAP FLASHING
ROOFING FLASHING
4" CANT

1½" RIGID INSULATION
1½" METAL DECKING
24 W BEAM CANTILEVERED OVER TRUSS @ 8'-0" O.C.

18 W BEAM SECURED TO CANTILEVERED BEAMS
18 W BEAM CUT TO RECEIVE BEAM HANGER & PRE-CAST FASCIA
9 W HANGER @ 8'-0" O.C. TO SUPPORT PRE-CAST CONC. FASCIA PANEL
6×8 CLIP ANGLE 6" LONG TO SECURE PRE-CAST PANEL TO BEAM HANGER

6×6 CLIP ANGLE 9" LONG
4×4 ANGLE HANGER
4×4 ANGLES @ 4'-0" O.C. SUPPORTING 1" STRIP HANGERS
6" CHANNEL SLOPED @ ANGLE OF HUNG CEILING SUPPORTED BY 4×4 ANGLE HANGER

9'-0" DEEP TRUSS SPANNING ENTRY TO SUPPORT CANTILEVERED BEAMS

ANGLE CLIPS TO SECURE PANELS

TWO 10" CHANNELS SUPPORT PRE-CAST FASCIA PANELS

THERMO-FORMED PAN TYPE PLASTIC CEILING
METAL DIVIDER STRIP TO RETAIN EDGE OF PLASTIC PAN
1" STRAP HANGER

4'-0" PRE-CAST CONC. PANEL

9'-0" DEEP TRUSS

¾" MARINE PLYWOOD SECURED TO CHANNEL HANGERS & METAL FURRING
¾" METAL FURRING @ 2'-0" O.C.
¾" CHANNEL RUNNER @ 16" O.C.
1½" MAIN CHANNEL @ 4'-0" O.C.

Fig. 4   A view of the upper entry soffit and parapet.

Problems related to condensation, moisture penetration, and corrosion are ever-present and had to be solved. The architects specified a simple but effective sealant system that matches the color of the concrete panels and affords long-term flexibility and adhesion. The polysulfide caulking material used in this installation is applied to all panel joints. A foam plastic backup rod is inserted into the joint before caulking. This step ensures optimum caulking depth for the joint and good adhesion for the sealant. The specifications must be written so that testing for leaks and ruptures of the caulking installation can be performed and faulty joints corrected before damage occurs.

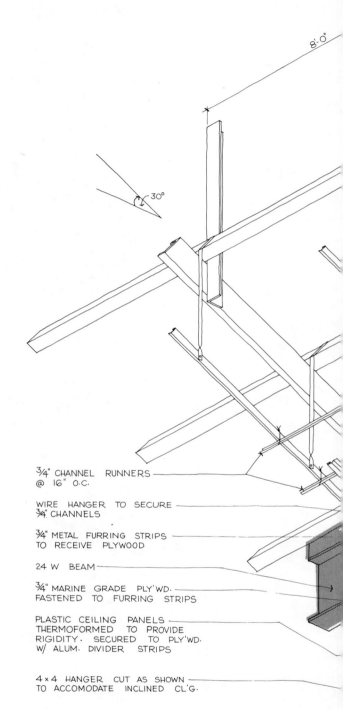

¾" CHANNEL RUNNERS @ 16" O.C.

WIRE HANGER TO SECURE ¾" CHANNELS

¾" METAL FURRING STRIPS TO RECEIVE PLYWOOD

24 W BEAM

¾" MARINE GRADE PLY'WD. FASTENED TO FURRING STRIPS

PLASTIC CEILING PANELS THERMOFORMED TO PROVIDE RIGIDITY. SECURED TO PLY'WD. W/ ALUM. DIVIDER STRIPS

4 × 4 HANGER CUT AS SHOWN TO ACCOMODATE INCLINED CL'G.

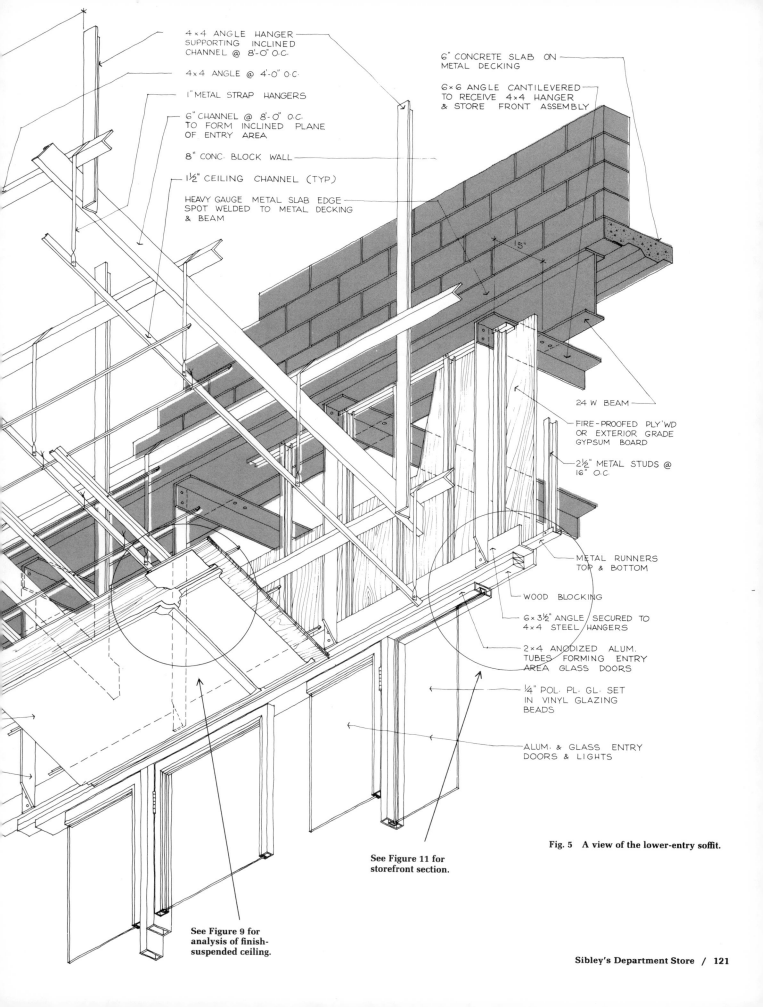

4×4 ANGLE HANGER
SUPPORTING INCLINED
CHANNEL @ 8'-0" O.C.

4×4 ANGLE @ 4'-0" O.C.

1" METAL STRAP HANGERS

6" CHANNEL @ 8'-0" O.C.
TO FORM INCLINED PLANE
OF ENTRY AREA

8" CONC. BLOCK WALL

1½" CEILING CHANNEL (TYP.)

HEAVY GAUGE METAL SLAB EDGE
SPOT WELDED TO METAL DECKING
& BEAM

6" CONCRETE SLAB ON
METAL DECKING

6×6 ANGLE CANTILEVERED
TO RECEIVE 4×4 HANGER
& STORE FRONT ASSEMBLY

15"

24 W BEAM

FIRE-PROOFED PLY'WD
OR EXTERIOR GRADE
GYPSUM BOARD

2½" METAL STUDS @
16" O.C.

METAL RUNNERS
TOP & BOTTOM

WOOD BLOCKING

6×3½" ANGLE SECURED TO
4×4 STEEL HANGERS

2×4 ANODIZED ALUM.
TUBES FORMING ENTRY
AREA GLASS DOORS

¼" POL. PL. GL. SET
IN VINYL GLAZING
BEADS

ALUM. & GLASS ENTRY
DOORS & LIGHTS

Fig. 5 A view of the lower-entry soffit.

See Figure 11 for
storefront section.

See Figure 9 for
analysis of finish-
suspended ceiling.

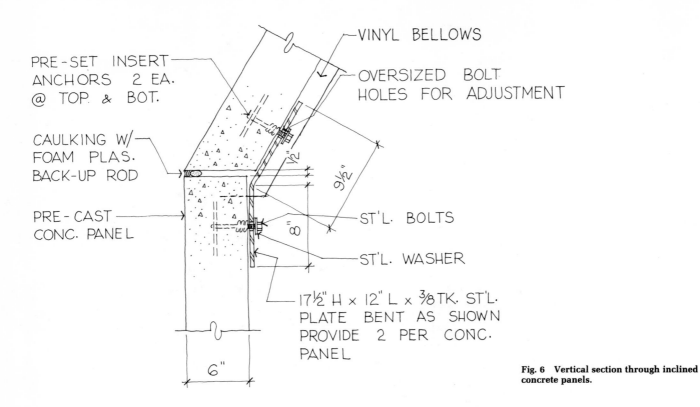

PRE-SET INSERT ANCHORS 2 EA. @ TOP. & BOT.

VINYL BELLOWS

OVERSIZED BOLT HOLES FOR ADJUSTMENT

CAULKING W/ FOAM PLAS. BACK-UP ROD

½"

9½"

PRE-CAST CONC. PANEL

8"

ST'L. BOLTS

ST'L. WASHER

17½" H × 12" L × ⅜ TK. ST'L. PLATE BENT AS SHOWN PROVIDE 2 PER CONC. PANEL

6"

Fig. 6   Vertical section through inclined concrete panels.

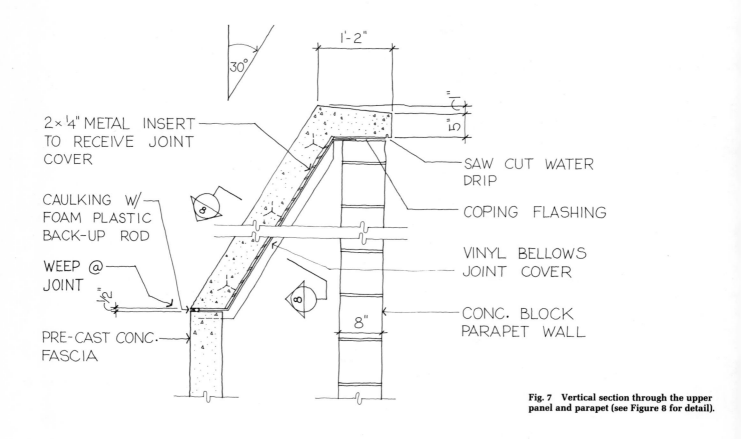

30°

1'-2"

1"

5"

2 × ¼" METAL INSERT TO RECEIVE JOINT COVER

8

SAW CUT WATER DRIP

CAULKING W/ FOAM PLASTIC BACK-UP ROD

COPING FLASHING

WEEP @ JOINT

½"

8

VINYL BELLOWS JOINT COVER

PRE-CAST CONC. FASCIA

8"

CONC. BLOCK PARAPET WALL

Fig. 7   Vertical section through the upper panel and parapet (see Figure 8 for detail).

Figure 6 indicates the connection used for horizontal joints between inclined and vertical panels. The two panels are positively secured to each other by a bent plate that is connected to anchors cast into the panel for this purpose. Vinyl bellows are installed at the inclined joint in order to waterproof this assembly. Figure 7 is a supplement to the preceding drawing and shows the upper panel of the parapet secured to the concrete block backup. A 2-by ¼-inch metal insert that receives the vinyl bellows discussed earlier is shown here. The vertical joint of the inclined plane is at best a difficult condition to deal with effectively with respect to water penetration. If the sealant fails, serious damage can be inflicted on assemblies below this point, and a standby system is required to prevent this from happening. Figure 8 is a plan section through the inclined joint and indicates the installation of the vinyl bellows that develop a channel for the conduction of moisture to weep holes at the horizontal joints. The vinyl bellows will provide the protection required if the sealant system were to fail along the inclined plane of the concrete panels. It is generally inappropriate to rely exclusively on sealants when detailing since their effectiveness depends upon the craftsmanship of the installer. Sealants may fail to perform properly, but backup systems such as stepped construction, interlocking of materials, and flashing should be considered wherever possible to minimize the damage sustained by a failed caulking application.

Figure 5 completes the view of the entry lobby as noted on Figure 3. Shown here is the termination of the sloped 6-inch channels and the suspended soffit assembly at the head of the lobby entry glass. The 24-inch beam supporting the second-floor slab and concrete block wall also secures the steel hanger and bracing angles for the entry vestibule construction. A series of 6-inch cantilevered angles are secured to 4-inch angle hangers for this purpose. The plastic pan soffit assembly shown in this drawing is enlarged for further study in Figure 9.

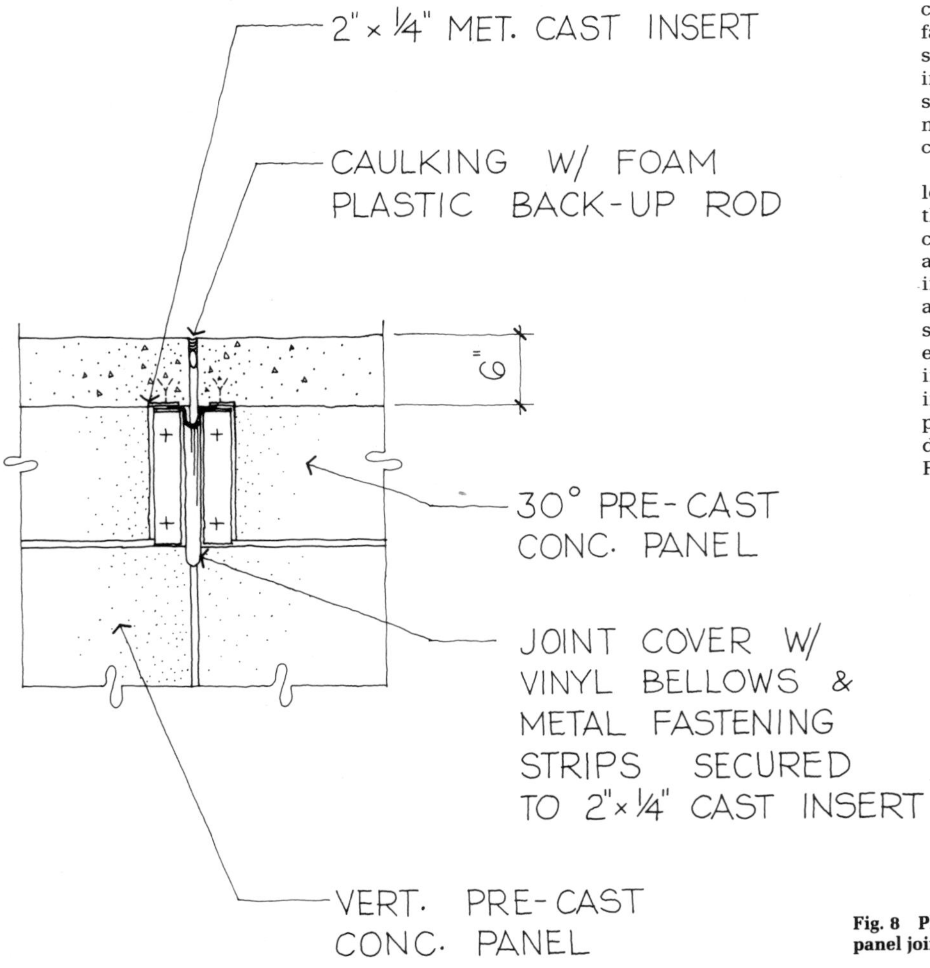

2" × ¼" MET. CAST INSERT

CAULKING W/ FOAM PLASTIC BACK-UP ROD

6"

30° PRE-CAST CONC. PANEL

JOINT COVER W/ VINYL BELLOWS & METAL FASTENING STRIPS SECURED TO 2" × ¼" CAST INSERT

VERT. PRE-CAST CONC. PANEL

Fig. 8 Plan section through the inclined panel joint.

The plastic panels that are used in this installation are formed by a vacuum-and-heat process that draws the heated plastic material into a special mold. Although the illuminated inclined plane at the entry becomes spectacular at night and may appear to be complex, the system and its details are simplicity itself. Ceiling channels support runners and furring strips at regular intervals. The furring strips receive ¾-inch fire-retarded marine-grade plywood which forms the inclined plane that receives the thermoformed plastic panels and the canopy lights. The plywood is attached to the furring with self-tapping screws. Aluminum divider strips are installed on the plywood in a modular arrangement that echoes the perimeter of each plastic pan. The lip of the plastic panel engages the four sides of the divider strip. The corner of each pan is molded to accept and be secured by the canopy light fixture. These light fixtures are individually connected to electric junction boxes set into the plywood before the installation of the plastic pans. Figure 10 illustrates the relation of the 2¼-inch aluminum divider strip, the plastic pan, and the plywood. The plastic pan has a certain degree of

flexibility that allows it to be snapped into position without breaking.

Figure 11 is a vertical section through the various elements forming the main entry lobby. Two views are presented in this drawing. The left side of the detail shows the exterior vestibule and the entry glass at the lobby, and the right side of the detail develops the section through the interior doors, the saddle, and the recessed rubber entry mat. The lobby construction is secured to the 24-inch beam located at the second floor. Figure 3 illustrates this construction in an unbroken view of the various assemblies. The interior suspended ceiling is composed of a simple gypsum board installation on furring channels which are used for screw or nail attachment. This furring is secured to channel runners supported by wire hangers. Wood blocking is shown frequently in these drawings, and this material is fireproofed in accordance with the code. However, a large variety of metal furring that is available for framing purposes can be installed instead of wood blocking and does conform to the most stringent fire codes.

Fig. 9   Entry soffit ceiling assembly

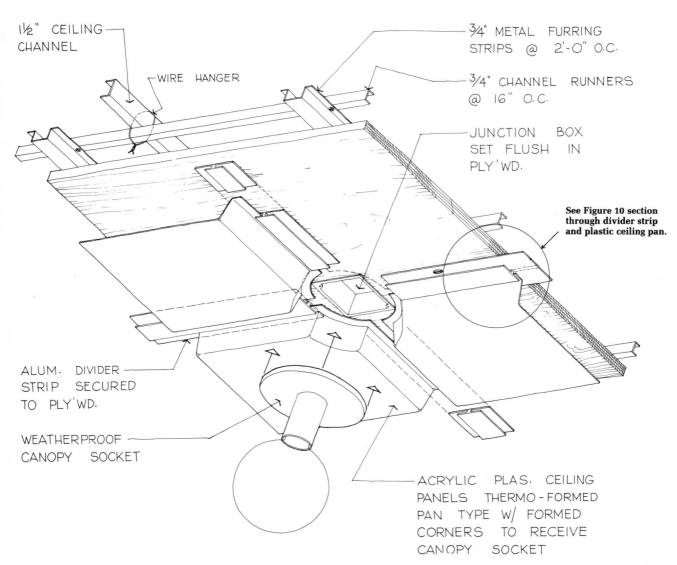

1½" CEILING CHANNEL

WIRE HANGER

¾" METAL FURRING STRIPS @ 2'-0" O.C.

¾" CHANNEL RUNNERS @ 16" O.C.

JUNCTION BOX SET FLUSH IN PLY'WD.

See Figure 10 section through divider strip and plastic ceiling pan.

ALUM. DIVIDER STRIP SECURED TO PLY'WD.

WEATHERPROOF CANOPY SOCKET

ACRYLIC PLAS. CEILING PANELS THERMO-FORMED PAN TYPE W/ FORMED CORNERS TO RECEIVE CANOPY SOCKET

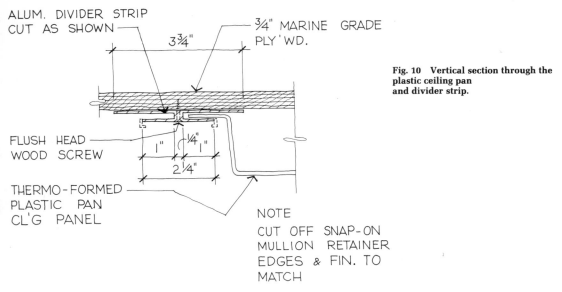

ALUM. DIVIDER STRIP
CUT AS SHOWN

3¾"

¾" MARINE GRADE
PLY'WD.

**Fig. 10 Vertical section through the
plastic ceiling pan
and divider strip.**

FLUSH HEAD
WOOD SCREW

1"   ¼"   ¼"

2¼"

THERMO-FORMED
PLASTIC PAN
CL'G PANEL

NOTE
CUT OFF SNAP-ON
MULLION RETAINER
EDGES & FIN. TO
MATCH

**Fig. 11 Vertical section through the
entry vestibule and lobby.**

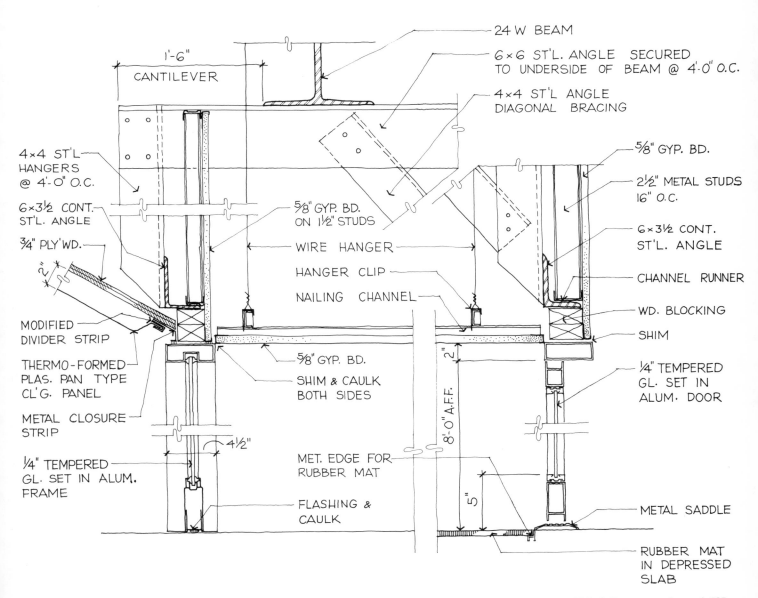

24 W BEAM

6×6 ST'L. ANGLE SECURED
TO UNDERSIDE OF BEAM @ 4'-0" O.C.

4×4 ST'L ANGLE
DIAGONAL BRACING

1'-6"
CANTILEVER

⅝" GYP. BD.

4×4 ST'L
HANGERS
@ 4'-0" O.C.

2½" METAL STUDS
16" O.C.

6×3½ CONT.
ST'L. ANGLE

6×3½ CONT.
ST'L. ANGLE

⅝" GYP. BD.
ON 1½" STUDS

¾" PLY'WD.

2"

CHANNEL RUNNER

WIRE HANGER

MODIFIED
DIVIDER STRIP

HANGER CLIP

WD. BLOCKING

NAILING CHANNEL

SHIM

THERMO-FORMED
PLAS. PAN TYPE
CL'G. PANEL

⅝" GYP. BD.

2"

¼" TEMPERED
GL. SET IN
ALUM. DOOR

METAL CLOSURE
STRIP

SHIM & CAULK
BOTH SIDES

8'-0" A.F.F.

4½"

¼" TEMPERED
GL. SET IN ALUM.
FRAME

MET. EDGE FOR
RUBBER MAT

5"

FLASHING &
CAULK

METAL SADDLE

RUBBER MAT
IN DEPRESSED
SLAB

8 Radio Corporation of America (RCA) Factory

Circleville, Ohio   ARCHITECTS: Haines Lundberg Waehler

Fig. 1   The office wing and one of the industrial units. *(Gil Amiaga.)*

Located in Circleville, Ohio, this extensive facility built for RCA encompasses a full range of industrial uses, including fabrication and assembly, material receiving and shipping, research, storage, and administration. The plant is more than 900 feet long and 350 feet wide and is sited on several acres of level plain. The complex is composed of one- and two-story structures as well as a manufacturing building that is 90 feet tall. Color is used sparingly in order to unify this complex of buildings, and the architects have chosen three basic types of metal siding to be used throughout.

Haines Lundberg Waehler is the architectural firm that developed this project, and no doubt the firm's extensive in-house engineering services were a critical factor in providing the comprehensive planning required by the owner. The architects were able to create a campuslike feeling that relieves the industrial bulk normally associated with this type of structure.

The selection of materials was a crucial factor in organizing the textural quality of the building facades. Deeply indented corrugated panels establish a background from which smooth projected planes of flush siding are juxtaposed. White, blue, and earth colors are used for continuity throughout the project. The offices are sheathed in a combination of glass and the most finely textured paneling to be found in the complex. The variety of texture, color, and form selected by the architects dignify the rather modest materials that are used. There is a unity evident in this project, in fact, a kind of legitimation of materials that have for the better part of the century been associated with rusty sheds and jerry-built structures—in short, one of the most aesthetically unpleasing building materials an industrial system can provide.

There are quite a number of late-nineteenth-century industrial buildings that were poorly designed with respect to space utilization, natural illumination, and ventilation, buildings that dehumanized the observer and the occupant alike. These buildings did not have the architectural integrity of the early New England mills with their austere brick facades sited against streams and rivers. In contrast, the seemingly endless progression of drab factories, warehouses, and sheds that exists today convinces the observer that corrugated metal siding is a material to be used only for the most marginal industrial applications.

Ironically, the aesthetic drawbacks of the material did nothing to diminish its use. The very demand for metal siding induced more manufacturers to enter the field, and competition combined with technological advances saw the development of a superior material. Metal siding and roofing have been a part of the American scene since the latter part of the nineteenth century. Sheds, factories, and other utilitarian structures, unseen or unlooked at, have been the beneficiaries of this highly economical material application. The fact that most of these buildings had little to recommend them with respect to design created for the material an almost permanent niche as one of the cheapest and most unlovely materials in use in the United States. By the end of World War II, metal siding was extensively in use on Quonset huts, factories, farm buildings, and a few very undesirable shantytowns in and around the world's industrial centers.

Some of our earliest colonial structures were roofed in terneplate, sheet iron that had been given a coating of 25 percent tin and 75 percent lead. In order to acquire a possible thirty- to fifty-year life span, this material had to be finished with leaded paint. Terneplate should not be confused with "tin roofing," which is actually galvanized steel sheeting and a product of the modern steel rolling process. The burgeoning auto industry in the 1920s and 1930s called for very large amounts of sheet steel for auto body parts such as fenders, hoods, and door panels. The technology that produced auto bodies also produced corrugated and stamped steel sheets, which were used with maximum economy for industrial construction. The demand for this type of material grew, and with it pressure for product refinement which would allow a greater degree of design flexibility. Henry Ford once quipped that you could get a Model T in any color as long as it was black. When technological developments made it economical to apply baked enamel to metal sheeting in a wide spectrum of colors, the use of the material broadened considerably. The advent and expansion of suburban areas and the development of decentralized industry brought living communities into close proximity to production areas. The somber hues of lead, tin, and galvanized metal were replaced with color, very often garish, but opening the door to new concepts in the aesthetics of industrial building.

The large-scale development of the aluminum industry after World War II introduced a material that could compete with steel as building siding. The development of new insulating materials and refinements in assembly techniques made metal siding a more effective and satisfying building material to work with.

It is possible today to purchase siding in virtually any color and in a variety of finishes such as baked enamel, fluorocarbon enamels, and variations of zinc and aluminum coatings. Metal siding comes in a variety of configurations that allows a designer to create smooth or strongly textured facades and an infinite variety of elevation treatments. The refinement of fastening devices has kept pace with the building industry. Self-tapping screws with built-in weather-protected neoprene gaskets and washers allow a remarkable ease of fabrication. Such a device can drill a hole, thread it, and make a watertight connection in one attachment step. Angled walls, suspended soffits, mansards, and sculptural shapes are now possible. Facelifts for existing building facades have become very simple to accomplish with lightweight metal siding. Tertiary structural elements such as lightweight angles and channels that secure siding to a structure can be secured to an existing building as easily as to a new one. It is somewhat poignant to see a fine old masonry building covered with a material once used only for chicken coops and sheds.

In Figure 1 a view of the RCA Factory's office wing can be seen in relation to one of the industrial units forming the complex. A strong contrast exists between the office wing, constructed on pilotis, and the massive factory part of the complex with its large planes of white metal siding, which serve as a billboard for the company logo. The vertical metal siding used on the factory buildings gives this campuslike complex a sense of scale and of relief from the demanding horizontal quality of the buildings. Figure 2 illustrates how the various materials relate to each other and demonstrates their respective uses. Siding type A, a corrugated and deeply folded material used on the facades of the industrial units, expresses the building parapets. The portion of the wall that is cantilevered outward is covered with siding type B, a 12-inch-wide tongue-and-groove component that creates a pleasant surface relieved by a thin vertical channel groove at every element. Operable vents in the intermediate soffits found throughout much of this project provide a necessary environmental function and an aesthetic theme. The office wing of this factory is appropriately detailed with flush, narrow vertical siding on its facade, soffits, and column covers.

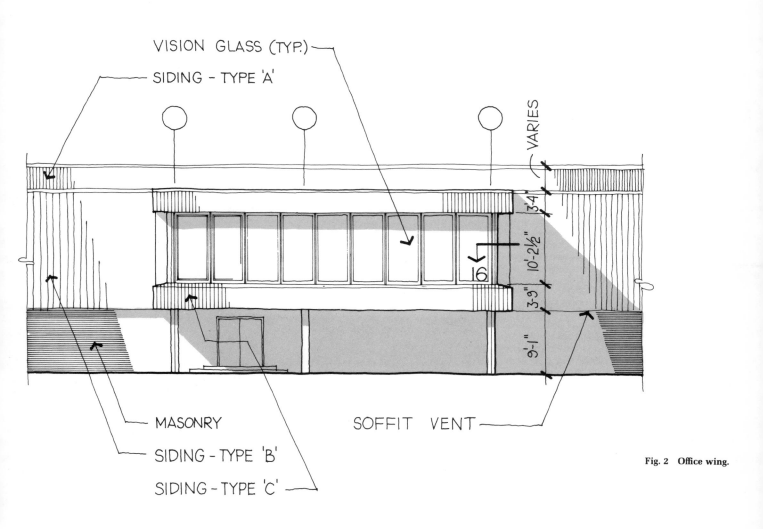

VISION GLASS (TYP.)

SIDING - TYPE 'A'

VARIES

3'-4"

10'-2½"

16

3'-9"

9'-1"

MASONRY

SIDING - TYPE 'B'

SIDING - TYPE 'C'

SOFFIT VENT

Fig. 2 Office wing.

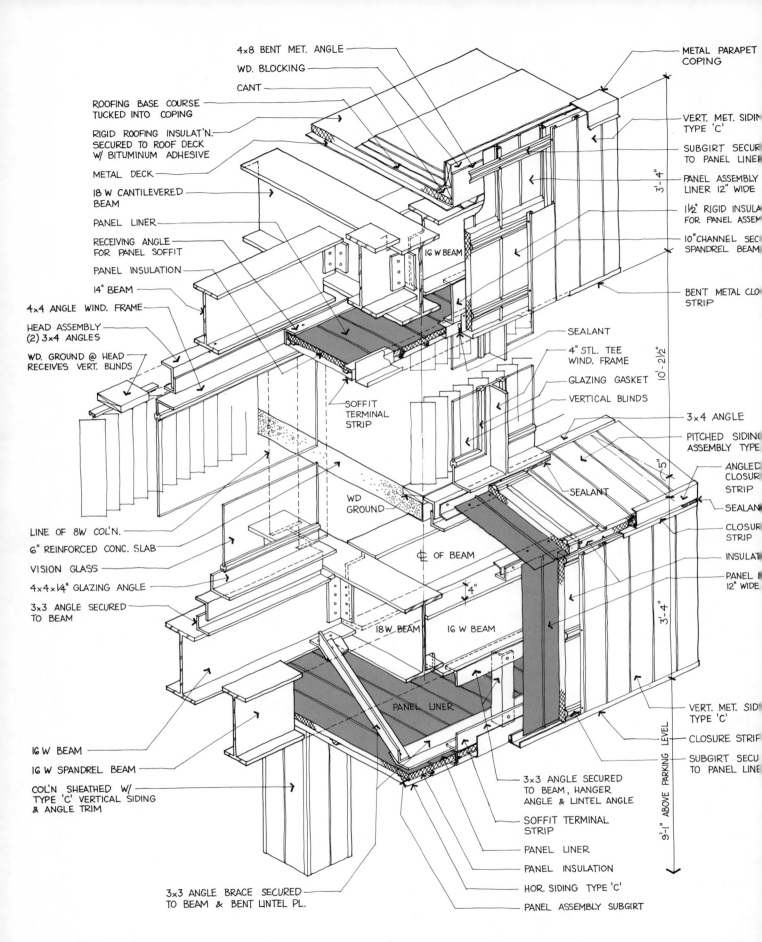

4×8 BENT MET. ANGLE

WD. BLOCKING

CANT

ROOFING BASE COURSE TUCKED INTO COPING

RIGID ROOFING INSULAT'N. SECURED TO ROOF DECK W/ BITUMINUM ADHESIVE

METAL DECK

18 W CANTILEVERED BEAM

PANEL LINER

RECEIVING ANGLE FOR PANEL SOFFIT

PANEL INSULATION

14" BEAM

4×4 ANGLE WIND. FRAME

HEAD ASSEMBLY (2) 3×4 ANGLES

WD. GROUND @ HEAD RECEIVES VERT. BLINDS

LINE OF 8W COL'N.

6" REINFORCED CONC. SLAB

VISION GLASS

4×4×¼" GLAZING ANGLE

3×3 ANGLE SECURED TO BEAM

16 W BEAM

16 W SPANDREL BEAM

COL'N SHEATHED W/ TYPE 'C' VERTICAL SIDING & ANGLE TRIM

3×3 ANGLE BRACE SECURED TO BEAM & BENT LINTEL PL.

METAL PARAPET COPING

VERT. MET. SIDIN TYPE 'C'

SUBGIRT SECUR TO PANEL LINE

PANEL ASSEMBLY LINER 12" WIDE

1½" RIGID INSULA FOR PANEL ASSEM

10"CHANNEL SEC SPANDREL BEAM

BENT METAL CLO STRIP

SEALANT

4" STL. TEE WIND. FRAME

GLAZING GASKET

VERTICAL BLINDS

3×4 ANGLE

PITCHED SIDIN ASSEMBLY TYPE

ANGLED CLOSUR STRIP

SEALAN

CLOSUR STRIP

INSULAT

PANEL 12" WIDE

VERT. MET. SID TYPE 'C'

CLOSURE STRIF

SUBGIRT SECU TO PANEL LINE

SOFFIT TERMINAL STRIP

WD GROUND

Ç OF BEAM

16 W BEAM

18 W BEAM

4"

PANEL LINER

3×3 ANGLE SECURED TO BEAM, HANGER ANGLE & LINTEL ANGLE

SOFFIT TERMINAL STRIP

PANEL LINER

PANEL INSULATION

HOR. SIDING TYPE 'C'

PANEL ASSEMBLY SUBGIRT

3'-4"

10'- 2½"

5"

3'-4"

9'-1" ABOVE PARKING LEVEL

Fig. 3 A view of the office wing, structure, and cladding system.

Figure 3 is an isometric view of part of the office wing, illustrating the connection of metal siding and glass to the structural steel frame. A detailed examination of this drawing indicates that the building is far from simple and that the recessed glass called for some well-thought-out details. The head of the vision glass is secured to two 3- by 4-inch angles and attached to the 18-inch beam. This connection also provides the support for the metal paneling used as a soffit. A watertight transition between vertical and horizontal surfaces is accomplished by closure strips and sealant. Figure 4 is a vertical section through this assembly and further explains the relation

of the various components. The vertical glass panels are set approximately 2 feet back from the face of the building and are protected from the sun by the resultant overhang. The soffit material forming the overhang and the sill is siding type C. The coordination of this siding requires alignment on horizontal, vertical, and angled surfaces. The head detail receives wood blocking that secures the vertical blinds. A gypsum board soffit and fascia, formed by metal stud hangers suspended from the deck, are shown. These in turn pick up horizontal metal joists that support either a soffit or a ceiling.

This project incorporates several different

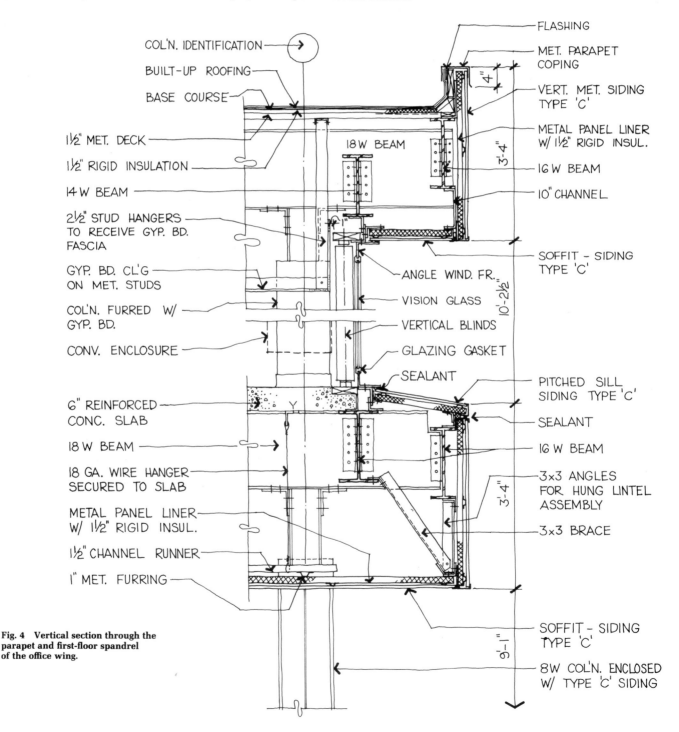

Fig. 4 Vertical section through the parapet and first-floor spandrel of the office wing.

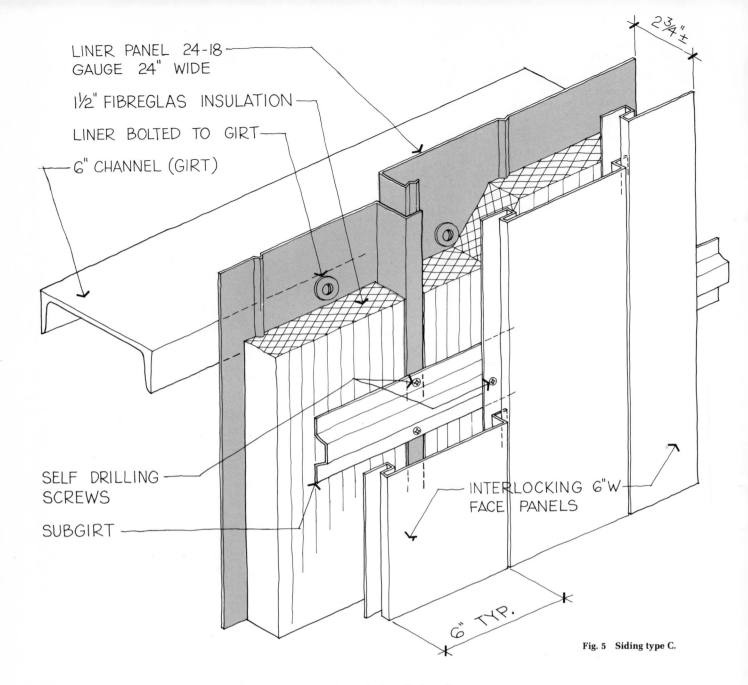

LINER PANEL 24-18 GAUGE 24" WIDE

1½" FIBREGLAS INSULATION

LINER BOLTED TO GIRT

6" CHANNEL (GIRT)

SELF DRILLING SCREWS

SUBGIRT

INTERLOCKING 6"W FACE PANELS

6" TYP.

2¾" ±

Fig. 5   Siding type C.

types of siding that should be examined carefully, since distinct differences exist between them. Metal siding systems generally require a combination of several connecting elements in order to be assembled. Siding types A and C are vertical panels composed of an exterior metal skin and an interior metal liner made of sheet steel or aluminum. The liner is approximately 24 inches wide with folded edges that form a shallow pan at least 1½ inches deep. Fiberglass insulation fills this inner cavity, and subgirts, or furring, are installed horizontally across the liner assembly in order to hold the insulation in place and receive the finish siding. Figure 5

illustrates the typical method used to secure siding to the intermediate structural element; in this case a 6-inch horizontal channel is used as a girt that receives the metal panel liner. Vertical spans up to 30 feet are possible depending on the gauge and configuration of the panel liner. The metal liner, which actually carries the exterior wall "skin," is attached to girts, or channels, that are secured to the main structure.

The office wing pilotis are 3 feet on center from the face of the building, as shown in Figures 4 and 6. This structural placement permits the horizontal plane of glass to be set back, forming an unbroken line of glazing. The structure is cantilevered past the column in order to pick up the projected parapet and sill. The conventionally reinforced 6-inch-thick concrete slab supports the hangers that carry the metal soffit. Note the brace that ties the hung lintel assembly back to the structure. The simple angles that receive the glazing must be cut in order to develop a firm connection with the H-shaped gaskets.

Although the horizontal band of vision glass wraps around most of the office unit, it is relieved by flush metal sections at the intersection of the office wing and the industrial units and at the building corner.

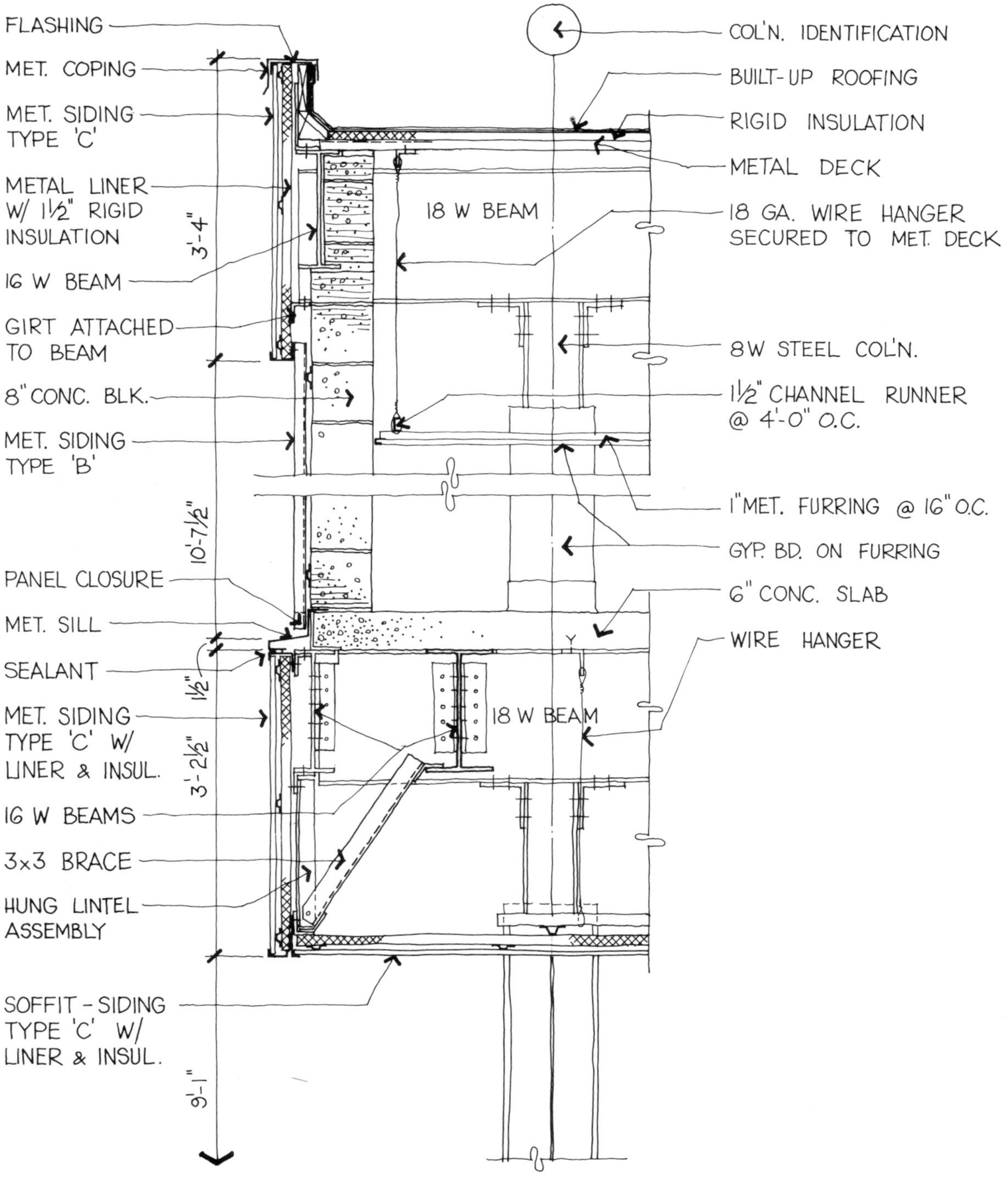

FLASHING
MET. COPING
MET. SIDING TYPE 'C'
METAL LINER W/ 1½" RIGID INSULATION
16 W BEAM
GIRT ATTACHED TO BEAM
8" CONC. BLK.
MET. SIDING TYPE 'B'
PANEL CLOSURE
MET. SILL
SEALANT
MET. SIDING TYPE 'C' W/ LINER & INSUL.
16 W BEAMS
3x3 BRACE
HUNG LINTEL ASSEMBLY
SOFFIT - SIDING TYPE 'C' W/ LINER & INSUL.
3'-4"
10'-7½"
1½"
3'-2½"
9'-1"
C
COL'N. IDENTIFICATION
BUILT-UP ROOFING
RIGID INSULATION
METAL DECK
18 W BEAM
18 GA. WIRE HANGER SECURED TO MET. DECK
8W STEEL COL'N.
1½" CHANNEL RUNNER @ 4'-0" O.C.
1" MET. FURRING @ 16" O.C.
GYP. BD. ON FURRING
6" CONC. SLAB
WIRE HANGER
18 W BEAM

This condition can be studied in the isometric view shown in Figure 7. The parapet and the vertical surface below the roof spandrel are similar to those shown in Figure 3. Siding type B is shown set back slightly, forming an opaque wall backed with concrete block at this point. Figure 6 is a vertical section through this assembly that illustrates the relation of material and structure. The 8-inch-thick concrete block wall shown here receives the siding girts. These girts or furring strips are just anchored to the wall. If this project were being built today, I have no doubt that additional insulation would be installed between the liner and the wall. This detail shows a variation of hung ceiling construction that is in common use throughout the United States. An 18-gauge wire hanger supports a 1½-inch channel runner located on 4-foot centers. To these are secured 1-inch furring strips at 16 inches on center designed to receive the gypsum board ceiling. Local building codes should be consulted to verify the legality of certain types of construction; for instance, wire hangers are not legal in New York City. The selection of a detail always requires a measure of caution with respect to local codes and safety.

Figure 2 shows the office wing set against the backdrop of the factory. In elevation and photograph, the industrial units of this factory appear to be relatively simple, especially in comparison with the more intricate design of the office unit. Upon further analysis it becomes apparent that the reason for the visual success of this building complex is the artful combination of building massing and materials. This has resulted in an expression of industrial construction in which an extremely cost-effective and potentially handsome material has been used effectively to create a satisfying design. In Chapter 5 we observe how extruded aluminum siding strips, a derivation of traditional storefront construction, are used to form spandrel and column covers for a high-rise urban office building. The RCA Factory illustrates how corrugated metal siding in its various configurations has been used to enclose an entire building complex.

An examination of the factory construction reveals some interesting points about design and simplicity. The

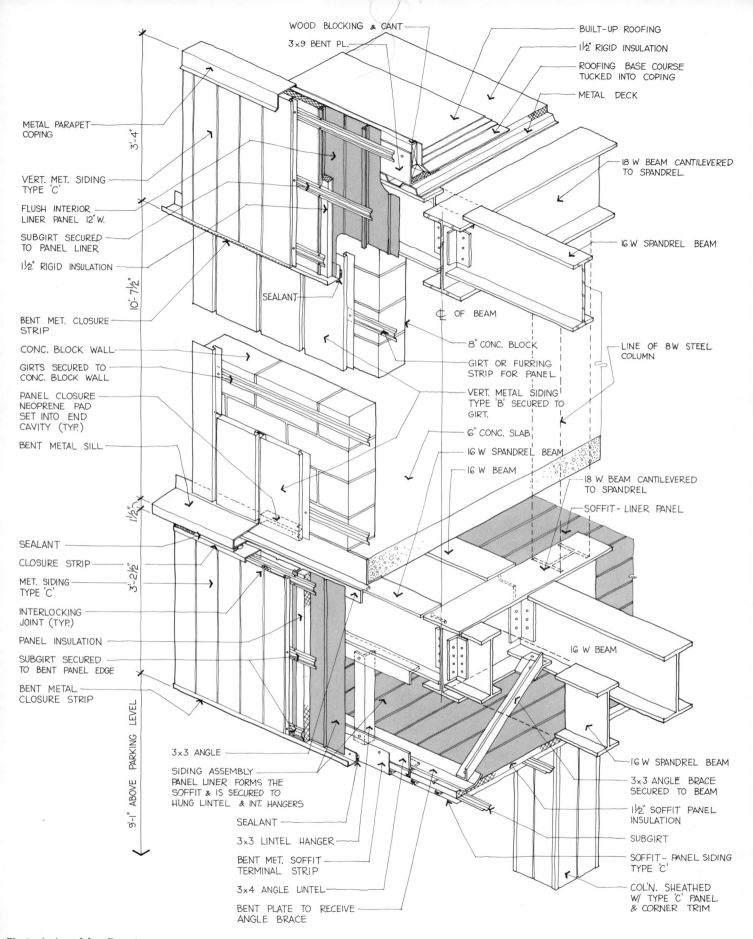

WOOD BLOCKING & CANT

3×9 BENT PL.

BUILT-UP ROOFING

1½" RIGID INSULATION

ROOFING BASE COURSE TUCKED INTO COPING

METAL DECK

METAL PARAPET COPING

3'-4"

VERT. MET. SIDING TYPE 'C'

FLUSH INTERIOR LINER PANEL 12" W.

SUBGIRT SECURED TO PANEL LINER

1½" RIGID INSULATION

10'-7½"

SEALANT

18 W BEAM CANTILEVERED TO SPANDREL

16 W SPANDREL BEAM

℄ OF BEAM

BENT MET. CLOSURE STRIP

CONC. BLOCK WALL

GIRTS SECURED TO CONC. BLOCK WALL

PANEL CLOSURE NEOPRENE PAD SET INTO END CAVITY (TYP.)

BENT METAL SILL

8" CONC. BLOCK

GIRT OR FURRING STRIP FOR PANEL

VERT. METAL SIDING TYPE 'B' SECURED TO GIRT.

LINE OF 8W STEEL COLUMN

6" CONC. SLAB

16 W SPANDREL BEAM

16 W BEAM

18 W BEAM CANTILEVERED TO SPANDREL

SOFFIT - LINER PANEL

1½"

SEALANT

CLOSURE STRIP

MET. SIDING TYPE 'C'

3'-2½"

INTERLOCKING JOINT (TYP.)

PANEL INSULATION

SUBGIRT SECURED TO BENT PANEL EDGE

BENT METAL CLOSURE STRIP

16 W BEAM

9'-1" ABOVE PARKING LEVEL

16 W SPANDREL BEAM

3×3 ANGLE BRACE SECURED TO BEAM

1½" SOFFIT PANEL INSULATION

SUBGIRT

SOFFIT - PANEL SIDING TYPE 'C'

COL'N. SHEATHED W/ TYPE 'C' PANEL & CORNER TRIM

3×3 ANGLE

SIDING ASSEMBLY PANEL LINER FORMS THE SOFFIT & IS SECURED TO HUNG LINTEL & INT. HANGERS

SEALANT

3×3 LINTEL HANGER

BENT MET. SOFFIT TERMINAL STRIP

3×4 ANGLE LINTEL

BENT PLATE TO RECEIVE ANGLE BRACE

Fig. 7 A view of the office wing and cladding.

Fig. 8 Roof and parapet assembly of a typical factory unit.

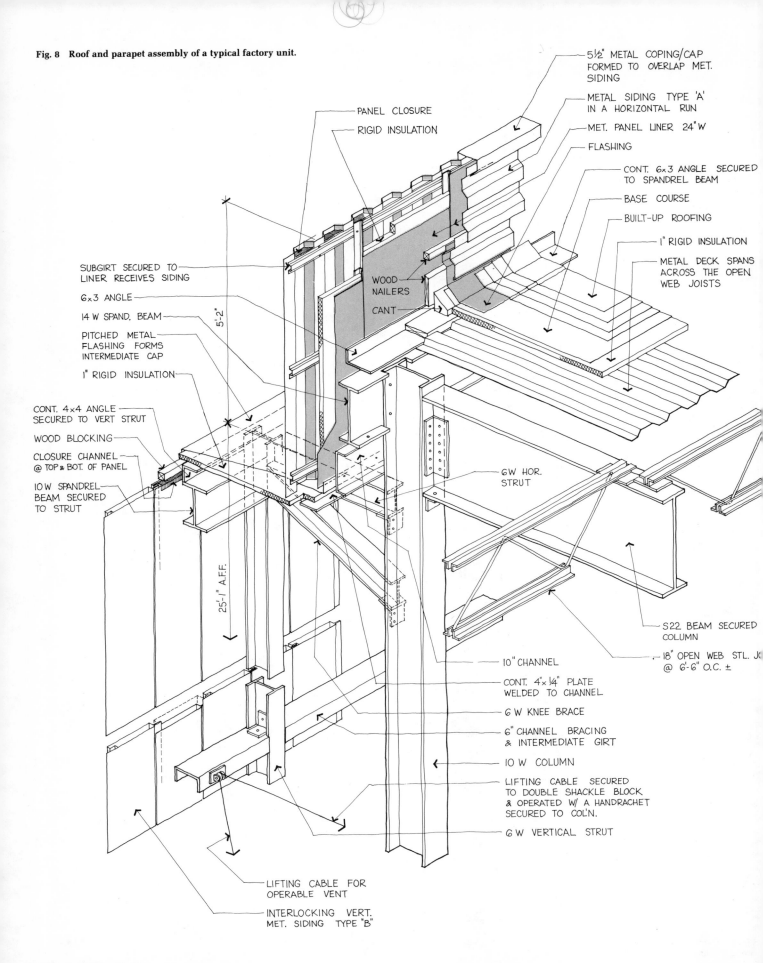

5½" METAL COPING/CAP
FORMED TO OVERLAP MET.
SIDING

METAL SIDING TYPE 'A'
IN A HORIZONTAL RUN

MET. PANEL LINER 24"W

FLASHING

CONT. 6x3 ANGLE SECURED
TO SPANDREL BEAM

BASE COURSE

BUILT-UP ROOFING

1" RIGID INSULATION

METAL DECK SPANS
ACROSS THE OPEN
WEB JOISTS

PANEL CLOSURE

RIGID INSULATION

WOOD
NAILERS

CANT

SUBGIRT SECURED TO
LINER RECEIVES SIDING

6x3 ANGLE

14 W SPAND. BEAM

PITCHED METAL
FLASHING FORMS
INTERMEDIATE CAP

1" RIGID INSULATION

5'-2"

CONT. 4x4 ANGLE
SECURED TO VERT STRUT

WOOD BLOCKING

CLOSURE CHANNEL
@ TOP & BOT. OF PANEL

10 W SPANDREL
BEAM SECURED
TO STRUT

25'-1" A.F.F.

6 W HOR.
STRUT

S22 BEAM SECURED
COLUMN

18" OPEN WEB STL. J(
@ 6'-6" O.C. ±

10" CHANNEL

CONT. 4"x ¼" PLATE
WELDED TO CHANNEL

6 W KNEE BRACE

6" CHANNEL BRACING
& INTERMEDIATE GIRT

10 W COLUMN

LIFTING CABLE SECURED
TO DOUBLE SHACKLE BLOCK
& OPERATED W/ A HANDRACHET
SECURED TO COL'N.

6 W VERTICAL STRUT

LIFTING CABLE FOR
OPERABLE VENT

INTERLOCKING VERT.
MET. SIDING TYPE "B"

upper portion of one unit is studied in Figure 8. This 30-foot-high structure is formed with steel beams, steel columns, and open web steel joists. The environmental specifications of this building require operable vents set approximately 8 feet above the floor slab. The architects have resolved this functional requirement by developing a secondary structure that projects approximately 2 feet past the main framing members. This structure is composed of angles and channels that are actually the girts that support and receive the siding components.

The basic cladding element described here, siding type B, is actually a composite of similar sidings on the market today. These single vertical panels interlock structurally and are composed of an inner and an outer metal skin with a core of rigid insulation. The panels are available in a variety of lengths, and there is usually a protected thermal break in the metal that minimizes heat loss and gain. The interlocking panels create a condition in which air infiltration is eliminated.

The parapet assembly is detailed simply and uses the type A siding vertically on the outside of the parapet and horizontally on the inside of the coping line. Figure 9 is a vertical section through the coping and indicates the relation of the parapet, flashing, and roofing system. The metal liner used throughout this complex as a backup for siding types A and B actually forms the vertical parapet structure and receives the facing material for the inner part of this assembly. Note the way in which the parapet flashing above the cant is bent into position to receive the horizontal siding.

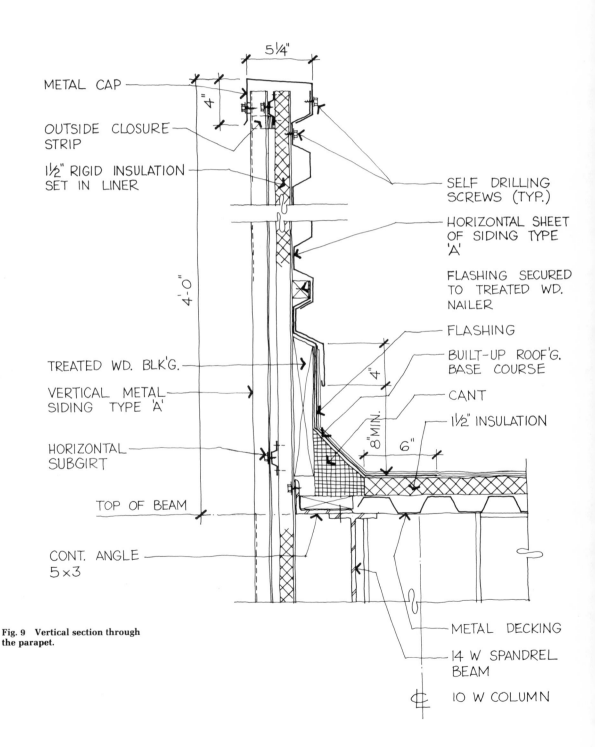

Fig. 9 Vertical section through the parapet.

Figure 10 illustrates the transition between the parapet and the main wall assembly. The secondary and tertiary structural elements are shown here. It is apparent that a number of accessory construction members are required to make this construction practicable. The closure strip, located at the vertical ends of the siding panels, is designed to seal the panels against air and moisture penetration. All the panel configurations used in this complex require the synthetic rubber closure strips provided by the manufacturer. Connecting devices are important since the speed of erection depends on the ease with which these elements can be attached to the structural frame.

Drywall construction and its reliance on metal studs have been instrumental in the development of a number of connecting devices that perform three major operations in one step, namely, drilling a hole, tapping a thread, and securing a weatherproof connection. The manufacturers of siding systems can be counted upon to provide a complete line of accessories designed to facilitate the use of their products.

The lower portion of the factory building corresponding to Figure 8 can be found in Figure 11. This illustration indicates the relation of the operable vent to the exterior wall system and the development of the secondary structural system. The 10-inch steel column supporting the main frame of the structure also braces the lower masonry

Fig. 10 Vertical section through the intermediate siding.

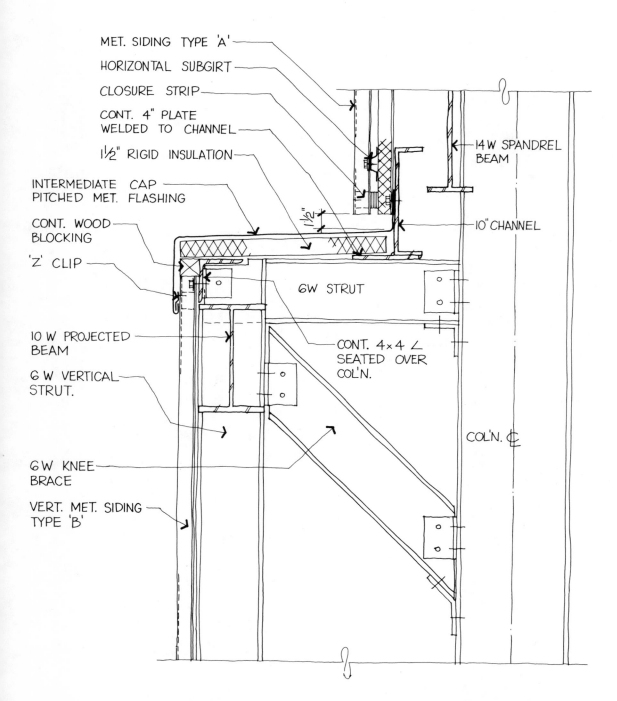

MET. SIDING TYPE 'A'

HORIZONTAL SUBGIRT

CLOSURE STRIP

CONT. 4" PLATE WELDED TO CHANNEL

1½" RIGID INSULATION

INTERMEDIATE CAP PITCHED MET. FLASHING

CONT. WOOD BLOCKING

'Z' CLIP

10 W PROJECTED BEAM

6 W VERTICAL STRUT.

6 W KNEE BRACE

VERT. MET. SIDING TYPE 'B'

14 W SPANDREL BEAM

10" CHANNEL

6 W STRUT

CONT. 4×4 ∠ SEATED OVER COL'N.

COL'N. ℄

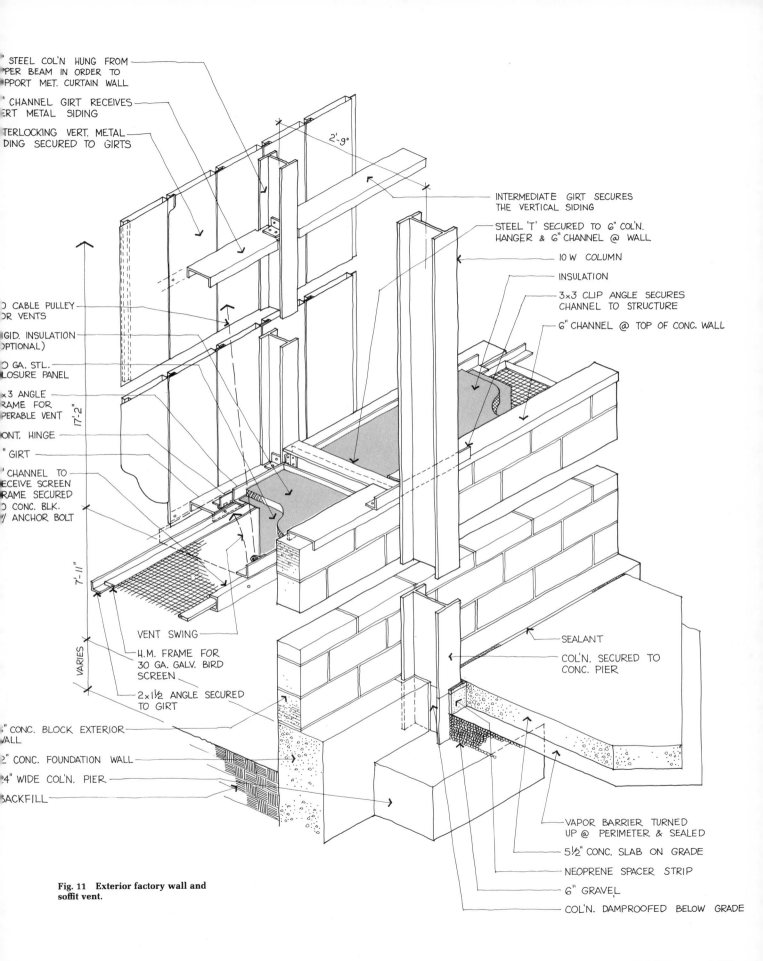

**STEEL COL'N HUNG FROM
PPER BEAM IN ORDER TO
PPORT MET. CURTAIN WALL**

**CHANNEL GIRT RECEIVES
ERT METAL SIDING**

**TERLOCKING VERT. METAL
DING SECURED TO GIRTS**

**CABLE PULLEY
OR VENTS**

**IGID. INSULATION
OPTIONAL)**

**GA. STL.
LOSURE PANEL**

**3 ANGLE
RAME FOR
PERABLE VENT**

ONT. HINGE

GIRT

**CHANNEL TO
ECEIVE SCREEN
RAME SECURED
O CONC. BLK.
/ ANCHOR BOLT**

17'-2"

7'-11"

VARIES

VENT SWING

**H.M. FRAME FOR
30 GA. GALV. BIRD
SCREEN**

**2×1½ ANGLE SECURED
TO GIRT**

**" CONC. BLOCK EXTERIOR
WALL**

2" CONC. FOUNDATION WALL

4" WIDE COL'N. PIER

BACKFILL

2'-9"

**INTERMEDIATE GIRT SECURES
THE VERTICAL SIDING**

**STEEL 'T' SECURED TO 6" COL'N.
HANGER & 6" CHANNEL @ WALL**

10 W COLUMN

INSULATION

**3×3 CLIP ANGLE SECURES
CHANNEL TO STRUCTURE**

6" CHANNEL @ TOP OF CONC. WALL

SEALANT

**COL'N. SECURED TO
CONC. PIER**

**VAPOR BARRIER TURNED
UP @ PERIMETER & SEALED**

5½" CONC. SLAB ON GRADE

NEOPRENE SPACER STRIP

6" GRAVEL

COL'N. DAMPROOFED BELOW GRADE

**Fig. 11   Exterior factory wall and
soffit vent.**

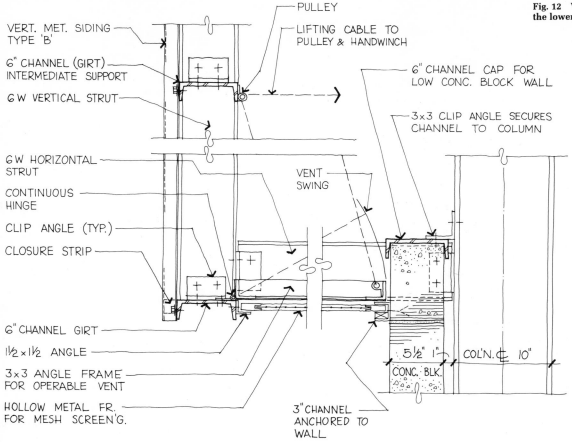

VERT. MET. SIDING TYPE 'B'

6" CHANNEL (GIRT) INTERMEDIATE SUPPORT

6 W VERTICAL STRUT

6 W HORIZONTAL STRUT

CONTINUOUS HINGE

CLIP ANGLE (TYP.)

CLOSURE STRIP

6" CHANNEL GIRT

1½ x 1½ ANGLE

3 x 3 ANGLE FRAME FOR OPERABLE VENT

HOLLOW METAL FR. FOR MESH SCREEN'G.

PULLEY

LIFTING CABLE TO PULLEY & HANDWINCH

6" CHANNEL CAP FOR LOW CONC. BLOCK WALL

3 x 3 CLIP ANGLE SECURES CHANNEL TO COLUMN

VENT SWING

5½" I", COL'N. ℄ 10"

CONC. BLK.

3" CHANNEL ANCHORED TO WALL

Fig. 12 Vertical section through the lower wall.

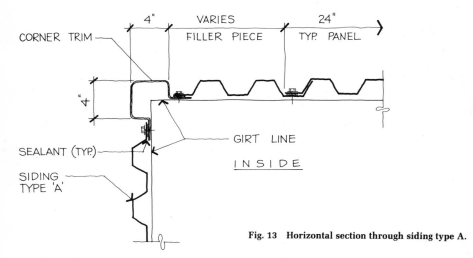

CORNER TRIM

4"   VARIES   24"
       FILLER PIECE   TYP. PANEL

4"

SEALANT (TYP.)

SIDING TYPE 'A'

GIRT LINE

I N S I D E

Fig. 13 Horizontal section through siding type A.

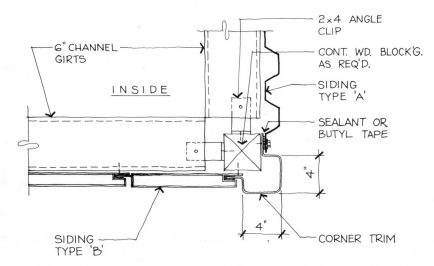

6" CHANNEL GIRTS

I N S I D E

2 x 4 ANGLE CLIP

CONT. WD. BLOCK'G. AS REQ'D.

SIDING TYPE 'A'

SEALANT OR BUTYL TAPE

4"

SIDING TYPE 'B'

4"

CORNER TRIM

Fig. 14 Horizontal section through siding types A and B.

wall. Figure 12 is a vertical section through the operable vent and the exterior wall. Here the bottom of a type B panel is secured to a girt, or 6-inch channel, and a closure strip is provided at the bottom of the siding. A fixed screen designed to keep out birds and small animals is located below the vent. The vent itself is operated through a system of pulleys, cables, and a hand winch mounted on the main column.

Figures 13, 14, and 15 illustrate how the various siding materials are used on corners, on points of transition, and in combination. Figure 13, a horizontal section through siding type A, describes a typical exterior corner at the parapet and shows the relation of the corner trim to the siding. This type of corrugated siding overlaps the connection for weather protection and is then sealed by butyl tape and a fastener secured through the panel to the girt. The corner trim can either be provided by the manufacturer or fabricated on the job. The continuity of color in this instance would demand the former. Figure 14 shows the intersection of types A and B siding at an outside corner. Wood blocking is used in this example to secure the panels and the corner trim. Figure 15 illustrates a type B corner detail. Note the special trim attached to the wood blocking by a Z clip that receives the siding.

An interesting transition of materials occurs at the corner column of the office wing. Figure 16 shows the relation of the column to the wraparound glazing and the column cover. Unlike the other columns of this wing, which are set back behind the

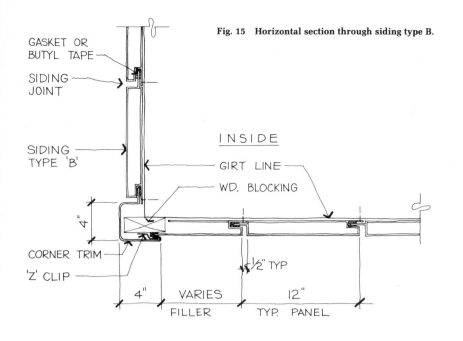

Fig. 15   Horizontal section through siding type B.

GASKET OR
BUTYL TAPE

SIDING
JOINT

SIDING
TYPE 'B'

INSIDE

GIRT LINE

WD. BLOCKING

4"

CORNER TRIM

'Z' CLIP

4"   VARIES   12"
       FILLER   TYP. PANEL

½" TYP

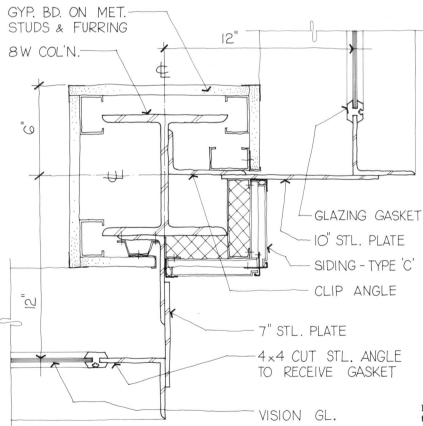

GYP. BD. ON MET.
STUDS & FURRING

8W COL'N.

12"

6"

12"

GLAZING GASKET

10" STL. PLATE

SIDING - TYPE 'C'

CLIP ANGLE

7" STL. PLATE

4×4 CUT STL. ANGLE
TO RECEIVE GASKET

VISION GL.

glass, this column has a quadrant which is exposed to the exterior and which must be faced with siding. The cut steel angles that receive the glazing gaskets are secured to the column with steel plates and clip angles welded together for additional rigidity and appearance's sake. The exterior quadrant receives type C siding secured to the insulated liner panel and subgirts. The part of the column inside the building is furred and covered with gypsum board.

Structural glazing gaskets were originally developed for the automobile industry and have been a part of building construction since the mid-1950s, when they were first used by Eero Saarinen in the General Motors Technical Center. Practical and economical, gaskets are manufactured to fit a large variety of glazing requirements. They are relatively easy to install using simple tools and techniques. The adhesive glue used with this material actually welds mitered joints and seams into a waterproof assembly. The chemically inert quality of neoprene allows the connection of glass to aluminum, steel, and other metals without promoting corrosion. The locking effect of the gasket seal results from the progressive insertion of a locking strip that places the entire gasket and glass assembly under compression. The locking strip is sometimes called a *zipper gasket*, a reflection of its closurelike action.

The RCA Factory and office wing serve as an example of coordinated technology, economy, and aesthetics. The complex illustrates the possibilities that exist when a basically economical material is used in an intelligent and consistent manner in conjunction with effective industrial planning.

Fig. 16   Horizontal section through the office corner column.

9 Spellman Halls
Princeton, New Jersey

ARCHITECTS: I. M. Pei & Partners

Fig. 1   View of
Spellman Halls
looking northeast
from the plaza.

Spellman Halls are dormitories for Princeton University undergraduates. They are located on a pleasant site overlooking the playing fields of the campus. An initial impression of engaging complexity and well-thought-out spatial relations heightens one's sense of discovery as the organization and construction of this project come into focus. The three- and four-story precast concrete buildings are linked to a T-shaped spine, as can be seen in Figure 2. Small triangular courtyards are located opposite the building entry areas and form "activity nodes" along the circulation spine. Precast concrete bridges used for fire safety and egress connect the dormitory units to each other and provide a strong sense of scale for this complex. Figure 1 shows a view of Spellman Halls looking northeast from the plaza. The juxtaposition of the dormitory units results in an exciting combination of faceted elevations that expresses great variations of light and shade; it is surprising that such variety could be derived from one building type. The basic dormitory unit for this project is a boldly conceived campus residence that is far from simple in either plan or structural concept.

The architects for this project, I. M. Pei & Partners, long associated with the creative use of precast concrete, have developed a strong statement of function and form in Spellman Halls. This complex was awarded several honors for design and the use of concrete. Seminal concepts introduced, for example, in Louis Kahn's Richards Medical Research Building, Medical & Biology Laboratories, Philadelphia, and Pier Luigi Nervi's Sports Palace, Rome, achieve a striking significance in these dormitories. There is, after all, much that can be said in favor of a structural system that also delivers integrated walls, floors, and window openings in a neat package with a high-quality concrete finish that closely resembles dressed limestone.

Figure 3 illustrates the relation of the internal traffic patterns of the living areas to the external circulation of the spine. Each floor of the dormitory is composed of two living units, each containing four private bedrooms; each unit has a galley kitchen, a bath, and a communal living room. A central stair capped by a skylight links all the building floors and provides a series of changing views for the occupants of each level (see Figures 4 and 5). The angled complexity and sculptural quality of the project are a function of a sophisticated process of structural and mechanical planning that utilizes twenty-four standard wall, slab, stair, and girder components that make up each floor of this project. A total of approximately 600 precast parts was required to assemble the eight units of

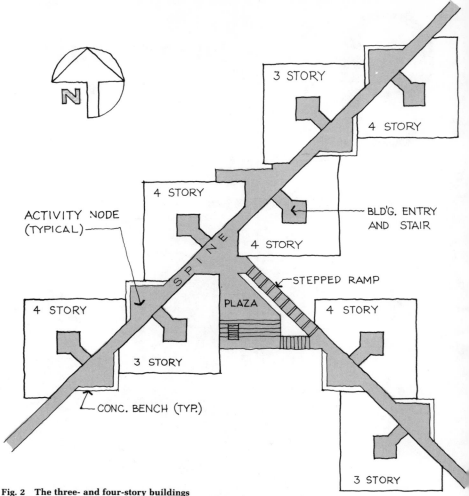

Fig. 2 The three- and four-story buildings are linked to a T-shaped spine.

Figs. 4 and 5 Views of the skylight.

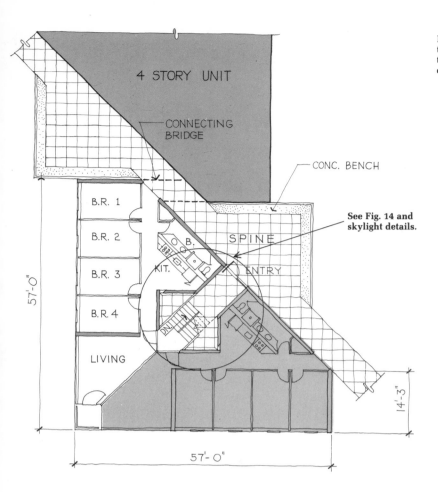

4 STORY UNIT

CONNECTING
BRIDGE

CONC. BENCH

See Fig. 14 and
skylight details.

B.R. 1

B.R. 2

SPINE

B.

KIT.

B.R. 3

ENTRY

DN.

B.R. 4

LIVING

57'-0"

57'- 0"

14'-3"

Fig. 3   Relation of internal
traffic patterns of living areas
to the external circulation
of the spine.

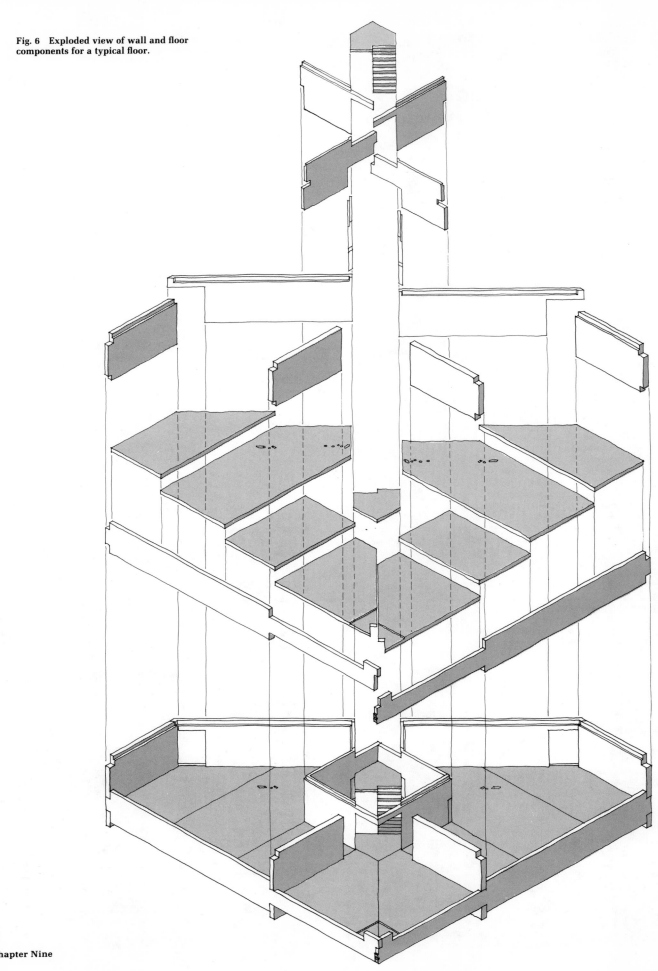

Fig. 6 Exploded view of wall and floor components for a typical floor.

this complex. Figure 6 is an isometric drawing showing an exploded view of the concrete components required for a typical floor of the dormitory unit. Wall panels, slabs, girders, and the stair assembly are shown falling into position at the bottom of the drawing. Plumbing and electrical roughing are provided for by precasting collars for pipes and conduit that are installed after the assembly of the structure. The interaction of elements shown here is indicative of an unusual degree of cooperation between the architect, the consulting engineers, and the contractor. Without the active collaboration and coordination of these participants in the construction process, a complex structural system of this type is impossible at any price. In fact, the concept was tested for economic viability by bidding the project against three other methods of construction, namely, conventional masonry and slab, precast plank and beam on load-bearing masonry, and cast-in-place concrete. The system actually used for construction was decidedly the most economical to build of the four proposals and was under the budget established for this project.

The procedures of industrial precasting differ markedly from those used for on-site poured concrete. The standardization of components such as wall sections allows the manufacturer to develop an economical assembly line production that ensures quality control with respect to the batching of ingredients, the water content, and the finish. The use of prestressed or posttensioned concrete and plastic-faced forms results in a degree of quality that is generally unavailable with on-site construction. The extensive formwork that would have been required for these buildings is made unnecessary by the precasting process. Wall sections, girders, and slabs are delivered to the site and fabricated in much the same way as a steel frame is. Simple structural connections are accomplished by welding and bolting components together. The ease with which this can be accomplished is illustrated in Figure 7. Shown here is a vertical section through the intersection of the typical slab and wall. A ¼-inch steel plate is welded to the anchor inserts of both the slab and the wall panels connecting these elements. The upper 8-inch wall section is then set on top of this intersection with mortar, stabilizing the assembly and concealing the connection. The intersection of a slab and a girder is shown in Figure 8; at this intersection an ordinary 2- by 2-inch steel angle is bolted to cast inserts that structurally secure these components.

It is important to note that the relative simplicity of construction requires intensive prior planning of the reinforcement and inserts. The necessary anchorage for connections must be provided in the locations called for by the construction requirements and must be designed in accordance with the overall structural specifications. An angled-corner

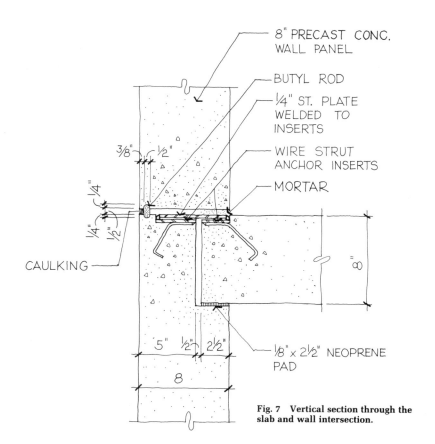

Fig. 7 Vertical section through the slab and wall intersection.

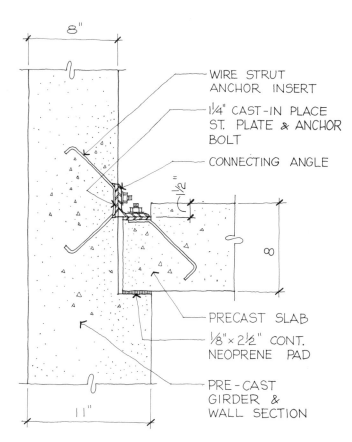

Fig. 8 Vertical section through the slab and girder intersection.

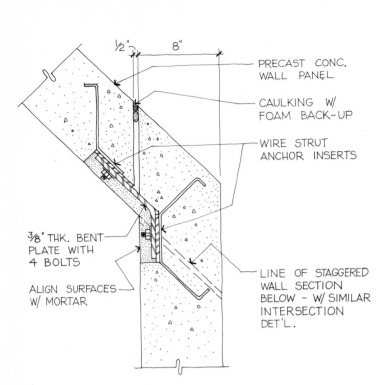

Fig. 9 Plan section at the angled corner wall intersection.

PRECAST CONC. WALL PANEL

CAULKING W/ FOAM BACK-UP

WIRE STRUT ANCHOR INSERTS

⅜" THK. BENT PLATE WITH 4 BOLTS

ALIGN SURFACES W/ MORTAR

LINE OF STAGGERED WALL SECTION BELOW - W/ SIMILAR INTERSECTION DET'L.

½" 8"

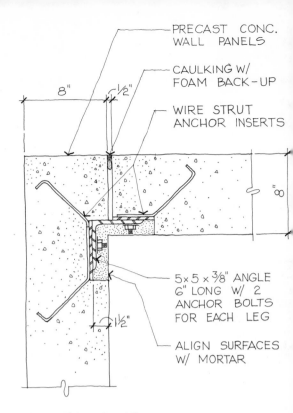

Fig. 10 Plan section at the building corner.

PRECAST CONC. WALL PANELS

CAULKING W/ FOAM BACK-UP

WIRE STRUT ANCHOR INSERTS

5 x 5 x ⅜" ANGLE 6" LONG W/ 2 ANCHOR BOLTS FOR EACH LEG

ALIGN SURFACES W/ MORTAR

8" ½" 8" 2½"

wall intersection is shown in Figure 9. Here a special bent steel plate designed to tie these two wall panels together is secured to the anchor inserts. This plan section indicates that the corner intersection is staggered from floor to floor of the building. Figure 10 indicates a right-angled wall connection in which the vertical panels are joined by a bolted 5- by 5-inch angle secured to the anchor inserts. Mortar is used to conceal the connection and align the wall surfaces. Figure 11 is a vertical section through the slab intersection showing the connecting plate and the anchor inserts for this assembly. Figure 12 is a view of the posttensioned cantilevered girders forming the right-angled corner of the dormitory balcony.

The underlying design logic of these buildings depends primarily on the architect's awareness of the industrial process and ability to humanize the interaction of form and function. There is a certain genius in being able to take simple components and incorporate them effectively into larger, more complex concepts. The glazing for this project is composed mainly of projected casement windows and fixed glass panels. The marriage of these popular and ubiquitous window units to the concrete panels takes place by the simple addition of a ⅜-inch metal bar that is secured to the window unit and is anchored to a reglet cast into the concrete for the purpose of receiving it.

Figure 13 delineates the refreshing simplicity of this detail and the natural way in which all these components interact. It would appear in this instance that the casement window was a unique development designed for this purpose only and not a standard component in use in thousands of other buildings. Simple details and inventive use of available components are complementary themes in the appreciation of this building. The addition of a ⅜-inch bar allowed the architects to use an utterly simple and available industrial unit for this highly sophisticated building type. The fixed glass is shown tied into the casement window at the jamb and set into the windowsill at the reglet so that fixed and movable sash interact. The casement window is modified by the addition of a metal stop that is secured to the window jamb. The wood sill, the insulation, and the gypsum board complete this fine statement of creative and practical detailing.

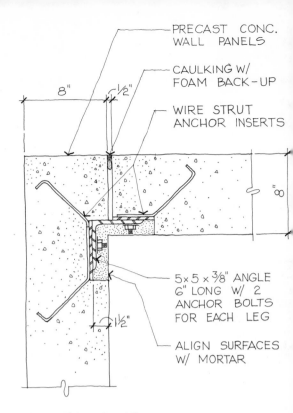

¼" ST. PLATE & ANCHOR BOLTS

CONC. FILL

WIRE STRUT ANCHOR INSERT WELDED TO CAST-IN PLACE ST. PL.

PRECAST CONC. SLAB

1" ½" 8" ½"

Fig. 11 Vertical section through the slab-slab connection.

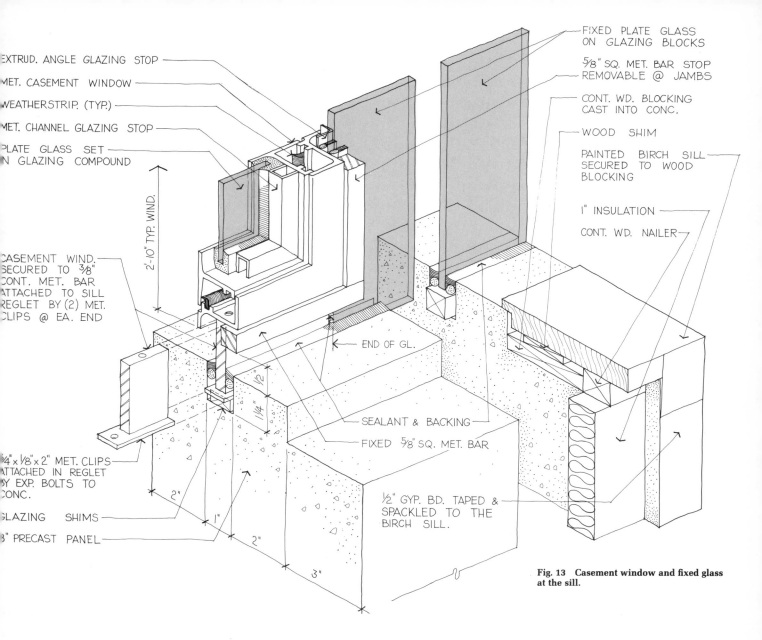

EXTRUD. ANGLE GLAZING STOP

MET. CASEMENT WINDOW

WEATHERSTRIP. (TYP.)

MET. CHANNEL GLAZING STOP

PLATE GLASS SET
IN GLAZING COMPOUND

CASEMENT WIND.
SECURED TO ³⁄₈"
CONT. MET. BAR
ATTACHED TO SILL
REGLET BY (2) MET.
CLIPS @ EA. END

³⁄₄" x ⅛" x 2" MET. CLIPS
ATTACHED IN REGLET
BY EXP. BOLTS TO
CONC.

GLAZING SHIMS

8" PRECAST PANEL

2'-10" TYP. WIND.

½"

¼"

2"

1"

2"

3"

FIXED PLATE GLASS
ON GLAZING BLOCKS

⁵⁄₈" SQ. MET. BAR STOP
REMOVABLE @ JAMBS

CONT. WD. BLOCKING
CAST INTO CONC.

WOOD SHIM

PAINTED BIRCH SILL
SECURED TO WOOD
BLOCKING

1" INSULATION

CONT. WD. NAILER

END OF GL.

SEALANT & BACKING

FIXED ⁵⁄₈" SQ. MET. BAR

½" GYP. BD. TAPED &
SPACKLED TO THE
BIRCH SILL.

Fig. 13   Casement window and fixed glass
at the sill.

Fig. 12   Posttensioned cantilevered
girders forming the right-angled
corner of the dormitory balcony.

Figure 14 describes a 3½-story entry lobby for a typical dormitory unit. Figure 4 is a view of this lobby taken from the courtyard opposite the building entry, and Figure 5 shows both a pleasant view available from the stair lobby and the skylight overhead. Figure 15 is a view of the skylight and its relation to the upper entry glass. Shown here is the intersection of the ⅜-inch vertical glass and the ¾-inch horizontal tempered glass of the skylight that spans the entry lobby. The metal side frame that sits astride the parapet panels is secured to the concrete with expansion

Fig. 14   A 3½-story entry lobby.

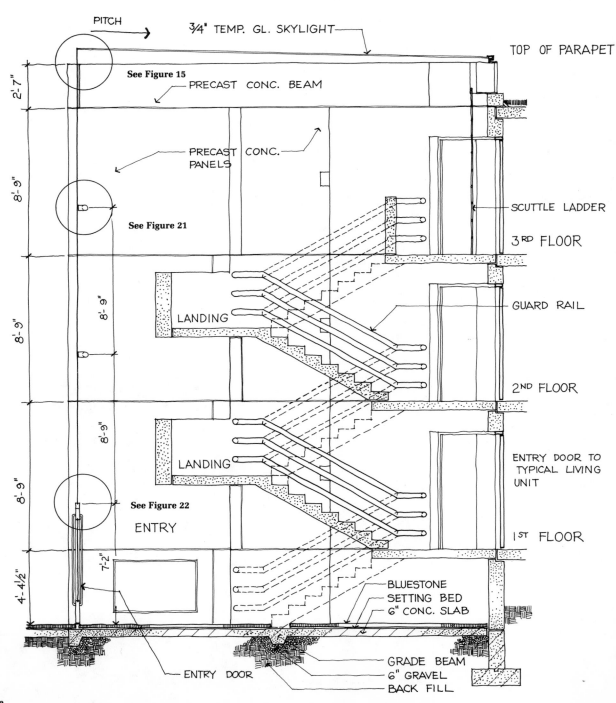

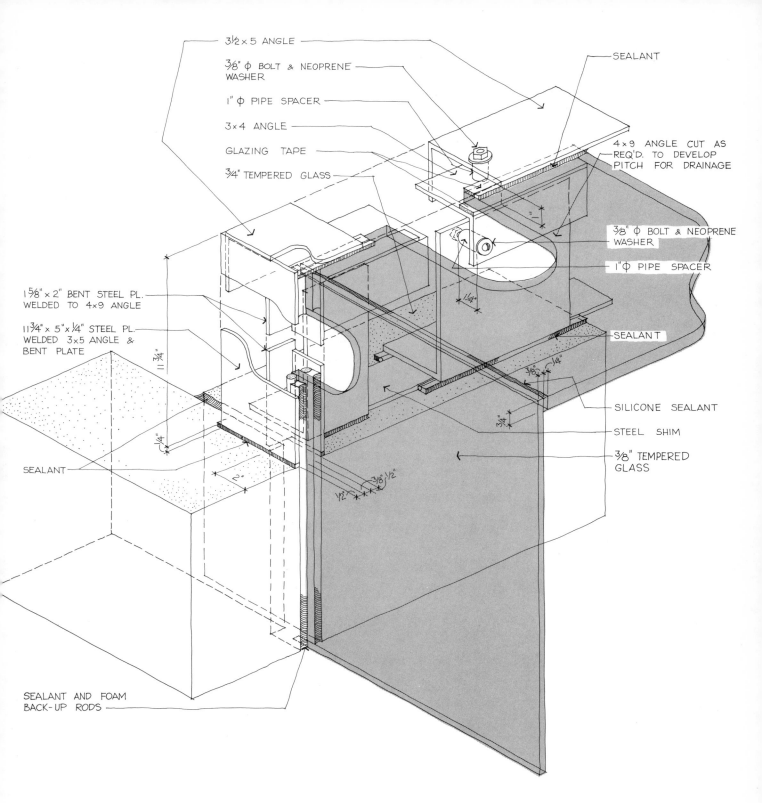

3½ × 5 ANGLE

⅜" ∅ BOLT & NEOPRENE WASHER

1" ∅ PIPE SPACER

3 × 4 ANGLE

GLAZING TAPE

¾" TEMPERED GLASS

SEALANT

4 × 9 ANGLE CUT AS REQ'D. TO DEVELOP PITCH FOR DRAINAGE

⅜" ∅ BOLT & NEOPRENE WASHER

1" ∅ PIPE SPACER

1⅝" × 2" BENT STEEL PL. WELDED TO 4×9 ANGLE

11¾" × 5" × ¼" STEEL PL. WELDED 3×5 ANGLE & BENT PLATE

SEALANT

11¾"

¼"

2"

SEALANT

⅜" ½"

½"

1¼"

¾"

⅜" ¼"

SEALANT

SILICONE SEALANT

STEEL SHIM

⅜" TEMPERED GLASS

SEALANT AND FOAM BACK-UP RODS

Fig. 15 Skylight detail at the entry.

bolts and anchors. Figure 16 is a part elevation study of the skylight and lobby glass viewed from the outside. The dotted vertical lines on the concrete and metal frame indicate the continuous vertical reglet that contains the entry glass. This elevation refers us to a detail that further explains the skylight system.

Figure 17 is a description of the vertical intersection of the skylight and the lobby glass. Note the silicone sealant used between the two glass elements, and restudy Figure 5 for the visual impact of this construction. Figure 18 is a plan section through the metal skylight assembly that indicates the reglet developed for the vertical entry glass. Figure 19 is similar but taken through the concrete panels. Figure 20 is a vertical section through the side frame of the skylight and indicates the three angles that form this construction. The 4- by 9-inch angle is cut to form a sloped section that provides the skylight with the necessary pitch for drainage. The 4- by 3-inch angle forms a flat surface that receives the ¾-inch skylight glass and follows the pitch developed by the larger angle. Finally, the 5- by 3½-inch angle is used to clamp the skylight glass securely in place.

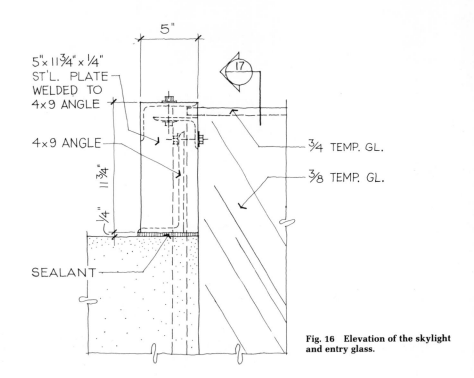

Fig. 16 Elevation of the skylight and entry glass.

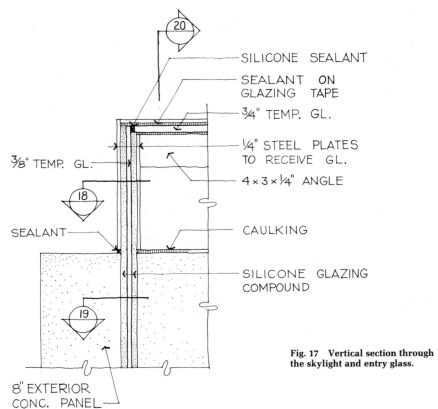

Fig. 17 Vertical section through the skylight and entry glass.

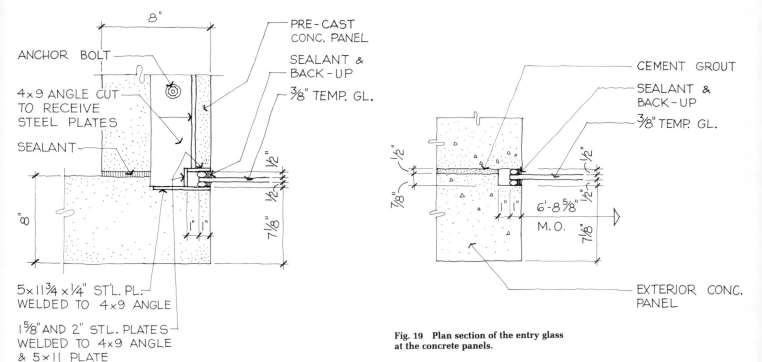

PRE-CAST
CONC. PANEL

SEALANT &
BACK-UP

3/8" TEMP. GL.

ANCHOR BOLT

4×9 ANGLE CUT
TO RECEIVE
STEEL PLATES

SEALANT

8"

8"

7/8"

1/2"

1/2"

1"   1"

5×11 3/4 ×1/4" ST'L. PL.
WELDED TO 4×9 ANGLE

1 5/8" AND 2" STL. PLATES
WELDED TO 4×9 ANGLE
& 5×11 PLATE

**Fig. 18   Plan section of the entry glass
at the skylight.**

CEMENT GROUT

SEALANT &
BACK-UP

3/8" TEMP. GL.

1/2"

7/8"

1/2"

1"   1"

6'-8 5/8"
M.O.

7/8"

EXTERIOR CONC.
PANEL

**Fig. 19   Plan section of the entry glass
at the concrete panels.**

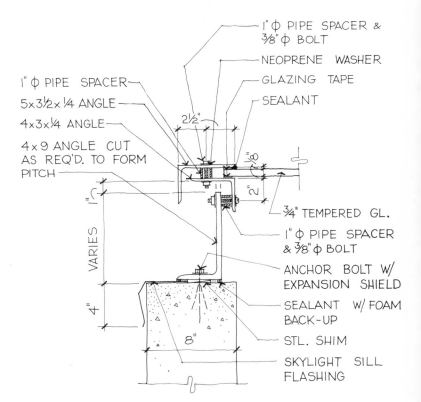

1" ⌀ PIPE SPACER &
3/8" ⌀ BOLT

NEOPRENE WASHER

GLAZING TAPE

SEALANT

1" ⌀ PIPE SPACER

5×3 1/2×1/4 ANGLE

4×3×1/4 ANGLE

4×9 ANGLE CUT
AS REQ'D. TO FORM
PITCH

2 1/2"

2 7/8"

2"

1"

VARIES

4"

8"

3/4" TEMPERED GL.

1" ⌀ PIPE SPACER
& 3/8"⌀ BOLT

ANCHOR BOLT W/
EXPANSION SHIELD

SEALANT W/ FOAM
BACK-UP

STL. SHIM

SKYLIGHT SILL
FLASHING

Fig. 20   Vertical section through the skylight.

Figure 21 continues the analysis of the entry lobby glass. Shown here is an intermediate supporting bracket for the lobby glass. Bracket elbows fabricated of 4-inch chrome steel pipe support the glass at approximately each floor level. The brackets permit the development of a seemingly large unbroken area of glass that effectively encloses the entry area physically but not visually. The bracket is securely anchored to the concrete side panel and is designed to receive the glass and finish fittings. Note that the lower glass is given a semicircular notch that is fitted around a steel spacer welded to the bracket. The spacer and the glazing tape are secured to the capped steel pipe. Another layer of glazing tape is applied to this assembly, effectively creating a sandwiched glass panel when the 4-inch-diameter steel clip is screwed into the elbow. The upper glass rests on the supported lower pane and is installed before the circular steel clip is attached. A bead of silicone separates the upper and lower glass panels from each other.

Figure 22 concludes the analysis of the entry glass and indicates the intersection of the glass and the door frame at the lobby level. The lowest panel of glass is supported by the hollow metal door frame, which has been reinforced with a tubular steel element at the head of the frame. The hollow metal door frame is mortared securely into place and is anchored to the reglet that runs up the entire height of the lobby. A view of this typical entry door may be studied in Figure 2.

Fig. 21 Entry area glass at support bracket.

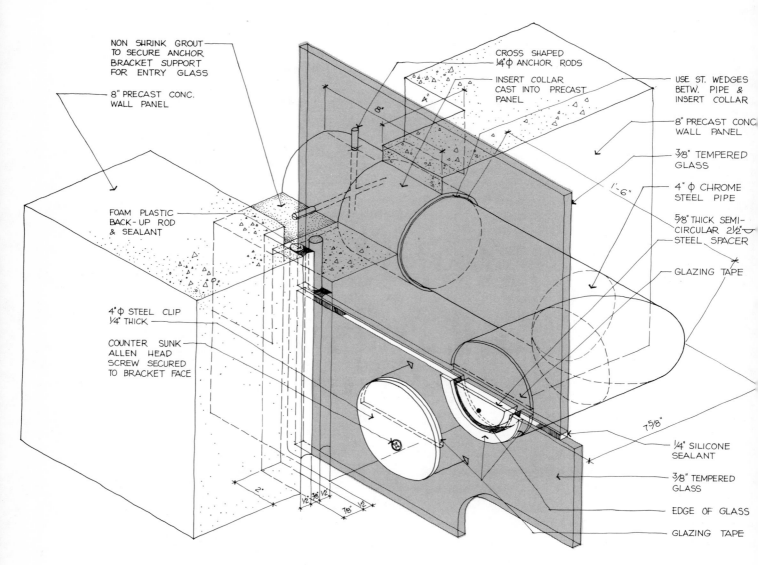

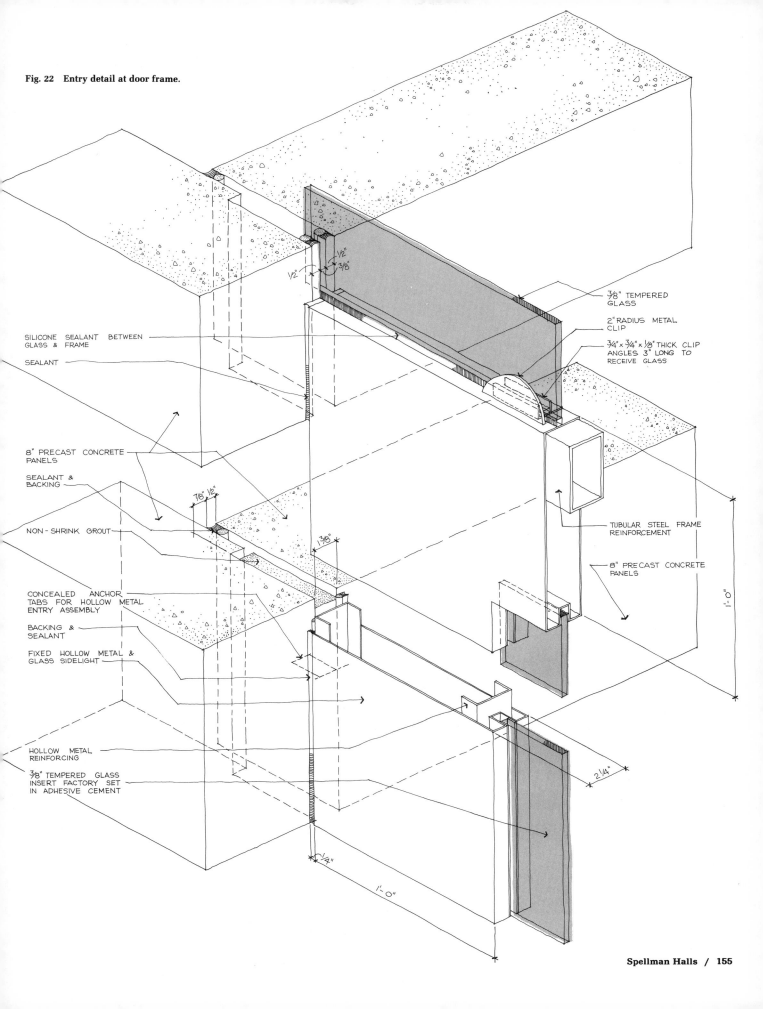

Fig. 22 Entry detail at door frame.

SILICONE SEALANT BETWEEN GLASS & FRAME

SEALANT

8" PRECAST CONCRETE PANELS

SEALANT & BACKING

NON - SHRINK GROUT

CONCEALED ANCHOR TABS FOR HOLLOW METAL ENTRY ASSEMBLY

BACKING & SEALANT

FIXED HOLLOW METAL & GLASS SIDELIGHT

HOLLOW METAL REINFORCING

3/8" TEMPERED GLASS INSERT FACTORY SET IN ADHESIVE CEMENT

3/8" TEMPERED GLASS

2" RADIUS METAL CLIP

3/4" x 3/4" x 1/8" THICK CLIP ANGLES 3" LONG TO RECEIVE GLASS

TUBULAR STEEL FRAME REINFORCEMENT

8" PRECAST CONCRETE PANELS

1/2"
3/8"
1/2"
7/8" 1/2"
3/8"
1'- 0"
2 1/4"
1/4"
1'- 0"

10
3 Park Avenue and Central Manhattan High School

New York, New York

ARCHITECTS: Shreve Lamb & Harmon Associates, PC Architects/Planners

Fig. 1   Variety of brick. *(Gil Amiaga.)*

A complex reinforced-concrete
structure approximately forty-two
stories high, 3 Park Avenue is sheathed in a
combination of metal and glass curtain
walls and brick and glass cavity wall
construction. The structure is one of New
York City's first multiuse buildings. It
houses the Central Manhattan High School
in its lower twelve stories, with a separate
entry for the school on 33d Street. A bank
is at street level on the corner facing 33d
Street and Park Avenue. The upper floors of
the building are devoted to office space. The
entry to the commercial section of the
building is at the intersection of Park
Avenue and 34th Street.

Shreve Lamb & Harmon Associates, PC
Architects/Planners, is the architectural
firm responsible for the development of the
design and contract documents for this
project. The building serves to remind us
how effective brick can be as an exterior
facing material. The massing of the
elevation as viewed in Figure 1 indicates
the variety of brick application available to
the designer and further demonstrates that
in this instance brick works aesthetically
well with its neighbors. Figure 2 provides a
view from the northwest corner of the
intersection looking at the building in a
southerly direction. The office tower breaks
free of the school at the twelfth-floor
mechanical equipment area and rises to the
top of the building, which is capped with a
penthouse defined by inclined brick piers.
The building contains a relatively large
variety of masonry and glass curtain wall
details. Individual windows set in masonry
cavity walls may be found side by side with
large expanses of metal and glass curtain
walls that may be seen in the tower portion
of the building.

Figure 3 is a view of a typical intersection
between the brick cavity wall and a
concrete spandrel beam. There is a
similarity to Figure 1 in the preface that
indicates the relation of cavity wall
construction to a steel frame. In this
instance the bottom of the concrete
spandrel beam is very close to the head of
the windows, eliminating the requirement
for a hung lintel. As in all forms of cavity
wall construction, the facing material
clears the structure as it rises to the top of
the building. The masonry backup is set
securely on the finished slab or deck. The
wedge insert, located approximately 1½
inches from the bottom of the spandrel
beam, is designed to receive a 5- by 5-inch
shelf angle. This steel angle is secured to
the structure every 3 feet on center,
providing the necessary support for the
shelf angle or relieving angle as it receives
the weight of face brick from the floor
above. The wedge insert is secured to the
concrete with reinforcing rods that are tied
back to the structural reinforcing of the
slab and the spandrel beam. This device is
cast into the structure when the concrete is
poured and becomes an integral part of the
building. The wedge insert is fabricated of
ductile iron that provides a sloped track, or
wedge, designed to eliminate slippage of
the shelf angle. When used with the proper
askew head bolts, the shelf angle may be
set at a given height with the assurance
that there will be no slippage after loading
occurs. The vertical track of the insert

Fig. 2   A view of the building from the
northwest corner of the intersection. *(Gil Amiaga.)*

provides the necessary adjustment for the
accurate vertical coursing of the face brick
without any special cutting. The 4-inch
concrete block backup is placed over
flashing designed to protect the shelf angle
assembly from structural damage due to
moisture.

Condensation in a curtain wall is a
problem that is solved in a variety of ways.
Architects, however, generally deal with
moisture and condensate in cavity walls in
a uniform way throughout a building. A 2-
inch-deep cavity is maintained between the
outer face brick and the inner masonry
backup wall. Rain-driven water and
condensate formed by a temperature
difference between the inner and the outer
skin of the building collects in the cavity
and is conducted to the exterior of the
building by weep holes built into the face
brick at the shelf angle. The flashing
mentioned earlier is very important because
it forms a water-resistant barrier that
conducts moisture away from the steel
angle to the exterior of the building
through weep holes. Much of the damage

sustained by buildings with masonry
curtain walls can be attributed to the
failure of flashing at the shelf angle and to
resultant corrosion of the masonry ties. If
the rusting cannot be arrested, the masonry
assembly must ultimately fail. Note the
masonry anchor ties that secure the face
brick to the backup wall. The tie is made of
corrosion-resistant material such as
stainless steel, and a V-shaped indent at its
center prevents water from being conducted
to the inner wall by capillary action, thus
eliminating another source of water
penetration in this type of construction. An
anchor tie is used for approximately every 2
square feet of face brick and usually
engages every other block course. It is
important to keep the cavity free of
construction debris. A horizontal wood two-
by-four is often used by brickmasons to
clear the cavity during construction. The
two-by-four is raised up every two block
courses before the anchor ties are installed
so that loose mortar and drippings are
removed before the next two courses of
block are installed.

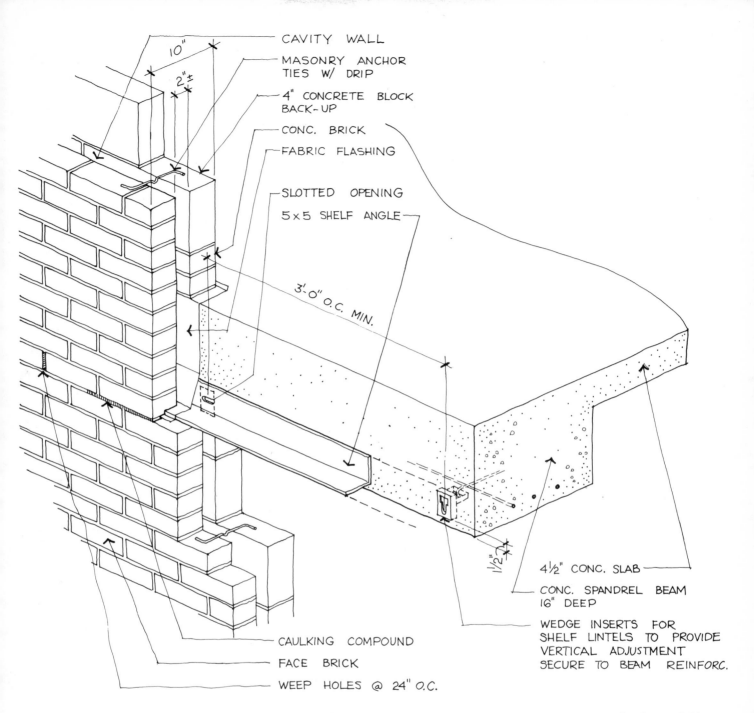

CAVITY WALL

MASONRY ANCHOR TIES W/ DRIP

4" CONCRETE BLOCK BACK-UP

CONC. BRICK

FABRIC FLASHING

SLOTTED OPENING

5 x 5 SHELF ANGLE

10"

2"±

3'-0" O.C. MIN.

1/2"

CAULKING COMPOUND

FACE BRICK

WEEP HOLES @ 24" O.C.

4½" CONC. SLAB

CONC. SPANDREL BEAM 16" DEEP

WEDGE INSERTS FOR SHELF LINTELS TO PROVIDE VERTICAL ADJUSTMENT SECURE TO BEAM REINFORC.

Fig. 3   Typical cavity wall at the spandrel beam.

Figure 4 is a vertical section through the spandrel assembly and indicates a variation of the flashing detail for a shelf angle in a concrete structure. A reglet cast into the concrete receives the flashing, and sealant is installed to make the connection watertight. The wedge insert is shown in dotted lines, and the attachment of the shelf angle can be studied. Note the askew head bolt projecting through the angle. The brick joint below the shelf angle is similar to that of Figure 1 of the preface. The shelf angle must transmit the accumulated loading of the face brick to the spandrel beam at this point. A sponge neoprene tape is used below the shelf angle to prevent the transmission of downward vertical forces below this point. If the face brick were allowed to transmit loading past the shelf angles, the brick would eventually become overstressed and fail. Horizontal mortar joints are uniformly approximately ½ inch thick. In order to maintain this dimension constant, the brick resting on the shelf angle is cut in a shape, as noted, to accommodate the requirements of this detail. The weep hole that conducts moisture to the exterior is shown in dotted lines; either it is a plastic tube with a diameter equal to the joint width, or the vertical joint at that point is kept clear of mortar to drain the cavity.

Figures 5 and 6 indicate the expansion joints that are required by the brick construction. Vertical expansion joints are usually called for at 20 feet on center. The joint itself is composed of a ⅜-inch neoprene filler finished with elastic sealant. The expansion joints are tooled to match the mortar and remain roughly the same size as the brick joints for the sake of consistency. They blend into the construction since the sealant material matches the mortar in color.

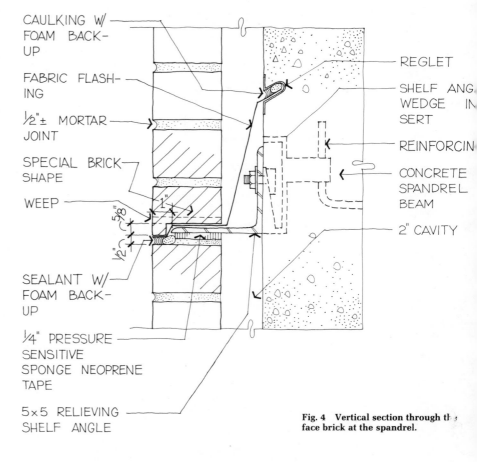

CAULKING W/ FOAM BACK-UP

FABRIC FLASH-ING

½"± MORTAR JOINT

SPECIAL BRICK SHAPE

WEEP

SEALANT W/ FOAM BACK-UP

¼" PRESSURE SENSITIVE SPONGE NEOPRENE TAPE

5×5 RELIEVING SHELF ANGLE

REGLET

SHELF ANG WEDGE IN SERT

REINFORCIN

CONCRETE SPANDREL BEAM

2" CAVITY

Fig. 4 Vertical section through th face brick at the spandrel.

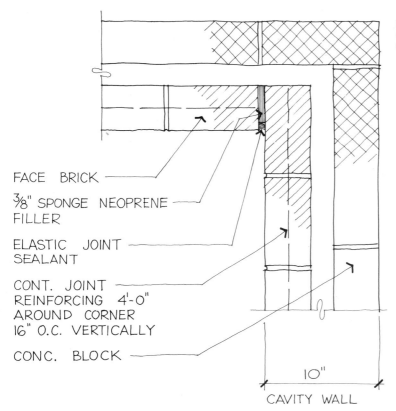

Fig. 5 Horizontal section through an expansion joint at the concave corner.

FACE BRICK

⅜" SPONGE NEOPRENE FILLER

ELASTIC JOINT SEALANT

CONT. JOINT REINFORCING 4'-0" AROUND CORNER 16" O.C. VERTICALLY

CONC. BLOCK

10"

CAVITY WALL

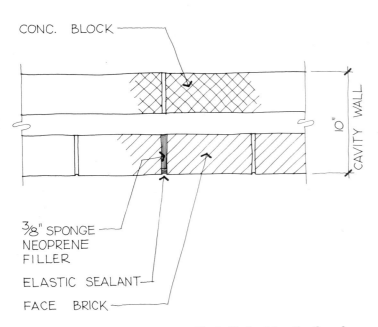

CONC. BLOCK

10" CAVITY WALL

⅜" SPONGE NEOPRENE FILLER

ELASTIC SEALANT

FACE BRICK

Fig. 6 Horizontal section through an expansion joint.

Figure 7 is a view taken through the school wing of this building and indicates the relation of the column to the brick wall and soffit. The face brick soldiers (vertically coursed brick elements) form a continuous accent here as well as on other portions of the building. The soldiers are specially cut and set on a hung lintel that also supports the soffit assembly. The fourth-floor spandrel beam is shown receiving the shelf angle. Vertical angle hangers are secured regularly to wedge inserts cast into the beam. A reglet receives the flashing at this point, and the construction here is similar to that shown in Figure 4. Several detail variations of this spandrel condition are worth pointing out. The brick is secured to the slab and the beam with a corrugated metal anchor strap attached to a dovetail slot cast into the concrete at the spandrel. The dovetail slot is filled with foam plastic to prevent it from being clogged with concrete during the pour. The foam plastic easily receives the anchor strap by simply being inserted into the slot and being twisted to engage the positive dovetail connection. Note the angle brace that stabilizes the hung lintel assembly. The angle brace is secured to the vertical hangers and is tied back to an angle clip at the slab that braces this assembly. The clip is secured to another insert that is designed to receive this construction. This adjustable insert differs from the wedge insert in the following way: It comes complete with its own integral track and a spring-loaded nut that slides back and forth, allowing up to 3 inches of adjustment for various connections. This anchor insert is ideal for horizontal installations and is secured to slabs and beams with reinforcing rods that are tied to the main structure.

The hung lintel assembly shown in Figure 7 supports the exterior face brick and the interior backup block. Fabric flashing that protects this connection is applied to the inner face of the backup block with bitumen adhesive, and the entire assembly is painted with an additional coating of bitumen. Aluminum trim is secured to the bottom of the lintels, and the transition to the mosaic tile soffit is

made by channels that support the wire lath and by cement plaster that receives the finished tile. A trim strip located at the recessed wall and secured to stainless steel clips completes the installation of the hung soffit.

The relation of the metal and glass curtain wall to the brick piers is shown in Figure 8. A cutaway view of this assembly shows the curtain wall spanning vertically from floor to floor. The spandrel beams in this view contain many of the accessories discussed earlier. Reglets that receive

flashing are shown, as are adjustable inserts that secure the curtain wall extrusions. Note the bent steel clip that is used to engage the head of the window frame. The vertical slot combined with the horizontal play of the adjustable insert allows a great deal of flexibility in the attachment of all sorts of accessories and hardware. The spandrel panels are faced with ⅜-inch-thick sheet aluminum plug-welded to perimeter aluminum extrusions. The spandrel panels are designed to receive the window frames. This building does not have a mullion and panel curtain wall system but a series of connected pivotal sashes that is used to enclose the structure wherever a metal and glass curtain wall is called for. The metal and glass panels are 28 feet wide and rise twenty-eight stories above the school unit on all four elevations of the tower.

Fig. 7   Hung lintel and soffit assembly at the lobby area.

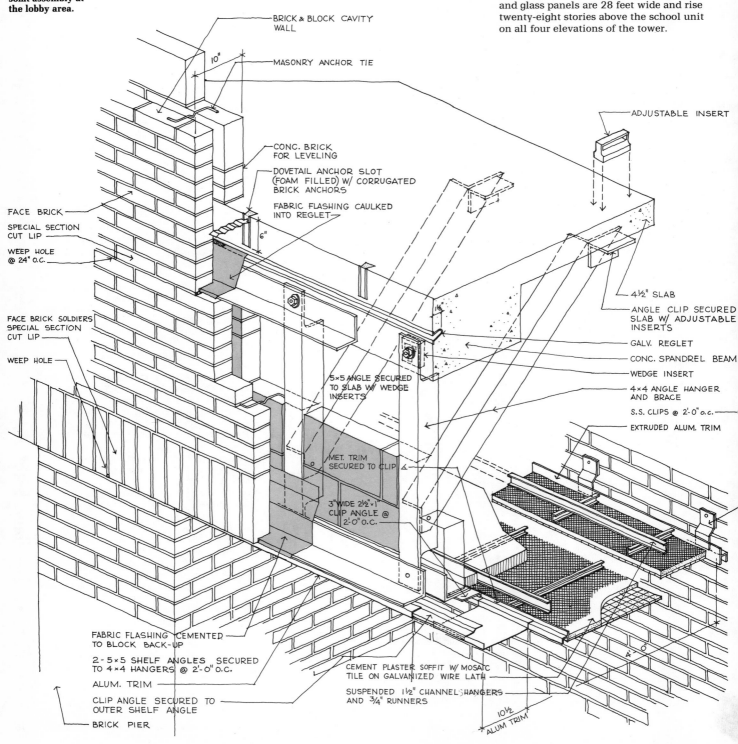

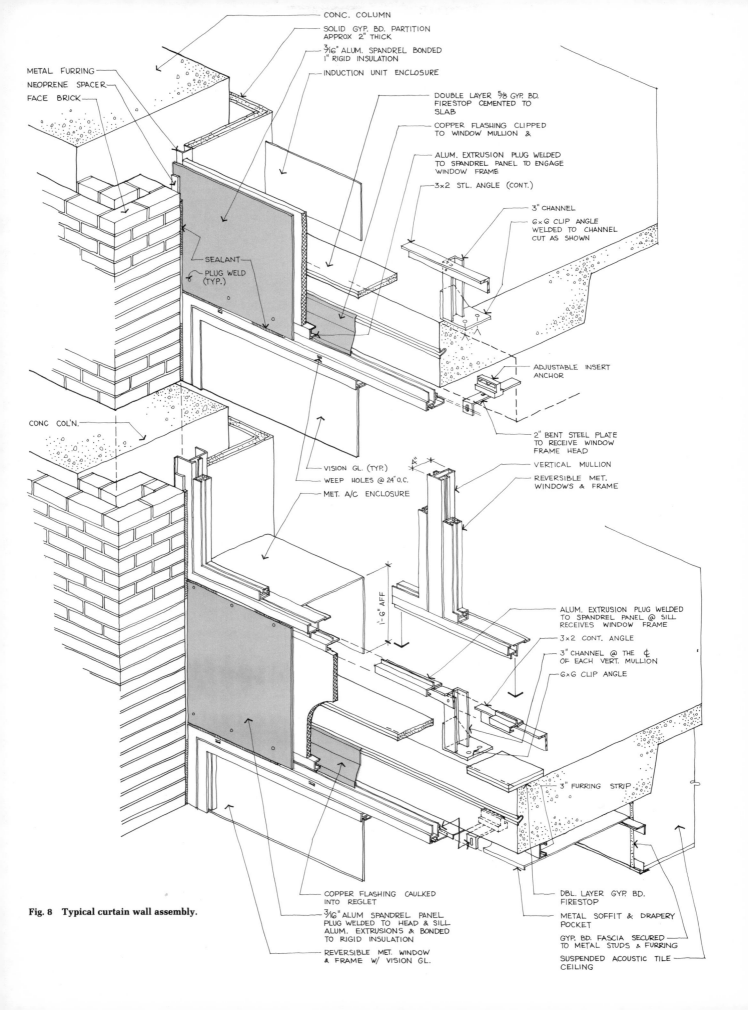

CONC. COLUMN

SOLID GYP. BD. PARTITION
APPROX 2" THICK

3/16" ALUM. SPANDREL BONDED
1" RIGID INSULATION

INDUCTION UNIT ENCLOSURE

DOUBLE LAYER 5/8 GYP. BD.
FIRESTOP CEMENTED TO
SLAB

COPPER FLASHING CLIPPED
TO WINDOW MULLION &

ALUM. EXTRUSION PLUG WELDED
TO SPANDREL PANEL TO ENGAGE
WINDOW FRAME

3×2 STL. ANGLE (CONT.)

3" CHANNEL

6×6 CLIP ANGLE
WELDED TO CHANNEL
CUT AS SHOWN

METAL FURRING
NEOPRENE SPACER
FACE BRICK

SEALANT

PLUG WELD
(TYP.)

ADJUSTABLE INSERT
ANCHOR

2" BENT STEEL PLATE
TO RECEIVE WINDOW
FRAME HEAD

CONC. COL'N.

VISION GL. (TYP.)
WEEP HOLES @ 24" O.C.

MET. A/C ENCLOSURE

4"

1'-6" AFF

VERTICAL MULLION

REVERSIBLE MET.
WINDOWS & FRAME

ALUM. EXTRUSION PLUG WELDED
TO SPANDREL PANEL @ SILL
RECEIVES WINDOW FRAME

3×2 CONT. ANGLE

3" CHANNEL @ THE ℄
OF EACH VERT. MULLION

6×6 CLIP ANGLE

3" FURRING STRIP

DBL. LAYER GYP. BD.
FIRESTOP

METAL SOFFIT & DRAPERY
POCKET

GYP. BD. FASCIA SECURED
TO METAL STUDS & FURRING

SUSPENDED ACOUSTIC TILE
CEILING

COPPER FLASHING CAULKED
INTO REGLET

3/16" ALUM SPANDREL PANEL
PLUG WELDED TO HEAD & SILL
ALUM. EXTRUSIONS & BONDED
TO RIGID INSULATION

REVERSIBLE MET. WINDOW
& FRAME' W/ VISION GL.

Fig. 8 Typical curtain wall assembly.

Figure 9 is a view of the typical curtain wall system, indicating the floor-to-floor height of the slabs and the height of the windowsill above the finished floor. Vertical and horizontal section cuts are noted for further study and analysis. Figure 10 indicates the relation of the spandrel panel to the concrete beam. The head and sill details for the pivotal sash are shown here engaging the spandrel panel. Heavy aluminum extrusions at the top and bottom of the spandrel panel are secured to the slab by an anchor clip at the slab and by a 3- by 2-inch continuous horizontal angle mounted below the sill and secured to the channel uprights. Note the attachment of the vertical 3-inch channels to 6- by 6-inch clip angles secured to the slab. The space between the edge of the slab and the inside face of the spandrel panel is sealed with a double layer of horizontal ⅝-inch gypsum board that serves as a fire-stop for this cladding system. The adjustable anchor insert is shown in dotted lines at the bottom of the slab. The 2-inch-wide anchor clip shown in Figure 8 is shown here engaging the head of the pivotal sash.

Figure 11 is a horizontal section through the cladding system and illustrates the relation of the window frame to the masonry piers and to the intermediate window mullion. Note the solid 2-inch gypsum board partition that forms the inside cover of the columns. A horizontal section through the spandrel cover and the brick piers is shown in Figure 12. The aluminum spandrel panel and the insulation are terminated at the brick pier, and the seam between them is filled with a neoprene spacer and a sealant. The gypsum board partition is a continuation of the one shown in Figure 11.

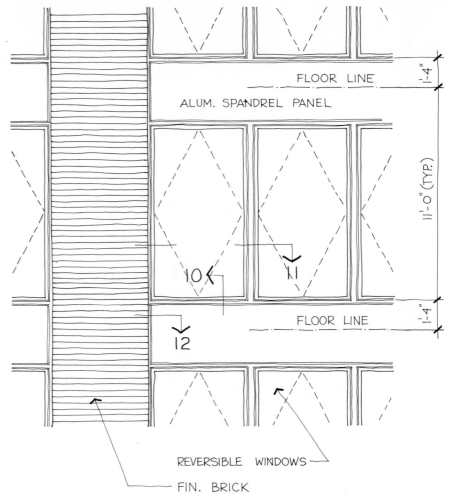

Fig. 9 Typical curtain wall system showing floor-to-floor height of slabs and height of windowsill above the finished floor.

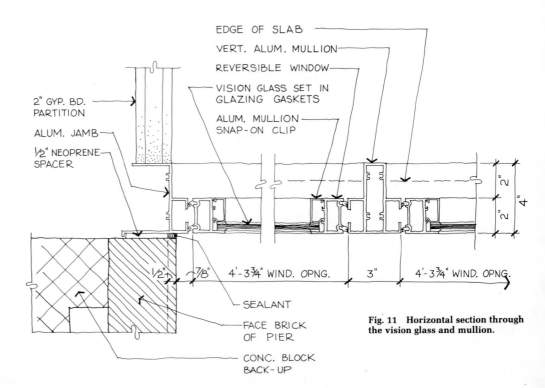

Fig. 11 Horizontal section through the vision glass and mullion.

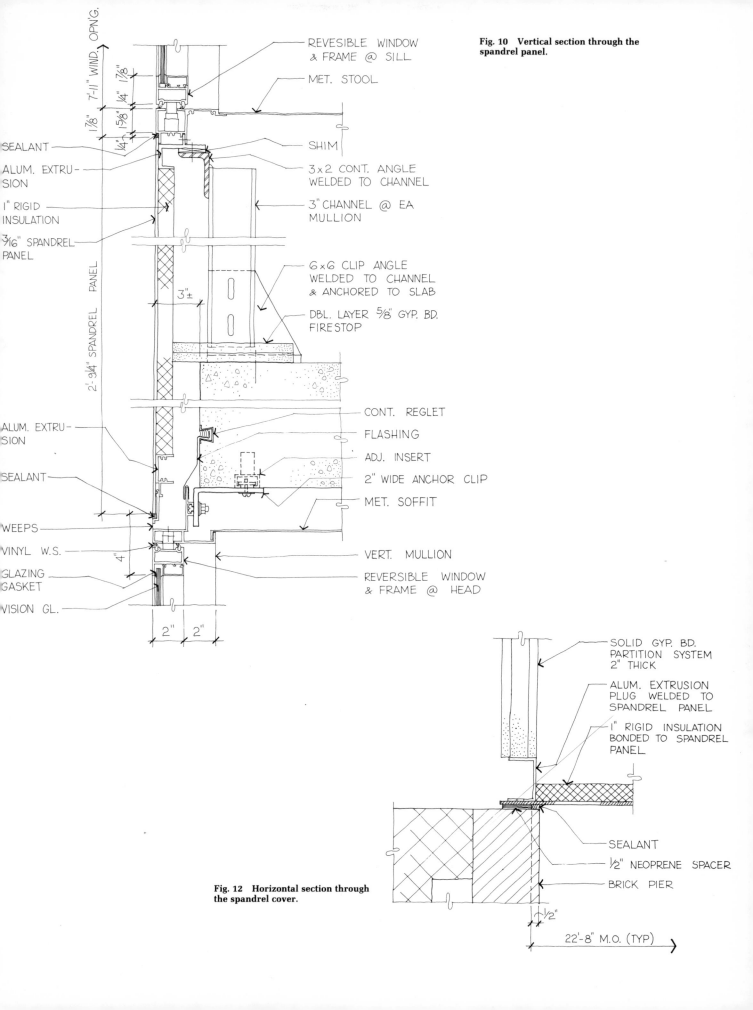

Fig. 10   Vertical section through the spandrel panel.

7'-11" WIND. OPN'G.

1⅞"
¼"
5⅝"
¼"
1⅞"

SEALANT

ALUM. EXTRU-SION

1" RIGID INSULATION

³⁄₁₆" SPANDREL PANEL

2'-9¼" SPANDREL PANEL

ALUM. EXTRU-SION

SEALANT

WEEPS

VINYL W.S.

GLAZING GASKET

VISION GL.

4"

2"   2"

3"±

3"±

REVESIBLE WINDOW & FRAME @ SILL

MET. STOOL

SHIM

3 x 2 CONT. ANGLE WELDED TO CHANNEL

3" CHANNEL @ EA MULLION

6 x 6 CLIP ANGLE WELDED TO CHANNEL & ANCHORED TO SLAB

DBL. LAYER ⅝" GYP. BD. FIRESTOP

CONT. REGLET

FLASHING

ADJ. INSERT

2" WIDE ANCHOR CLIP

MET. SOFFIT

VERT. MULLION

REVERSIBLE WINDOW & FRAME @ HEAD

Fig. 12   Horizontal section through the spandrel cover.

SOLID GYP. BD. PARTITION SYSTEM 2" THICK

ALUM. EXTRUSION PLUG WELDED TO SPANDREL PANEL

1" RIGID INSULATION BONDED TO SPANDREL PANEL

SEALANT

½" NEOPRENE SPACER

BRICK PIER

½"

22'-8" M.O. (TYP)

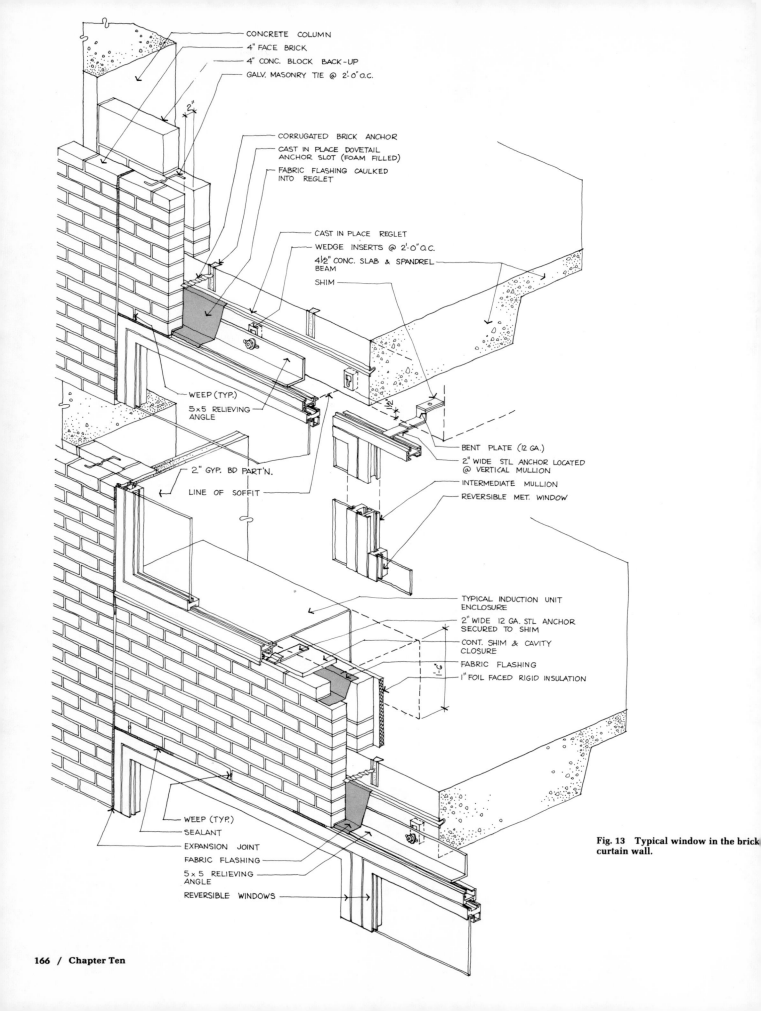

CONCRETE COLUMN
4" FACE BRICK
4" CONC. BLOCK BACK-UP
GALV. MASONRY TIE @ 2'-0" O.C.

CORRUGATED BRICK ANCHOR
CAST IN PLACE DOVETAIL ANCHOR SLOT (FOAM FILLED)
FABRIC FLASHING CAULKED INTO REGLET

CAST IN PLACE REGLET
WEDGE INSERTS @ 2'-0" O.C.
4½" CONC. SLAB & SPANDREL BEAM
SHIM

2"

WEEP (TYP.)
5x5 RELIEVING ANGLE

BENT PLATE (12 GA.)
2" WIDE STL ANCHOR LOCATED @ VERTICAL MULLION

2" GYP. BD PART'N.
LINE OF SOFFIT

INTERMEDIATE MULLION
REVERSIBLE MET. WINDOW

TYPICAL INDUCTION UNIT ENCLOSURE
2" WIDE 12 GA. STL ANCHOR SECURED TO SHIM
CONT. SHIM & CAVITY CLOSURE
FABRIC FLASHING
1" FOIL FACED RIGID INSULATION

WEEP (TYP.)
SEALANT
EXPANSION JOINT
FABRIC FLASHING
5 x 5 RELIEVING ANGLE
REVERSIBLE WINDOWS

Fig. 13 Typical window in the brick curtain wall.

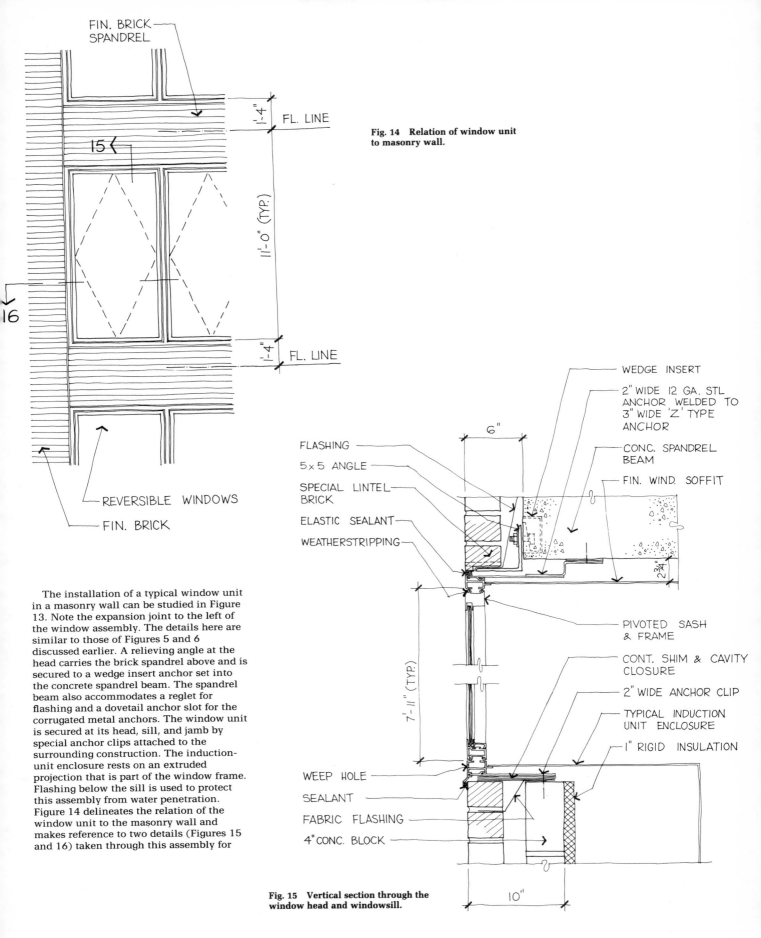

FIN. BRICK
SPANDREL

1'-4"

FL. LINE

Fig. 14 Relation of window unit
to masonry wall.

15

11'-0" (TYP.)

16

1'-4"

FL. LINE

REVERSIBLE WINDOWS

FIN. BRICK

6"

WEDGE INSERT

2" WIDE 12 GA. STL
ANCHOR WELDED TO
3" WIDE 'Z' TYPE
ANCHOR

FLASHING

5 x 5 ANGLE

SPECIAL LINTEL
BRICK

ELASTIC SEALANT

WEATHERSTRIPPING

CONC. SPANDREL
BEAM

FIN. WIND. SOFFIT

2¾"

PIVOTED SASH
& FRAME

CONT. SHIM & CAVITY
CLOSURE

2" WIDE ANCHOR CLIP

TYPICAL INDUCTION
UNIT ENCLOSURE

1" RIGID INSULATION

7'-11" (TYP.)

WEEP HOLE

SEALANT

FABRIC FLASHING

4" CONC. BLOCK

10"

The installation of a typical window unit in a masonry wall can be studied in Figure 13. Note the expansion joint to the left of the window assembly. The details here are similar to those of Figures 5 and 6 discussed earlier. A relieving angle at the head carries the brick spandrel above and is secured to a wedge insert anchor set into the concrete spandrel beam. The spandrel beam also accommodates a reglet for flashing and a dovetail anchor slot for the corrugated metal anchors. The window unit is secured at its head, sill, and jamb by special anchor clips attached to the surrounding construction. The induction-unit enclosure rests on an extruded projection that is part of the window frame. Flashing below the sill is used to protect this assembly from water penetration. Figure 14 delineates the relation of the window unit to the masonry wall and makes reference to two details (Figures 15 and 16) taken through this assembly for

Fig. 15 Vertical section through the
window head and windowsill.

further analysis. Figure 15 is a vertical section through the pivotal window, indicating the head and sill details for this assembly. This two-dimensional drawing indicates the parts of this assembly that are required for the successful installation of the pivotal sash. Note the metal soffit at the head of the window.

Figure 16 is a horizontal section through the window jamb and the masonry pier. A special 2-inch-wide anchor clip is shown secured to the column assembly receiving the window frame. Since this window assembly is composed of two units of sash approximately 4 feet wide, the intermediate mullion is smaller than the mullion shown in Figure 11; that assembly spans approximately 28 feet.

Figure 17 is a view of a typical single window set into the masonry curtain wall of the school building, referring to three details (Figures 18, 19, and 20) through the head, sill, and jamb of the window unit. The typical pivotal sash is used here as it is throughout the rest of the building. Figure 18 is a horizontal section through the window jamb, indicating the attachment of the window frame to the masonry construction. The special anchor clip, typical for this building, is designed to engage the extruded projections of the window frame. The clip is then anchored to the masonry wall by expansion anchors. Shims are used to make the window assembly plumb. The plaster-on-wire lath shown here is in accordance with the requirements of the New York City Board of Education. Note the vinyl gaskets that are attached to the window itself and protect the assembly from water penetration.

Figure 19 is a vertical section through the window head that indicates the shelf angle and the window attachment. Note the weep holes provided at the brick cavity wall and in the head of the window frame. The finish brick is cut to a special shape to conceal the shelf angle, and flashing is used to protect this assembly. The flashing terminates at the frame of the window and is sealed into the window assembly as shown. The window head is secured to a bent steel plate that is attached to the shelf angle. Glazing gaskets that are uniform for this project receive the vision glass and are held in place by aluminum snap-on trim at the window head, the window jamb, and the windowsill.

The sill detail for this assembly is shown in Figure 20. This vertical section illustrates the relation of the window frame to the metal stool and sill assembly. A steel anchor designed to engage the metal frame of the window is secured to the masonry backup wall and carries the metal stool as well. Moisture trapped by the window frame is weeped to the exterior by a series of holes provided by the manufacturer in the head and sill sections of the window assembly. The lowest portion of the frame forms a drip cap over the brick masonry and completes the sill detail.

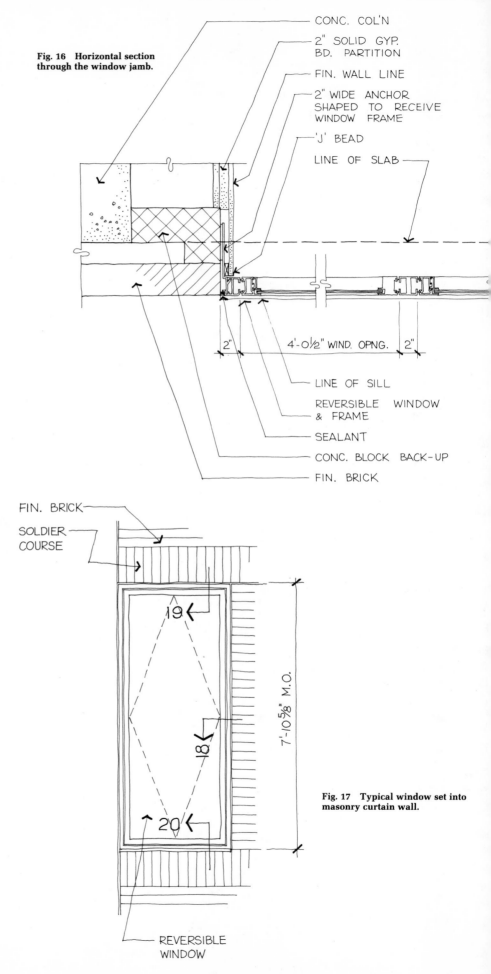

Fig. 16 Horizontal section through the window jamb.

CONC. COL'N
2" SOLID GYP. BD. PARTITION
FIN. WALL LINE
2" WIDE ANCHOR SHAPED TO RECEIVE WINDOW FRAME
'J' BEAD
LINE OF SLAB
2"
4'-0½" WIND. OPNG.
2"
LINE OF SILL
REVERSIBLE WINDOW & FRAME
SEALANT
CONC. BLOCK BACK-UP
FIN. BRICK

FIN. BRICK
SOLDIER COURSE
19
18
20
7'-10⅝" M.O.

Fig. 17 Typical window set into masonry curtain wall.

REVERSIBLE WINDOW

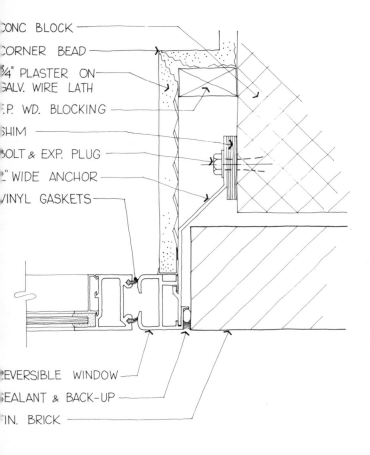

CONC BLOCK

CORNER BEAD

¾" PLASTER ON
GALV. WIRE LATH

F.P. WD. BLOCKING

SHIM

BOLT & EXP. PLUG

2" WIDE ANCHOR

VINYL GASKETS

REVERSIBLE WINDOW

SEALANT & BACK-UP

FIN. BRICK

Fig. 18 Horizontal section through
the window jamb.

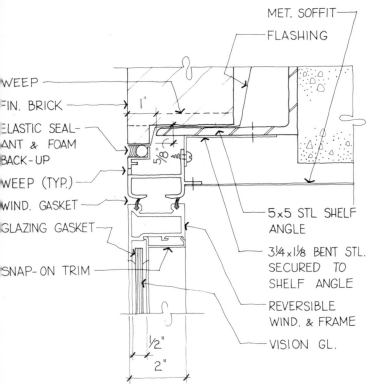

MET. SOFFIT

FLASHING

WEEP

FIN. BRICK

ELASTIC SEAL-
ANT & FOAM
BACK-UP

WEEP (TYP.)

WIND. GASKET

GLAZING GASKET

SNAP-ON TRIM

1"

⅝"

½"

2"

5x5 STL SHELF
ANGLE

3¼ x 1⅛ BENT STL.
SECURED TO
SHELF ANGLE

REVERSIBLE
WIND. & FRAME

VISION GL.

Fig. 19 Vertical section through
the window head.

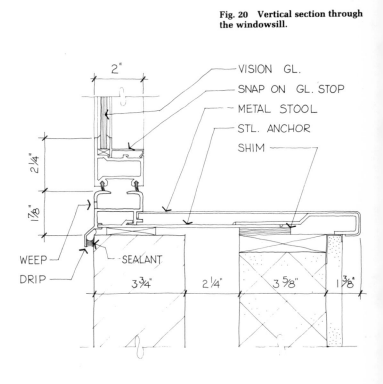

Fig. 20 Vertical section through
the windowsill.

VISION GL.

SNAP ON GL. STOP

METAL STOOL

STL. ANCHOR

SHIM

2"

2¼"

1⅞"

WEEP

DRIP

SEALANT

3¾"   2¼"   3⅝"   1⅜"

Figure 21 describes a typical parapet wall assembly found in the school building at the twelfth-floor roof. The parapet itself is strengthened by the extension of reinforcing rods projected from the roof slab into a 2-inch vertical plane of concrete mortar. The parapet is composed of three layers of brick, with a cavity between the first and second brick layer and a vertical 2-inch-thick plane of concrete mortar between the middle and inside brick wall face. It is this concrete mortar that receives the reinforcing rods that strengthen this assembly. The face brick rests on the relieving angle and is secured to the spandrel slab with corrugated galvanized anchors that engage cast-in-place dovetail slots. Copper cap flashing is installed through the parapet and projects over the copper base flashing. The base flashing is seated on the base course of the roofing,

and all subsequent layers of roofing are installed over the base course and base flashing to create a waterproof sandwich of these materials adjacent to the inside face of the parapet. The roofing is applied to a horizontal layer of 2-inch-thick rigid insulation that is cemented to lightweight concrete fill.

The window section is secured to the relieving angle as noted in Figure 19. The coping that terminates the parapet assembly is fabricated of ⅛-inch-thick sheet metal that is bent into the required shape and secured to the parapet with a steel angle at approximately every 4 feet on center; ¼-inch steel bolts anchored into concrete mortar receive the coping assembly. A 4-inch-wide metal trim strip in the same shape as the coping is used to seal the intersection of the coping sections. It is set in sealant and screwed into place.

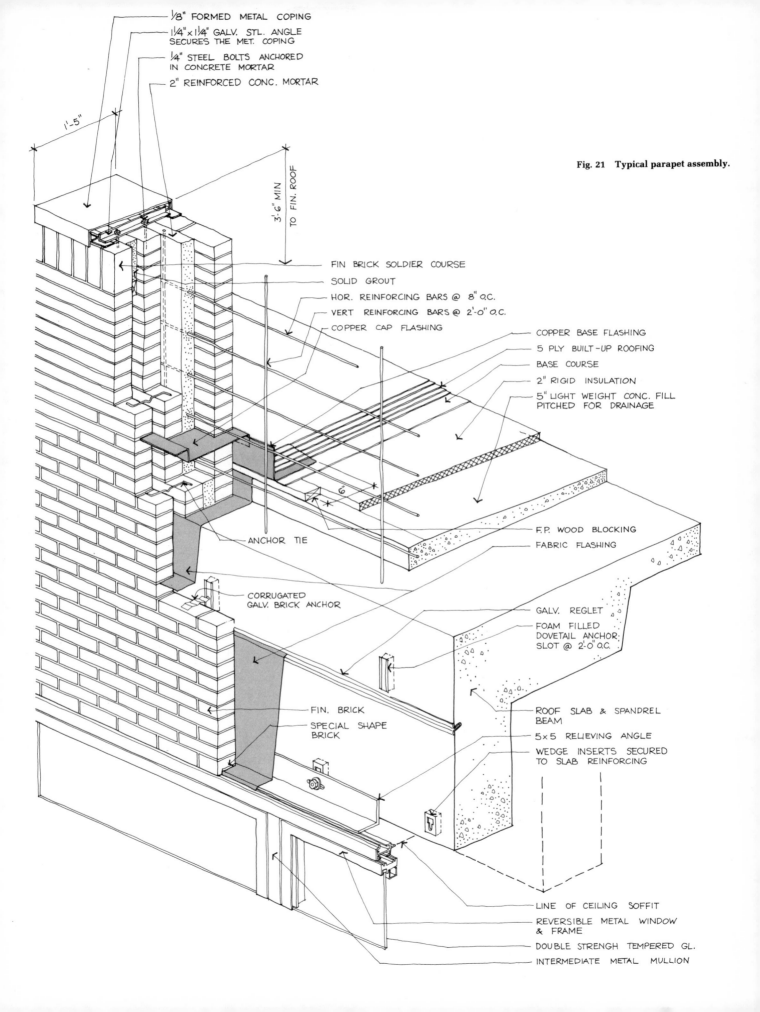

⅛" FORMED METAL COPING

1¼"×1¼" GALV. STL. ANGLE SECURES THE MET. COPING

¼" STEEL BOLTS ANCHORED IN CONCRETE MORTAR

2" REINFORCED CONC. MORTAR

1'-5"

3'-6" MIN TO FIN. ROOF

FIN BRICK SOLDIER COURSE

SOLID GROUT

HOR. REINFORCING BARS @ 8" O.C.

VERT. REINFORCING BARS @ 2'-0" O.C.

COPPER CAP FLASHING

COPPER BASE FLASHING

5 PLY BUILT-UP ROOFING

BASE COURSE

2" RIGID INSULATION

5" LIGHT WEIGHT CONC. FILL PITCHED FOR DRAINAGE

ANCHOR TIE

F.P. WOOD BLOCKING

FABRIC FLASHING

CORRUGATED GALV. BRICK ANCHOR

GALV. REGLET

FOAM FILLED DOVETAIL ANCHOR SLOT @ 2'-0" O.C.

FIN. BRICK

SPECIAL SHAPE BRICK

ROOF SLAB & SPANDREL BEAM

5×5 RELIEVING ANGLE

WEDGE INSERTS SECURED TO SLAB REINFORCING

LINE OF CEILING SOFFIT

REVERSIBLE METAL WINDOW & FRAME

DOUBLE STRENGH TEMPERED GL.

INTERMEDIATE METAL MULLION

Fig. 21   Typical parapet assembly.

11 The Tower Building
Philadelphia, Pennsylvania

ARCHITECTS: Mitchell/Giurgola Architects

Fig. 1   A view of the building from the southeast.

In the United States it is not surprising to observe a high-rise commercial structure in which all four elevations are identical. This suggests that certain conditions determined its final appearance. We can speculate, for instance, that the building receives uniform sunlight throughout the day and year on all elevations and that the weather never changes. These suppositions are incorrect, of course. One might argue that when the building was constructed, energy costs were negligible and the owners could well afford to sacrifice orientation in order to maintain exterior uniformity. The design of many buildings built before the energy crunch of the early 1970s can be rationalized by the preceding argument, but there is absolutely no current justification for the continuation of this type of thinking. We simply cannot afford to be cavalier with respect to our energy resources.

In congested urban areas it is difficult to site a major high-rise building in ways that will optimize its orientation. A building's design is in lockstep with zoning requirements, density, and codes. If we rely exclusively on mechanical systems such as heating and air conditioning to provide a balanced internal environment, we function ineffectively with respect to economy and resources. Moreover, we ignore several basic lessons taught by the Roman architect Vitruvius regarding what can be done to maximize a building's performance with respect to its site. In countries where energy has always been a problem, structures have been designed to take advantage of the orientation and the prevailing winds in order to maximize interior comfort. It is not uncommon to find very small windows on the north elevation of buildings in frigid climes, nor is it unusual to encounter overhangs for southern elevations, and sunscreens facing the west, in the tropics and southern latitudes. These are highly rational responses to real problems, solutions that involve a minimal outlay of valuable energy resources. It therefore becomes a moment of great satisfaction to encounter a building in the United States that is not only rational, innovative, and technically superior, but handsome as well. The Tower Building, commissioned by the Insurance Company of North America, located in downtown Philadelphia, Pennsylvania, and designed by the firm of Mitchell/Giurgola Architects, is an architectural work of reason and delight that makes an important statement with respect to design and conservation.

Figure 1 is a view of the building as seen from the southeast. By virtue of its metal skin and unconventional appearance, the Tower Building is in strong contrast to its neighbors. The north elevation, with its curtain wall of flush glass and metal, rises to the roof, twenty-eight stories above the street, broken only by the huge air scoops at the fifteenth-floor mechanical-equipment room. Immediately to the east of the tower we encounter a traditional prewar building in the Georgian revival style. At the

Fig. 2 A view of the main building entry from the street level.

eighteenth floor, the east elevation breaks free of its adjacent neighbor and we are faced with an unusual juxtaposition of elevations. The single most striking element is the deeply inset windows that are protected from the sun on that elevation. The solid wall projection of the stair tower is a logical expression for the service core of the building, since the remaining three elevations are unencumbered by adjacent buildings and are exposed to the street.

Figure 2 is a view of the main building entry from the street level and shows a setback two stories high merging with an impressive four-story-high arcade. The west elevation above the fourth floor, as seen in Figure 3, is composed of deeply inset windows that are uniform for this elevation as well as for the south and east elevations. Figure 4 shows a close-up view of the deeply recessed windows formed by the sunscreen assembly. In spite of the elevation variations throughout the structure, there is a consistency that holds the building together as a three-dimensional design entity. The metal curtain walls, the column covers, the trim, and color are used with great skill in order to create a total architectural statement. The highly articulated exterior skin of this building has been developed as a logical reflection of orientation and energy conservation.

The architects of the Tower Building acknowledge the invaluable assistance provided by the Cupples Products Division of the H. H. Robertson Company in the development of the final detailing and in the fabrication of the aluminum curtain

Fig. 3 The west elevation above the fourth floor.

Fig. 4 Close-up view of the deeply recessed windows.

wall panels and accessory components. It was primarily their shop drawings that I used to develop the sketches that accompany this text. The architects' drawings for the curtain wall were executed within a design format, and they do not necessarily deal with "nuts and bolts." The specifications for the cladding system were written for performance. The successful bidder on the job, Cupples Products, submitted a performance package which required them to work closely with the architects' technical team in order to develop the necessary contract documents. They submitted an extensive set of shop drawings that became the basis of a construction agreement.

It is important to understand the variation of professional services rendered in this particular instance. The subcontractor became a consultant for the architect on a limited basis. It was the subcontractor's input that took care of detail problems, coordination, and installation procedures for the project. The architects, on the other hand, were freed to develop the design parameters for the curtain wall, the structure, and other systems. Both the architects and the contractor were able to contribute effectively in a way that most closely paralleled their area of competence. Once the overall criteria for the performance of the curtain wall were established, it was not necessary for the architect to supply highly involved and possibly nongermane details that would be subsequently replaced by the contractor's own and certainly more pertinent proposal. In Chapter 6 a similar contractual situation is described in which precast concrete was used for the curtain wall system. The situation with the Tower Building is more complex, however, as the panel system for this building was not a standard manufactured item in the early 1970s, although it derives from a metal pan system that was commonly in use on commercial buildings in the 1930s and early postwar years. The technical problems inherent in this type of construction were not ironed out until the completion of the Tower Building. The innovative use of the material, the proven capability of the contractor, and the well-earned reputation of the architects combined to make this system work well for the client. I would not, however, recommend that this type of contractual arrangement be used by an architect on a regular basis without a great deal of technical, design, and legal advice.

A striking factor in the facade of this building is its feeling of continuity and craftsmanship. The joints separating the panels seem to be part of the decorative pattern of the glass and from a distance appear to be a tracery of fine elevation lines. The white polyvinyl-fluoride finish on the metal panels has weathered well since the mid-1970s and reinforces the sleek appearance of the building. The panels form a flush exterior surface that conceals their method of fastening to the

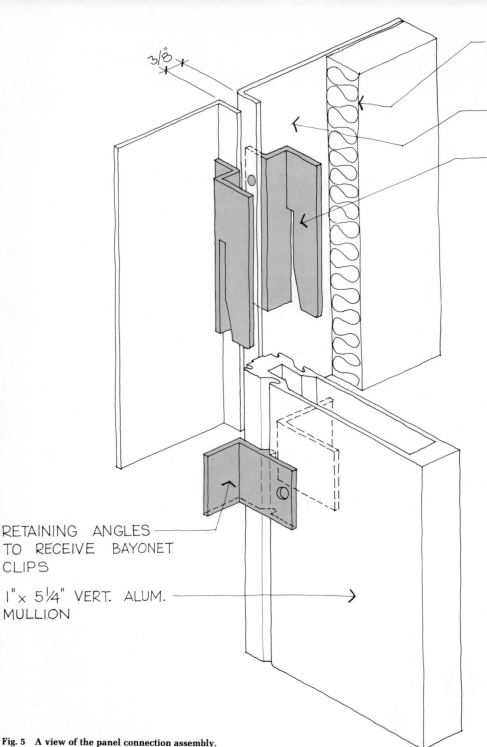

1" INSULATION BATT
GLUED TO ALUM.
PANEL

ALUM SPANDREL PANEL
W/ INTEGRAL LIP

BAYONET CLIP SECURED
TO PANEL & DESIGNED
TO ENGAGE THE VERT.
MULLION – 2 PER
PANEL SIDE

RETAINING ANGLES
TO RECEIVE BAYONET
CLIPS

1" x 5¼" VERT. ALUM.
MULLION

Fig. 5 A view of the panel connection assembly.

building structure. The mullion and grid curtain wall systems that are in use today generally require a combination of vertical and horizontal members to contain the wall panels and enclose the building.

The design and construction team on this project developed an interesting panel and mullion system that is the basis of the curtain wall system. The cladding material is sheet aluminum approximately ³⁄₁₆ inch thick with formed edges; it develops a pan-shaped panel that is extremely resistant to *oil canning*, in which flush metal panels appear to form ripples and dents along their surfaces. A polyvinyl-fluoride finish is applied in two coats, each baked separately, and is used on panels, vertical mullions, and all curtain wall accessories. Figure 5 is an enlarged isometric drawing that explains the interaction of the panel and mullion system. We are able to identify the bayonet clips that are secured to the formed panel edges. The bayonet clips are designed to engage the retaining angle clips that are machine-screwed to the vertical mullions. This system provides proper alignment, uniform joint width, and concealed fastening. It also allows a panel to be removed at any time for replacement or repair.

The following vertical and horizontal sections taken through the curtain wall are very similar to the drawings that were prepared by the architects in order to establish the design standards for the project. Figure 6 is an analysis of the northern wall of the building. It shows typical floor-to-floor heights and other basic dimensioning information. In addition, the relationship of the vertical mullion to the slabs and the spandrel panels is shown, as are the induction unit and cover. Figure 7 is a response to a different set of design conditions related to the building's solar orientation. The aluminum mullion is set back from the face of the building and is no longer continuous. It receives the convex panels at the sill line and, as seen in Figure 8, secures the concave portion of the sunscreen at the head of the vision glass.

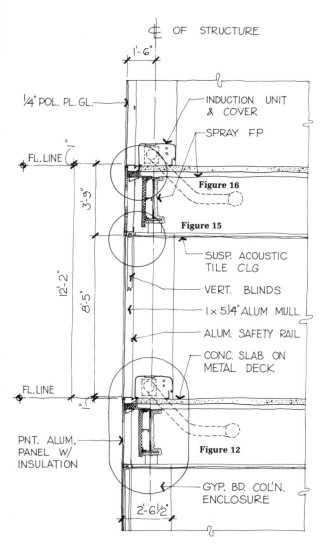

⊄ OF STRUCTURE

1'-6"

¼" POL. PL. GL.

INDUCTION UNIT
& COVER

SPRAY FP

FL. LINE

Figure 16

Figure 15

3'-9"

SUSP. ACOUSTIC
TILE CLG

VERT. BLINDS

12'-2"

8'-5"

I × 5¼" ALUM MULL.

ALUM. SAFETY RAIL

CONC. SLAB ON
METAL DECK

FL. LINE

Figure 12

PNT. ALUM.
PANEL W/
INSULATION

GYP. BD. COL'N.
ENCLOSURE

2'-6½"

**Fig. 6   Flat wall, or typical
north wall.**

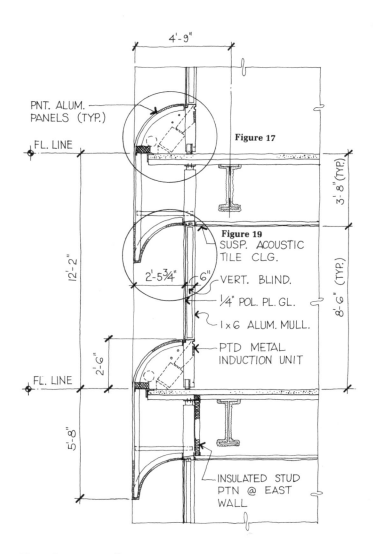

4'-9"

PNT. ALUM.
PANELS (TYP.)

Figure 17

FL. LINE

3'-8" (TYP.)

Figure 19

12'-2"

SUSP. ACOUSTIC
TILE CLG.

2'-5¾"   6"

VERT. BLIND.

¼" POL. PL. GL.

I × 6 ALUM. MULL.

8'-6" (TYP.)

2'-6"

PTD METAL
INDUCTION UNIT

FL. LINE

5'-8"

INSULATED STUD
PTN @ EAST
WALL

Fig. 7   Sunscreen wall.

**Fig. 8   Aluminum mullion secures
concave portion of sunscreen
head of vision glass.**

Figure 9 indicates the transition between both elevations. The carefully articulated corner with its sculptural relationship of recessed glass and curved panels makes the intersection of the building planes work gracefully. An enlarged view of this intersection occurs in Figure 10. Here the structure and its relation to the curtain wall section are expressed in greater detail, with materials and dimensions shown.

The Tower Building structure is composed of a steel frame and a composite slab of concrete and metal decking. The penthouse is an interesting development of a two-story greenhouse that may be studied in Figure 11. The greenhouse skylight is formed by the extension of the typical vertical mullion that is the basis of the panel cladding system. Note the curve that is developed as the vertical mullion returns to the set-back face of the penthouse. This variety of elevation variations is achieved with a relatively simple palette of cladding details.

The typical flat wall of the north elevation is the most appropriate place to start an examination of the building's curtain wall system. Here the vertical mullions are continuous and secured to the edge of the slab. A typical spandrel

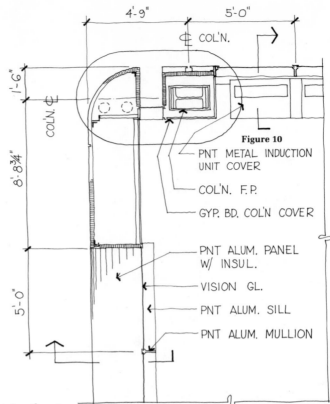

PNT METAL INDUCTION UNIT COVER

COL'N. F.P.

GYP. BD. COL'N COVER

PNT ALUM. PANEL W/ INSUL.

VISION GL.

PNT ALUM. SILL

PNT ALUM. MULLION

Fig. 9   Part plan of northwest corner.

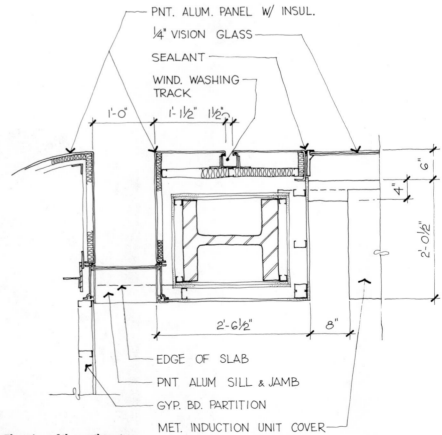

PNT. ALUM. PANEL W/ INSUL.

¼" VISION GLASS

SEALANT

WIND. WASHING TRACK

EDGE OF SLAB

PNT ALUM SILL & JAMB

GYP. BD. PARTITION

MET. INDUCTION UNIT COVER

Fig. 10   Plan view of the northwest corner.

Fig. 11   The penthouse.

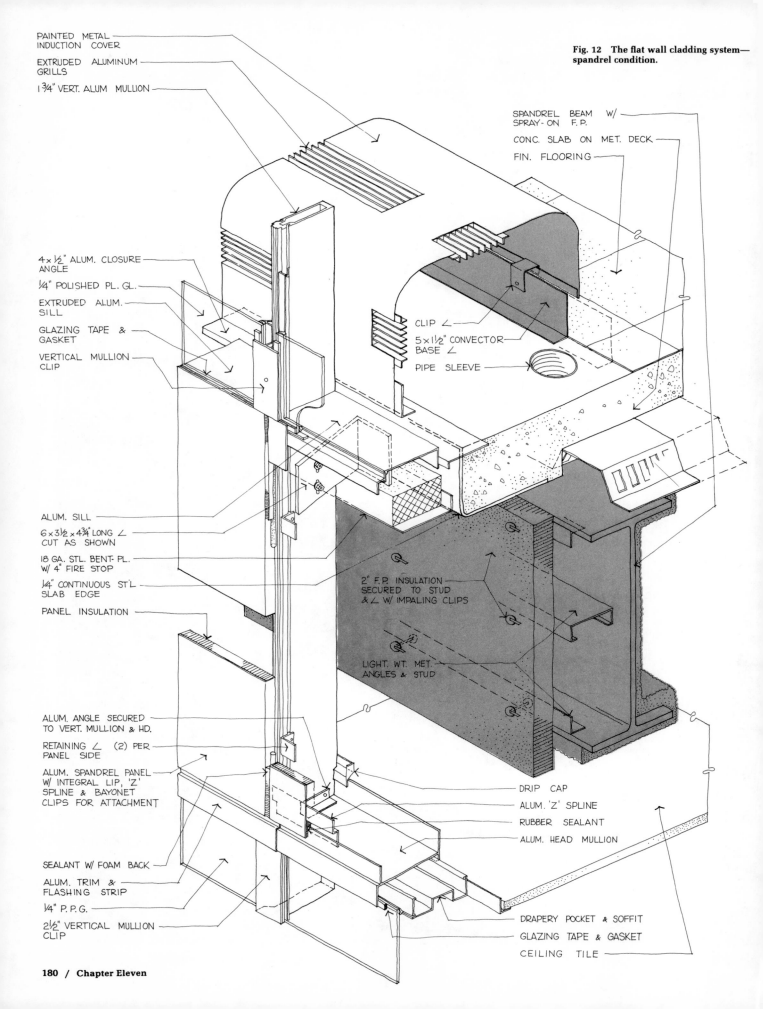

PAINTED METAL
INDUCTION COVER

EXTRUDED ALUMINUM
GRILLS

1 ¾" VERT. ALUM MULLION

4 × ½" ALUM. CLOSURE
ANGLE

¼" POLISHED PL. GL.

EXTRUDED ALUM.
SILL

GLAZING TAPE &
GASKET

VERTICAL MULLION
CLIP

ALUM. SILL

6 × 3½ × 4¾ LONG ∠
CUT AS SHOWN

18 GA. STL. BENT- PL.
W/ 4" FIRE STOP

¼" CONTINUOUS ST'L
SLAB EDGE

PANEL INSULATION

ALUM. ANGLE SECURED
TO VERT. MULLION & HD.

RETAINING ∠ (2) PER
PANEL SIDE

ALUM. SPANDREL PANEL
W/ INTEGRAL LIP, 'Z'
SPLINE & BAYONET
CLIPS FOR ATTACHMENT

SEALANT W/ FOAM BACK

ALUM. TRIM &
FLASHING STRIP

¼" P. P. G.

2½" VERTICAL MULLION
CLIP

**Fig. 12   The flat wall cladding system—
spandrel condition.**

SPANDREL BEAM W/
SPRAY- ON F. P.

CONC. SLAB ON MET. DECK

FIN. FLOORING

CLIP ∠

5 × 1½" CONVECTOR
BASE ∠

PIPE SLEEVE

2" F. P. INSULATION
SECURED TO STUD
& ∠ W/ IMPALING CLIPS

LIGHT. WT. MET.
ANGLES & STUD

DRIP CAP

ALUM. 'Z' SPLINE

RUBBER SEALANT

ALUM. HEAD MULLION

DRAPERY POCKET & SOFFIT

GLAZING TAPE & GASKET

CEILING TILE

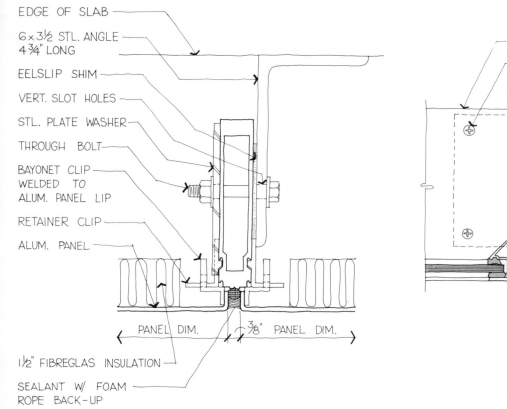

EDGE OF SLAB

6 × 3½ STL. ANGLE 4¾" LONG

EELSLIP SHIM

VERT. SLOT HOLES

STL. PLATE WASHER

THROUGH BOLT

BAYONET CLIP WELDED TO ALUM. PANEL LIP

RETAINER CLIP

ALUM. PANEL

PANEL DIM.

⅜"

PANEL DIM.

1½" FIBREGLAS INSULATION

SEALANT W/ FOAM ROPE BACK-UP

Fig. 13 Flat wall system at the spandrel.

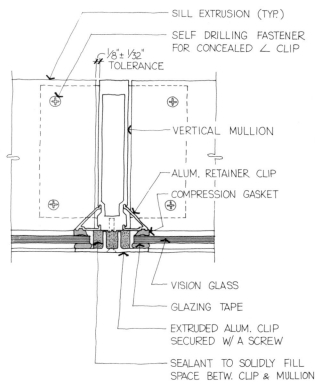

SILL EXTRUSION (TYP.)

SELF DRILLING FASTENER FOR CONCEALED ∠ CLIP

⅛" ± 1/32" TOLERANCE

VERTICAL MULLION

ALUM. RETAINER CLIP

COMPRESSION GASKET

VISION GLASS

GLAZING TAPE

EXTRUDED ALUM. CLIP SECURED W/ A SCREW

SEALANT TO SOLIDLY FILL SPACE BETW. CLIP & MULLION

Fig. 14 Flat wall system

condition is shown in Figure 12, in which we are able to study the components and methods of assembly in the system. The vertical mullion is secured to the slab by a cut angle that has been welded to the steel slab edging. At this location all other connections and components with the exception of the induction cover are attached to the mullion. Figure 13 indicates the relationship of the vertical mullion to the spandrel panels and slab. The bayonet clips and retaining angle clips shown here in plan are a reflection of the material indicated in Figure 5.

The edge of the slab as shown in Figure 12 requires some study with respect to fire and safety codes. There is usually a space between the slab and the curtain wall panel that must be sealed against the spread of fire. In this particular instance, the building code allowed the installation of a rigid inorganic fire-stop that provides the required fire rating and rests on a bent metal plate that receives it. The spandrel beam is fireproofed in two ways. Between the curtain wall and the beam a 2-inch layer of rigid fireproofing insulation is secured by impaling clips to light metal sections provided for that purpose. The side of the beam facing the ceiling plenum is fireproofed with a cementitious spray-on material that is used throughout the rest of the building.

The extruded sill and head mullions are

clipped to the vertical mullion with small concealed angles. Four retaining angles are required by each panel's bayonet mounts. The retaining angles are secured to the mullion in grooves designed to receive them. When the panels are in place, the upper lip at the sill forms the retainer that holds the glass in place horizontally. The vision glass is secured at the top by the interaction of the head mullion and the extruded drapery pocket. Glazing tape and compression gaskets are used throughout in order to seal the glass installation properly. The glass is secured vertically with continuous clip retainers that engage the vertical mullion and are designed to receive the glazing materials. Figure 14 is a plan section of this assembly and is drawn in large scale for further examination.

Caulking and sealants have improved considerably since the days when chalk and linseed oil were mixed together to form putty, a substance that dried out quickly and had to be replaced frequently. Most of the materials used for glazing on the Tower Building are synthetic substances with a long life and novel applications. The vision glass is secured to mullions by glazing tape that has double-sided sticky surfaces that grip the glass and metal glazing stops. The interior of the glass is held in place by a compression gasket that is received by the extrusions forming the mullions. In many ways the large-scale use of glass as an

exterior curtain wall material depended upon the development of highly advanced sealants. In fact, one of the most popularly used sealants is a spin-off of the space industry, originally used to provide a stable material base for solid-fuel rocket boosters. As a practical matter, the sealant bead should be about as deep as it is wide, approximately ¼ to ½ inch. The size of the bead is controlled by inserting a foam plastic backer rod to the proper depth. Once this is done, the caulking installation can proceed with optimum conditions ensured.

You will note that the concrete slab is equipped with sleeves in order to receive piping and other mechanical accessories. A drip cap is secured to the mullion at the head in order to capture condensate formed by temperature differentials between the curtain wall and the interior spaces of the building. All panels are provided with 1½-inch foil-backed semirigid insulation that is secured to the panels by impaling clips. The clip requires modern adhesives in order to function effectively. It is composed of a long stem brazed or soldered to a metal disk. The clip is glued to the inside of the panel approximately 1 foot on center, and the insulation sheets are pushed over the stem, or impaled; a washer is slipped over the stem, and it is then bent at a right angle to hold the insulation in place. An epoxy glue is used to make the installation of the impaling clips possible.

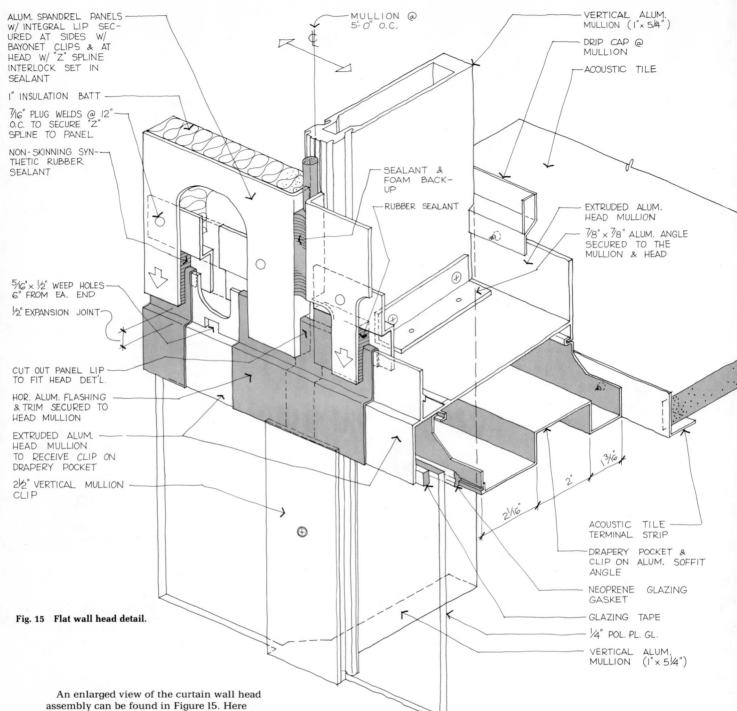

ALUM. SPANDREL PANELS W/ INTEGRAL LIP SECURED AT SIDES W/ BAYONET CLIPS & AT HEAD W/ "Z" SPLINE INTERLOCK SET IN SEALANT

1" INSULATION BATT

7/16" PLUG WELDS @ 12" O.C. TO SECURE "Z" SPLINE TO PANEL

NON-SKINNING SYNTHETIC RUBBER SEALANT

5/16" x 1/2" WEEP HOLES 6" FROM EA. END

1/2" EXPANSION JOINT

CUT OUT PANEL LIP TO FIT HEAD DET'L.

HOR. ALUM. FLASHING & TRIM SECURED TO HEAD MULLION

EXTRUDED ALUM. HEAD MULLION TO RECEIVE CLIP ON DRAPERY POCKET

2 1/2" VERTICAL MULLION CLIP

MULLION @ 5'-0" O.C.

SEALANT & FOAM BACK-UP

RUBBER SEALANT

VERTICAL ALUM. MULLION (1" x 5 1/4")

DRIP CAP @ MULLION

ACOUSTIC TILE

EXTRUDED ALUM. HEAD MULLION

7/8" x 7/8" ALUM. ANGLE SECURED TO THE MULLION & HEAD

1 3/16"

2"

2 1/16"

ACOUSTIC TILE TERMINAL STRIP

DRAPERY POCKET & CLIP ON ALUM. SOFFIT ANGLE

NEOPRENE GLAZING GASKET

GLAZING TAPE

1/4" POL. PL. GL.

VERTICAL ALUM. MULLION (1" x 5 1/4")

Fig. 15 Flat wall head detail.

An enlarged view of the curtain wall head assembly can be found in Figure 15. Here the flat wall vertical mullion intersects the extruded aluminum head mullion. The configuration of this section indicates two continuous grooves on either side of the vertical mullion that pick up clip retainers for the vision glass below. The edge of the mullion facing the exterior is shaped to accommodate the aluminum panels and develop the necessary spacing between them for the sealant application.

When the question arises whether to flash or not to flash, the answer is invariably affirmative. In this instance aluminum flashing is installed over the head mullion in order to prevent moisture penetration, and the resultant condensate is conducted outside through weep holes located between the flashing and the head mullion. The panels are inserted over this

flashed head mullion and set into place, with sealant filling the voids formed by the assembly. The vision glass at the head is held in place by the interaction of the extruded head mullion and the soffit angle. Here one can see the glazing tape secured to the head and to the vision glass. A vertical mullion clip provides the exterior closure for the full height of the vision glass.

The glazing of the vision glass is best seen in Figure 16. This view of the sill explains the installation. The clip retainers, which are lightweight extruded aluminum angles, snap into the vertical mullion and are designed to receive the compression

gaskets which hold the glass in place. Glazing tape forms the exterior weather protection for this assembly, and in addition, liquid sealant is pumped into the cavity to form a watertight connection.

The sill extrusion receives the vision glass and allows the installation of the compression gaskets, the glazing stops, and additional sealant. In case some excess water should develop through condensation or leakage, weep holes are installed to conduct it away. The cut steel angle shown in Figure 16 secures the mullion to the slab at an angle that allows the clearance of the other cladding elements. The retaining angles that are designed to receive the

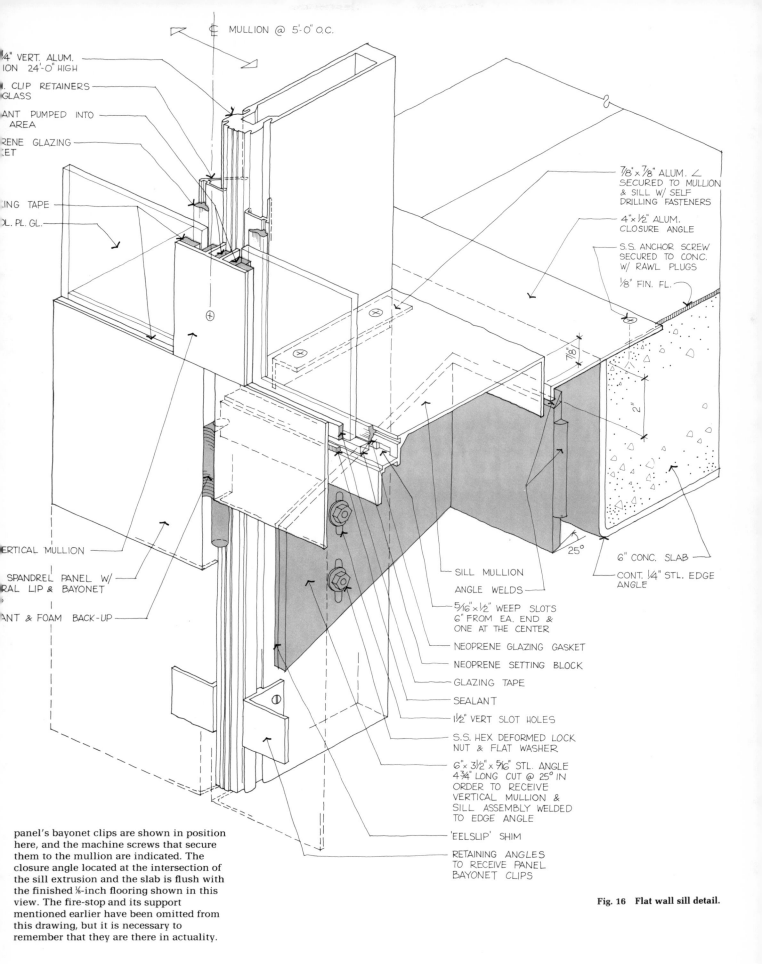

C MULLION @ 5'-0" O.C.

4" VERT. ALUM.
ION 24'-0" HIGH

CLIP RETAINERS
GLASS

ANT PUMPED INTO
AREA

RENE GLAZING
KET

ING TAPE

OL. PL. GL.

VERTICAL MULLION

SPANDREL PANEL W/
RAL LIP & BAYONET

ANT & FOAM BACK-UP

⅞" × ⅞" ALUM. ∠
SECURED TO MULLION
& SILL W/ SELF
DRILLING FASTENERS

4" × ½" ALUM.
CLOSURE ANGLE

S.S. ANCHOR SCREW
SECURED TO CONC.
W/ RAWL PLUGS

⅛" FIN. FL.

⅞"

2"

25°

6" CONC. SLAB

CONT. ¼" STL. EDGE
ANGLE

SILL MULLION

ANGLE WELDS

5⁄16" × ½" WEEP SLOTS
6" FROM EA. END &
ONE AT THE CENTER

NEOPRENE GLAZING GASKET

NEOPRENE SETTING BLOCK

GLAZING TAPE

SEALANT

1½" VERT SLOT HOLES

S.S. HEX DEFORMED LOCK
NUT & FLAT WASHER

6" × 3½" × 5⁄16" STL. ANGLE
4¾" LONG CUT @ 25° IN
ORDER TO RECEIVE
VERTICAL MULLION &
SILL ASSEMBLY WELDED
TO EDGE ANGLE

'EELSLIP' SHIM

RETAINING ANGLES
TO RECEIVE PANEL
BAYONET CLIPS

panel's bayonet clips are shown in position
here, and the machine screws that secure
them to the mullion are indicated. The
closure angle located at the intersection of
the sill extrusion and the slab is flush with
the finished ⅛-inch flooring shown in this
view. The fire-stop and its support
mentioned earlier have been omitted from
this drawing, but it is necessary to
remember that they are there in actuality.

Fig. 16   Flat wall sill detail.

Fig. 17 Sunscreen assembly and recessed windowsill.

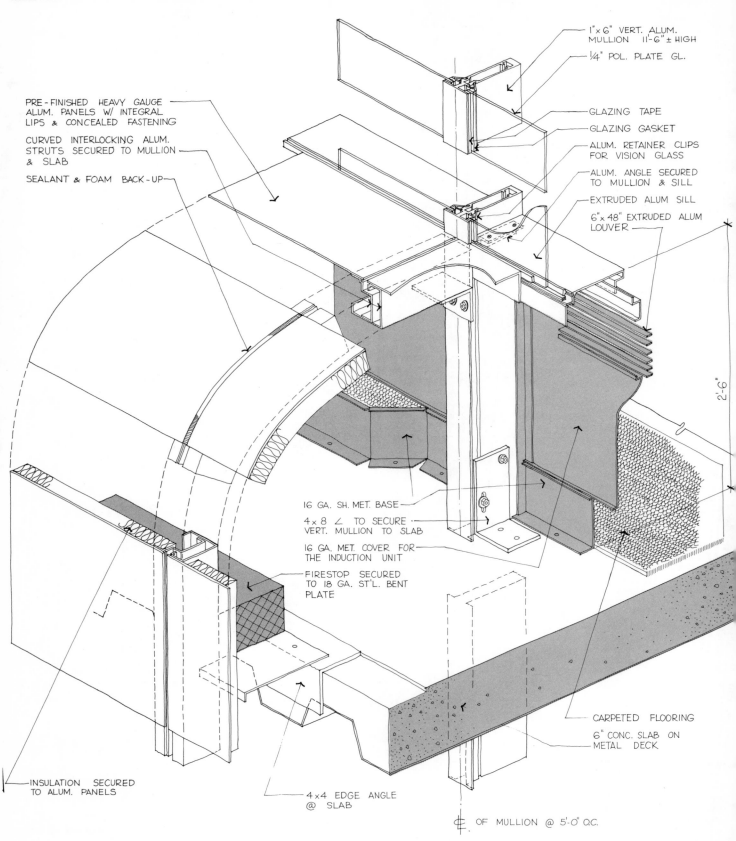

PRE-FINISHED HEAVY GAUGE ALUM. PANELS W/ INTEGRAL LIPS & CONCEALED FASTENING

CURVED INTERLOCKING ALUM. STRUTS SECURED TO MULLION & SLAB

SEALANT & FOAM BACK-UP

1"x 6" VERT. ALUM. MULLION 11-6" ± HIGH

1/4" POL. PLATE GL.

GLAZING TAPE

GLAZING GASKET

ALUM. RETAINER CLIPS FOR VISION GLASS

ALUM. ANGLE SECURED TO MULLION & SILL

EXTRUDED ALUM SILL

6"x 48" EXTRUDED ALUM LOUVER

2'-6"

16 GA. SH. MET. BASE

4 x 8 ∠ TO SECURE VERT. MULLION TO SLAB

16 GA. MET. COVER FOR THE INDUCTION UNIT

FIRESTOP SECURED TO 18 GA. ST'L. BENT PLATE

INSULATION SECURED TO ALUM. PANELS

4 x 4 EDGE ANGLE @ SLAB

CARPETED FLOORING

6" CONC. SLAB ON METAL DECK

℄ OF MULLION @ 5'-0" O.C.

The development of the sunscreen curtain wall on the south, east, and west elevations requires a modification of the technical approach used on the north face of the building. Figure 17 is an indication of the sill and spandrel section of this assembly. The vertical mullion used in the sunscreen is a variation of the one used in the flat wall section. Here the mullion is extruded in a T shape, and the extrusion is secured to the top of the slab and to the metal deck above. The convex curve of the spandrel is formed with the same heavy-gauge aluminum used throughout, and the material is bent downward to form a lip that intersects the sill. The curve for the remainder of the assembly is reinforced by extruded aluminum struts that have been curved to receive the panel and that interlock as part of the construction process. A clip angle secures these struts to the vertical mullion at the sill.

The extruded aluminum sill which forms the top of the cover for the induction unit is attached to the vertical mullion by a concealed clip angle. This extrusion and the panel lip form the pocket that receives the vision glass. The glazing tape, the compression gasket, and the setting block are shown in place with the glass. The interior face of the sill section receives the induction unit cover and the louver assembly. Figure 18 indicates the relation of the mullion to the vision glass, the sill, and the convex sunscreen in a plan section.

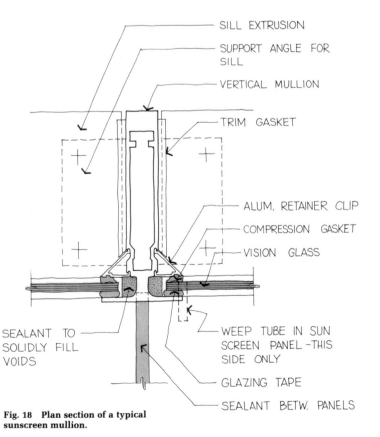

SILL EXTRUSION

SUPPORT ANGLE FOR SILL

VERTICAL MULLION

TRIM GASKET

ALUM. RETAINER CLIP

COMPRESSION GASKET

VISION GLASS

SEALANT TO SOLIDLY FILL VOIDS

WEEP TUBE IN SUN SCREEN PANEL –THIS SIDE ONLY

GLAZING TAPE

SEALANT BETW. PANELS

Fig. 18 Plan section of a typical sunscreen mullion.

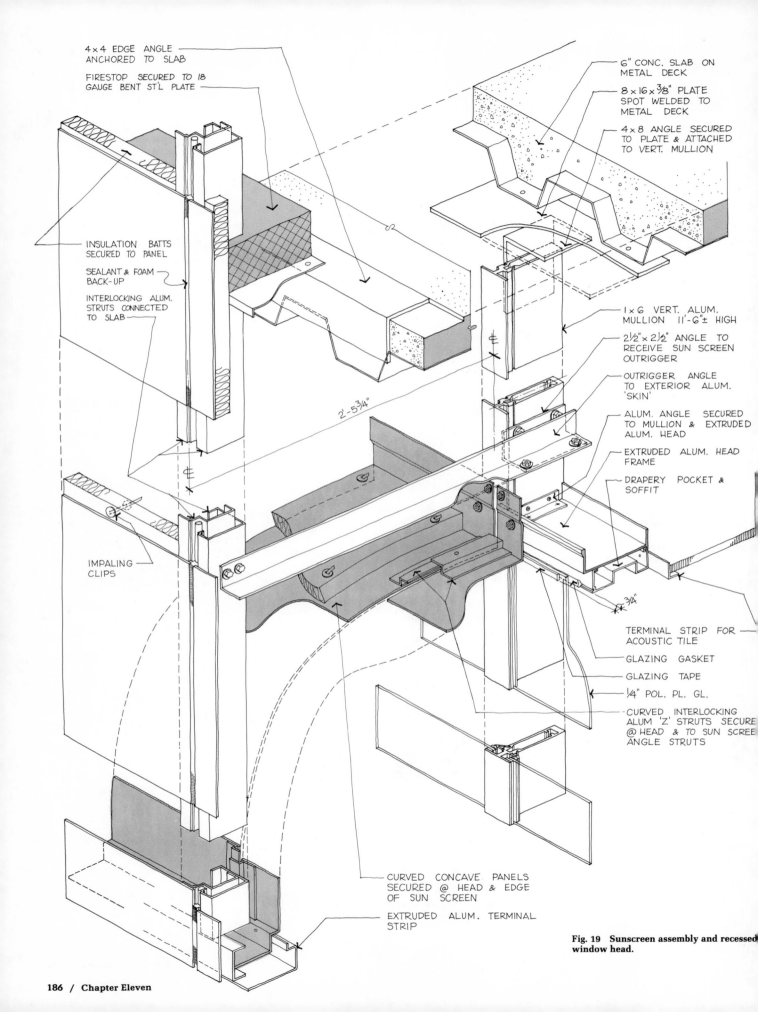

4 × 4 EDGE ANGLE
ANCHORED TO SLAB

FIRESTOP SECURED TO 18
GAUGE BENT ST'L PLATE

INSULATION BATTS
SECURED TO PANEL

SEALANT & FOAM
BACK-UP

INTERLOCKING ALUM.
STRUTS CONNECTED
TO SLAB

IMPALING
CLIPS

6" CONC. SLAB ON
METAL DECK

8 × 16 × 3/8" PLATE
SPOT WELDED TO
METAL DECK

4 × 8 ANGLE SECURED
TO PLATE & ATTACHED
TO VERT. MULLION

1 × 6 VERT. ALUM.
MULLION 11'-6"± HIGH

2½" × 2½" ANGLE TO
RECEIVE SUN SCREEN
OUTRIGGER

OUTRIGGER ANGLE
TO EXTERIOR ALUM.
'SKIN'

ALUM. ANGLE SECURED
TO MULLION & EXTRUDED
ALUM. HEAD

EXTRUDED ALUM. HEAD
FRAME

DRAPERY POCKET &
SOFFIT

3/4"

TERMINAL STRIP FOR
ACOUSTIC TILE

GLAZING GASKET

GLAZING TAPE

¼" POL. PL. GL.

CURVED INTERLOCKING
ALUM 'Z' STRUTS SECURE
@ HEAD & TO SUN SCREE
ANGLE STRUTS

2'-5¾"

CURVED CONCAVE PANELS
SECURED @ HEAD & EDGE
OF SUN SCREEN

EXTRUDED ALUM. TERMINAL
STRIP

**Fig. 19 Sunscreen assembly and recessed
window head.**

The curved panels that pass by the edge of the slab form a fluelike space that is closed with a combination of an incombustible, rated fire-stop and a bent steel plate that is secured to the slab edge angle. Semirigid insulation is secured to the panels with impaling clips as described earlier, and the installation is sealed to form a watertight assembly. The analysis of this detail continues in Figure 19. The interlocking struts that form the spandrel cover are secured to the vertical mullion by a horizontal "outrigger" angle brace. The support of the outer, concave spandrel cover is developed by the curved vertical mullion attached at the sill and through the outrigger angle secured to the head of this assembly.

The vertical mullion is secured to an 8-by 16-inch plate welded to the metal deck. Approximately 4 feet below this point, the concave panel forming the sunscreen begins its sweep to the exterior of the building curtain wall. Curved interlocking Z struts are plug-welded to the aluminum panels in order to reinforce the panels, and this assembly is terminated at the intersection with the vertical struts forming the exterior spandrel panel. The insulation for the panels is secured by impaling clips that are standard for this building. A view of the sunscreen from the interior can be seen in Figure 8. The drapery pocket, the suspended acoustic tile ceiling, and the beginning of the convex curve of the panel are neatly aligned. Figure 20 is a view of the space formed by the convex spandrel cover and indicates the curved strut, the insulation, and the heating, ventilating, and air conditioning (HVAC) pipes. The combination of the sunscreen and the heat-absorbing vision glass results in a pleasant and subdued interior light level that not only is restful but saves energy. The convex panel is given a bent lip upward in a complex configuration that intersects the drapery pocket and the soffit mullion. The panel is then connected to the vertical mullion and the soffit and forms part of the glazing pocket that receives the vision glass.

The following are the general notes submitted by Cupples Products as part of their shop drawings for the Tower Building. Although the notes are brief, they are complete and incisive. They should be reviewed in order to become acquainted with the material that a contractor believes is necessary for guidance during the fabrication and installation process.

1. Dimensions and details shown represent ideal material and erection conditions. Building conditions may necessitate detail modifications and dimensional variations.

2. Erector to notify the contractor . . . of building conditions and/or trade restrictions that do not permit proper curtain wall installation. Do not proceed without an approved alternate or relief.

3. All connections must be sound and in accordance with approved details. Weld lengths and fillet sizes must be maintained and performed by skilled craftsmen. Obtain approved weld profile changes from Cupples Engineering, if required, due to building tolerances or accessibility.

4. Insulation: foil backed semi-rigid Fiberglas, three lb. density, "K" factor = 23, 1 and ½ inches thick for spandrel and sunscreen panels, "U" = 137; 1" thick for col. covers and corner covers, "U" = 156.

5. Exterior Curtain Wall Sealant and/or Perimeter Wall Sealant: One part Acrylic terpolymer. Joint filler or back-up rod used in conjunction with this sealant to be ethafoam rods.

6. Curtain Wall Expansion and/or Concealed Joints: Non-skinning synthetic rubber.

7. Erector Note: All material is to be erected and sealed water tight in accordance with, but not limited to notes, details and dimensions contained in these drawings and in accordance with the best practice of the industry.

8. All exterior sealant joints are to be tooled and recessed min. ⅟₁₆" below metal surface.

These notes are representative of the cladding system installation only and do not describe other material prepared by the contractor for this project.

This chapter touches upon the main curtain wall systems that were designed for the Tower Building by Mitchell/Giurgola Architects and does not deal with the many additional details that went into the finished tower. I would be remiss not to point out that the entire building was developed with infinite care and intelligence. It is not a simple job to create a structure in which each of the elevations is treated as a separate entity designed to mesh with the larger concepts of the overall design. The control that makes this possible is evident throughout the tower. As one goes through these details, it is impossible not to admire the care and attention lavished on these assemblies in order to make them work effectively. Each groove of every extrusion becomes significant in terms of the overall installation, and the final results more than justify the effort of Cupples Products to satisfy the architects' design requirements. The inclusion of the contractor in the development of the design details and the response of the architects represented teamwork on the highest level. In this case it effectively solved the curtain wall problem. This procedure points in a direction of future cooperation between participants in the construction and design process; such cooperation can lead to the most expeditious and economical development of contract material for a building project.

Fig. 20 Space formed by convex spandrel cover.

Index

Page numbers in *italic* refer to illustrations.

About the Author

Herman Sands is Professor of Architectural Technology, New York City Technical College of the City University of New York. A graduate of Pratt Institute School of Architecture in 1960, he is a partner of Sands and Sperling Architects and has been active in design and project development for many institutional, commercial, and educational projects.